Presto! It's Piano Magic

Book 1

First Edition

Dennis Frayne

Presto! It's Music Magic Publications

Murrieta, CA
www.prestopianomagic.com
info@prestopianomagic.com

First Edition © 2018, Dennis Frayne

Presto! It's Piano Magic, Book 1, First Edition

Published by:

Presto! It's Music Magic Publications
Murrieta, CA
www.prestopianomagic.com

All rights reserved. No part of this book may be reproduced or transmitted in any form or by any means, electronic or mechanical, including photocopying, recording, or by any information storage and retrieval system without written permission from the author, except for the inclusion of brief quotations in a review.

© by Dennis Frayne
Printed in the United States of America

Library of Congress Cataloging in Publication Data

Frayne, Dennis
Presto! It's Piano Magic, Book 1, First Edition

ISBN-13: 978-1-7321254-1-4

LC

To The Teacher

Presto! It's Piano Magic, Book 1, is designed as an all-inclusive, holistic approach to teaching piano to beginning students.

This approach to teaching piano can be used successfully for children, youth, and adults. It can be used successfully for students who have never had a piano lesson, and for students who have had some lessons but are missing background information, are unable to read music, or have other gaps in music theory, musical understanding, or technical skill development.

Presto! It's Piano Magic, Book 1, is comprehensive. It contains lessons, theory, technique, and performance pieces, all in one book. One supplement you might consider as you work through *Book 1* is the *The Holiday and Special Occasion Studio Packet*. This add-on contains songs and pieces at all levels of student ability (through *Book 1* and *Book 2*) for use during holiday seasons and special occasions. The *The Holiday and Special Occasion Studio Packet* is a teacher or studio supplement – you can hand out individual songs and pieces to students. This can be great for student recitals.

Lessons are sequenced in a way that makes logical sense to a beginning learner. Each topic is introduced using clear, straight-forward, easy-to-read words, while using the language of music. Concepts and skills build on each other in a careful structure that is coherent and purposeful; they are not thrown out haphazardly, and students are not overwhelmed with too many new ideas at once.

Lessons are designed so that students develop technical facility while they learn to read music. Efforts to learn to *read* music will not hinder a student's ability to learn to *play* music on the piano. Arrangements of songs and pieces are developmentally appropriate, interesting, drawn from diverse cultures, genres, styles, and they *sound good*.

Lessons strive to teach the whole student as a well-rounded musician, in order to facilitate thorough musical development at the piano. *Book 1* introduces the piano keyboard and traditional music notation, and also embarks upon ear training, sight singing (including solfege), and rhythmic understanding – skills that will become more and more useful as students advance in reading, playing, improvising, and even composing music.

Best wishes to you and your students as each one begins their musical journey!

Presto! It's Piano Magic is dedicated to my wife, Grace Byeon,
who offered so much love, support, help, and quality assurance
during the development of my music series publications.

I further dedicate to, and wish to thank,

Ruth Stevenson Alling, who introduced me, many years ago, to some of the teaching strategies, curricula, and repertoire I employ and further develop here, with insights I gained learning her *Lo Kno Pla Approach to the Piano*.

Chizuko Asada, who helped me understand some important fundamentals to developing proper technique at the piano, including "ghost hands" and other strategies to achieve tension-free playing.

Michael Bartel, who opened my eyes to healthier and more successful approaches to practicing, replacing old, bad habits with new, good habits, memorization strategies, and selecting repertoire with developmental purpose and intention.

Table of Contents

The Piano Keyboard 3
Hot Cross Buns 6
Posture and Piano Hands 8
Hush-a-bye 12
The Piano: A Brief History 14
The Piano: How It Works 16
Posture: Sitting at the Piano 18
Hands and Finger Numbers 20
Merrily We Roll Along and *Mary Had a Little Lamb* 26
Go Tell Aunt Rhodie 30
Part One Completion Page 33

The Music Alphabet 34
The Music Alphabet and the Piano Keyboard 37
Twinkle Twinkle Little Star 44
Baa, Baa, Black Sheep, Pease Porridge Hot, The ABC Song 46
Introduction to Music Notation 48
Cuckoo Song 52
Hooray! 54
Scales, Keys, and Modes 58
Three Blind Mice 60
Un elefante 64
Balonku 66
Wayfaring Stranger 68
Part Two Review 72
Part Two Completion Page 75

Accidentals 76
The Wind 77
Half Steps and Whole Steps 78
Hush! Little Baby 80
Happy Birthday 82
America 86

Table of Contents (cont.)

First 5 Major Scales on the Piano Keyboard	88
La Raspa	92
La Cucaracha	94
Michael, Row the Boat Ashore	96
Part Three Review	101
Part Three Completion Page	105
Music Notation: The Staff	106
Music Notation: Clefs	108
Paw-Paw Patch	110
Treble Clef	112
Bass Clef	113
London Bridge	117
Los pollitos	124
The Grand Staff	126
Ledger Lines	127
Duérmete, mi niño	128
Au clair de la lune	132
Go Down, Moses	138
First 5 Major Scales: Two Octaves	145
Little Birdie	151
Rhythm	152
Song of Happiness	160
Bought Me a Cat	168
Pick Up Measure	171
The Herring Song	172
Dotted Notes and Ties	174
De colores	178
Part Four Review (Final Review)	181
For S/He's a Jolly Good Fellow	183
Part Four Completion Page	187
Certificate and Prize Order Form	189

My name is Presto, and I'm going to be your guide!

I'm a magician, and I'm also a musician!

Presto is a magic word, used by magicians all over the world!

And in music, *presto* means *very fast*.

Many musical terms, like *presto*, come from the Italian language.

And so, as we get started on our journey together, I, Presto the Magician Musician, welcome you to this book!

When you complete all four parts of the book and reach the finish, you will earn a prize!

I hope that you will enjoy learning how to play the piano!

You're going to learn how to play the piano!

The *piano* is a *keyboard instrument* that we play with the fingers of both of our hands.

There are many types of pianos and keyboards:

Grand Piano   Upright Piano

Electric Keyboard   Synthesizer

Pipe Organ   Harpsichord

Which ones will you play?

The Piano Keyboard

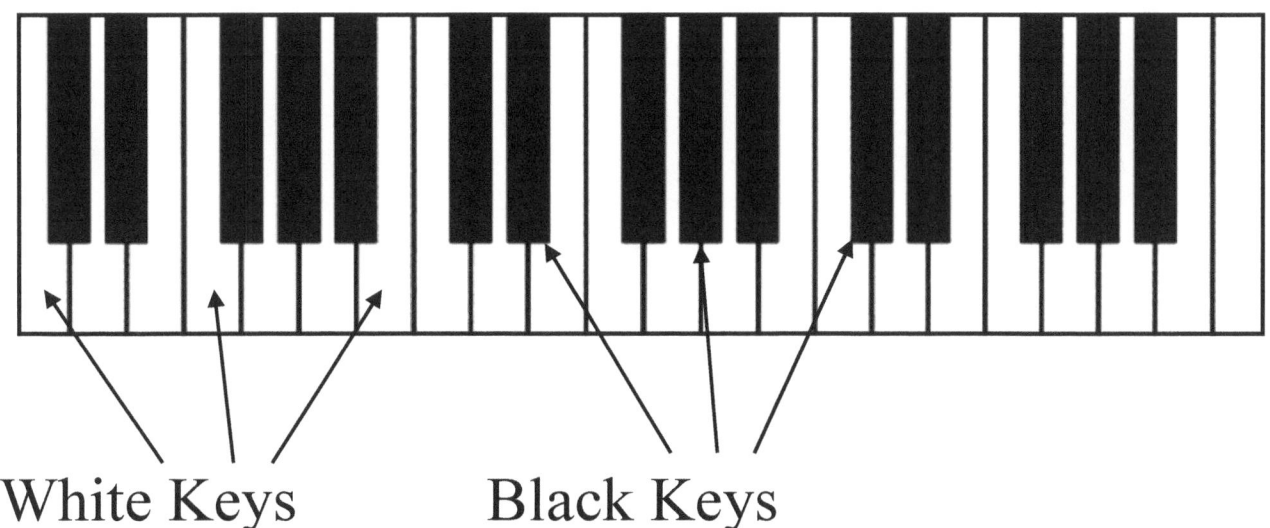

In music, *pitch* is the sound we hear when we play or sing a note.

Let's play some notes, or *pitches*, on the piano keyboard, by pressing some of the keys.

Notice how some notes sound higher, and some notes sound lower.

This is their pitch!

THE PIANO KEYBOARD (CONT.)

Pitch goes lower (to the left)   Pitch goes higher (to the right)

On the piano, pitch goes up (gets higher) as we go to the right, and pitch goes down (gets lower) as we go to the left.

Let's play some more pitches! Can you hear them get higher as you go to the right, and lower as you go to the left?

What are some other words for higher and lower?

<u>Lower → Higher Word List</u>

Lower	Higher
Low	High
Down	Up
Below	Above
Bottom	Top
Descending	Ascending

Examples:

A *higher* pitch is *above* a lower pitch.   Pitch going *up* is *ascending*.

The *lowest* note on the piano is at the *bottom* of the keyboard.

PITCH RECOGNITION GAME

Pitch goes lower (to the left) ← ———

Pitch goes higher (to the right) ——— →

↑ Middle C

Teacher: Play Middle C, and then play a second note on the piano keyboard.

Student: Is the second note (pitch) <u>higher</u> or <u>lower</u> than the first note (pitch)?
(Try a few of these to help train your ear.)

Circle the correct answer:

← ——— This direction is going higher/lower on the piano keyboard.

This direction is going higher/lower on the piano keyboard. ——— →

This note is _____ than this note.

Let's learn how to play our first song:
Hot Cross Buns!

First, let's sing the song:

*"Hot cross buns! Hot cross buns!
One a penny, two a penny!
Hot cross buns!"*

Can you tell, in this song, when the pitch goes up, when it goes down, and when it stays the same?

Next, let's clap our hands to the beat as we sing the song:

{
Hot	*cross*	*buns!*		*Hot*	*cross*	*buns!*	
Clap	*Clap*	*Clap*	*Clap*	**Clap**	*Clap*	*Clap*	*Clap*
1	*2*	*3*	*4*	*1*	*2*	*3*	*4*

{
One	*a*	*penny,*	*two a*	*penny!*	*Hot*	*cross*	*buns!*	
Clap	*Clap*	*Clap*	*Clap*	**Clap**	*Clap*	*Clap*	*Clap*	
1	*2*	*3*	*4*	*1*	*2*	*3*	*4*	

Next, let's learn to play the song on the piano!

Start with your Right Hand. Use your middle or tall finger to play all the notes. Curve your finger slightly, and play on the tip of your finger, like this:

Hot Cross Buns

Right Hand only.

Traditional

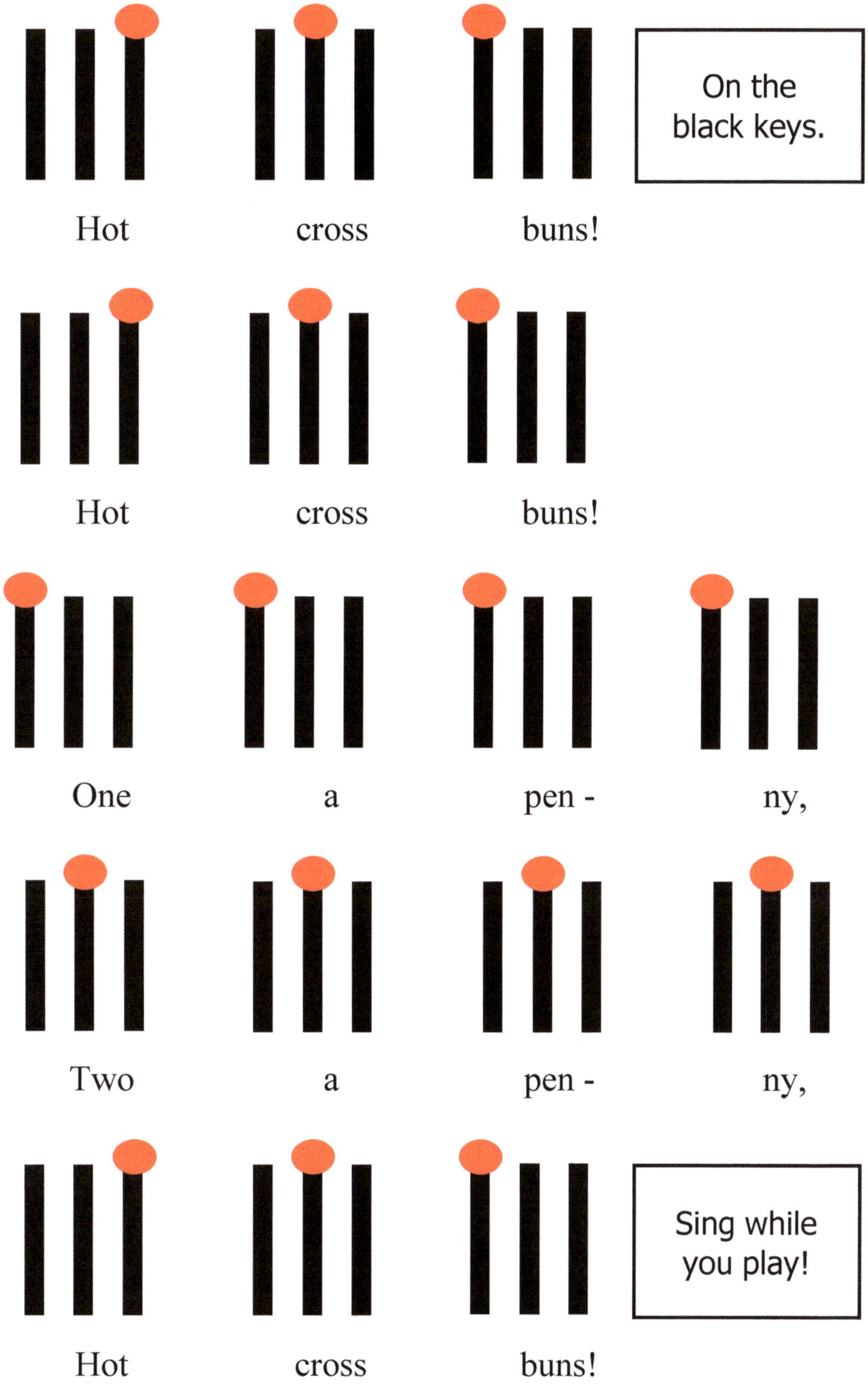

On the black keys.

Hot   cross   buns!

Hot   cross   buns!

One   a   pen -   ny,

Two   a   pen -   ny,

Hot   cross   buns!

Sing while you play!

LET'S LEARN ABOUT POSTURE AND PIANO HANDS

When we play the piano, we want our bodies, our arms and legs, our shoulders, our wrists and hands, to be *free of tension*.

Tension means tightness, which can cause discomfort, pain, and make it harder to play the piano enjoyably.

Think about good posture, sitting upright (not slouching), yet also remaining somewhat relaxed, loose, and tension-free.

"Ghost Hands"

Hold your arms up and let your hands hang down loosely, dangling, with no tension, kind of like a ghost:

Now, when you play the piano, pivot your "ghost hand" wrists up just slightly as you place your fingers gently on the keys.

You are ready to play the piano, tension-free!

Now let's add the Left Hand to *Hot Cross Buns*. Your Left Hand will play two notes. Use your thumb on the higher note and either your middle/tall finger or pinky finger on the lower note.

Memorize all your songs, and sing the words as you play!

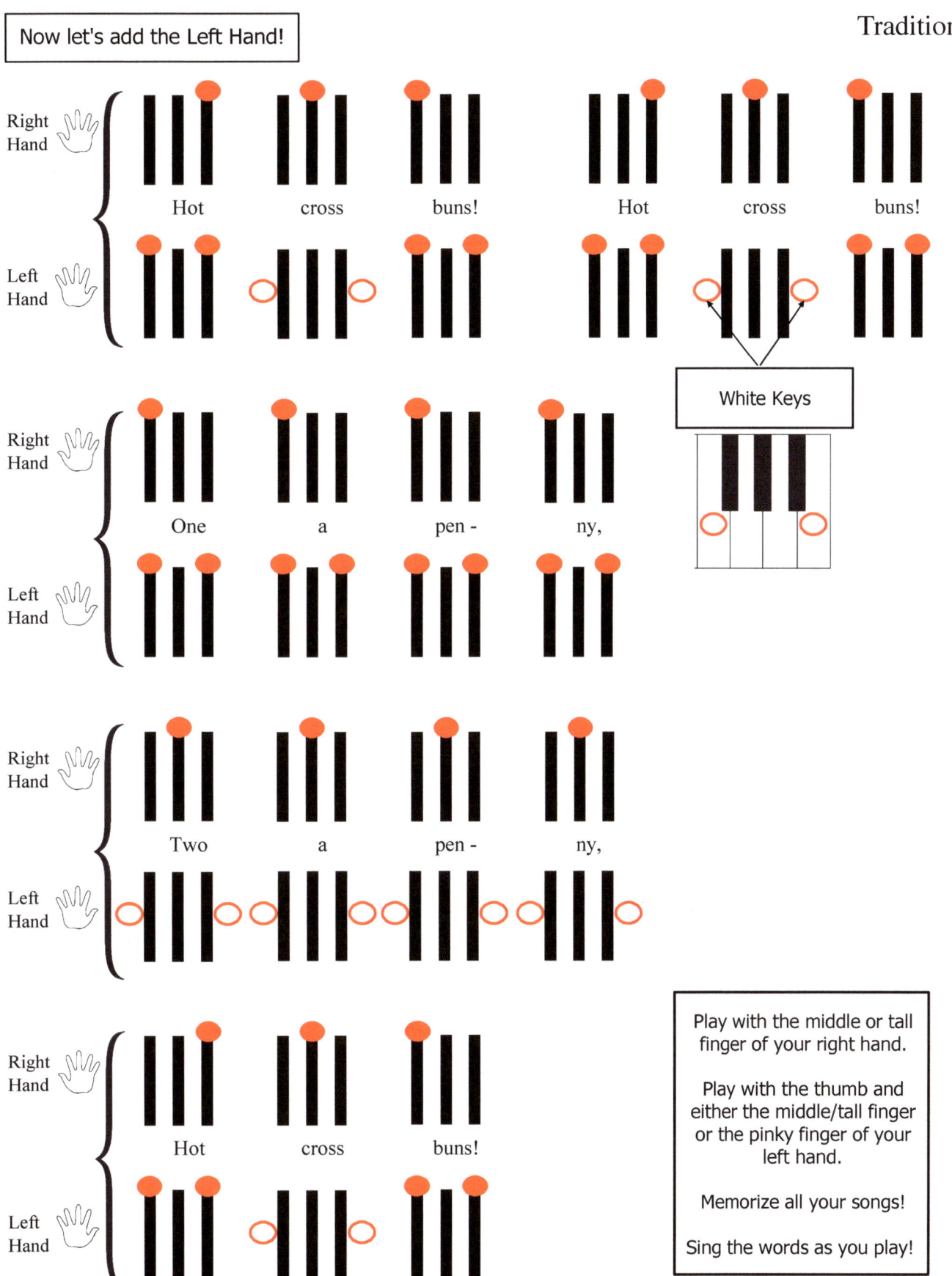

REVIEW PITCH DIRECTION AND PITCH RECOGNITION

*Draw an arrow going **up** the keyboard:*

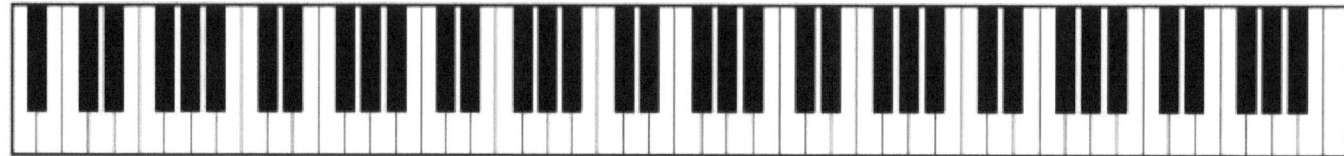

*Draw an arrow going **down** the keyboard:*

Circle one:

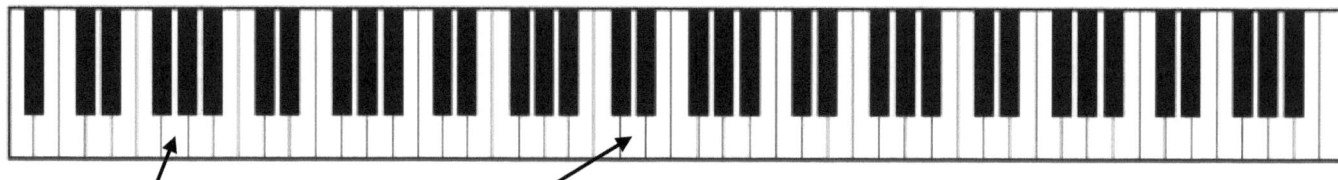

This key is **above/below** this key.

Circle one:

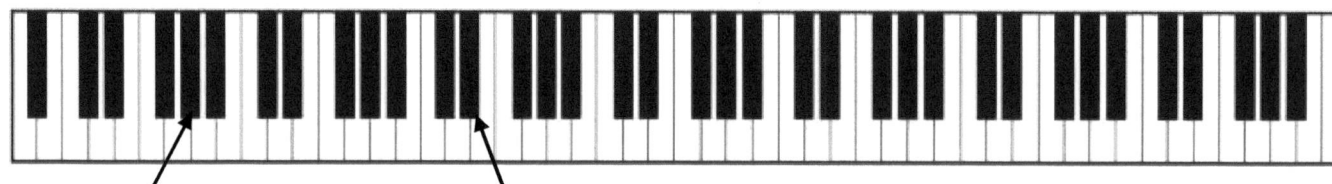

This key is **higher/lower** than this key.

Circle one:

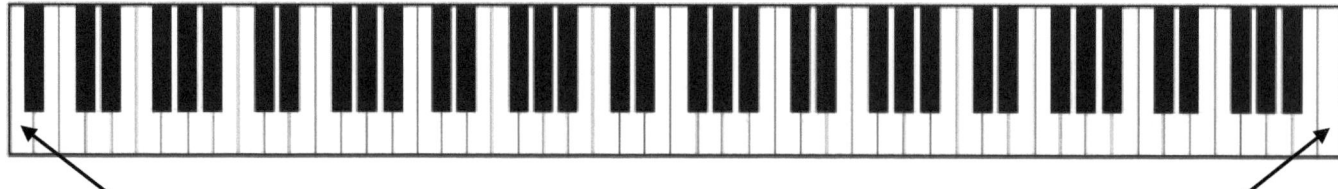

Top/bottom of the keyboard.   **Top/bottom** of the keyboard.

PITCH RECOGNITION GAME

Teacher: Place a soft object on the piano keyboard and ask student to play any key that is higher/lower than, or above/below, the object.

Specify whether student should play a black key or a white key.

REVIEW PITCH DIRECTION (CONT.)

*Draw an arrow going **up** the keyboard:*

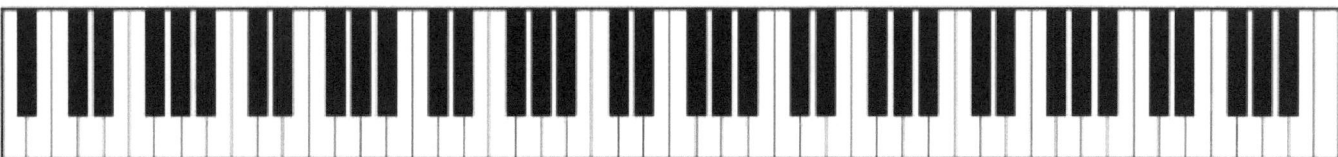

*Draw an arrow going **down** the keyboard:*

Circle one:

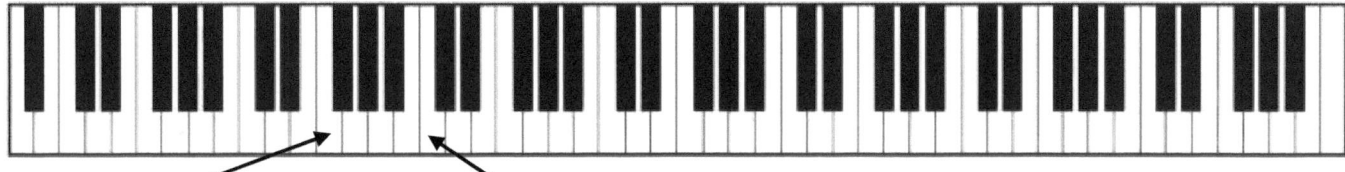

This key is **above/below** this key.

Circle one:

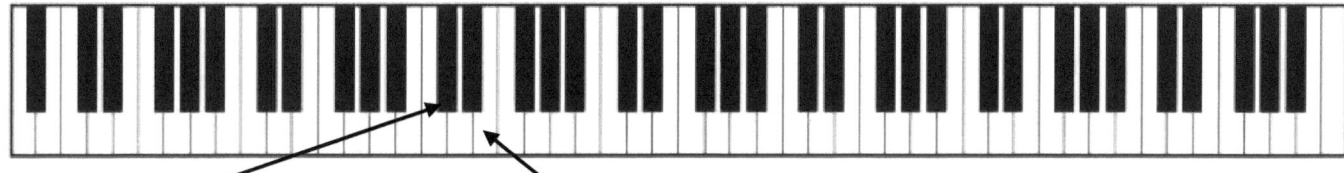

This key is **higher/lower** than this key.

Circle one:

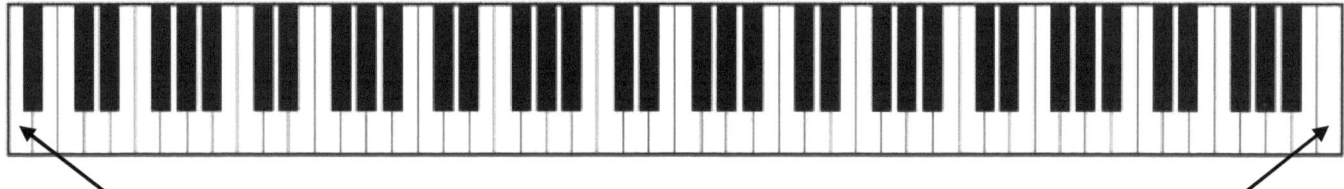

Top/bottom of the keyboard. **Top/bottom** of the keyboard.

Now let's learn to play our next song, *Hush-a-bye*. Just like *Hot Cross Buns*, play the Right Hand with your middle or tall finger only, keeping your playing finger slightly curved and tension-free (remember "ghost hands"). Play the Left Hand with your thumb and either your middle/tall finger or pinky finger.

Memorize all your songs, and sing the words as you play!

Let's learn how to play our next song: *Hush-a-bye!*

First, let's sing the song:

*"Hush-a-bye, baby,
On the tree-top,
When the wind blows,
The cradle will rock."*

Can you tell, in this song, when the pitch goes up, when it goes down, and when it stays the same?

Next, let's clap our hands to the beat as we sing the song:

{ *Hush - a - bye, ba   -   by,   On the tree - top,*
  Clap   Clap   **Clap**   Clap
  1   2   *1*   2

{ *When the wind blows,   The cra - dle will rock.*
  Clap   Clap   **Clap**   Clap
  1   2   *1*   2

Next, let's learn to play the song on the piano!

Start with your Right Hand. Use your middle or tall finger to play all the notes. Curve your finger slightly, and play on the tip of your finger.

After you learn the Right Hand, then add the Left Hand and play both hands together.

Memorize all your songs, and sing the words as you play!

Hush-A-Bye

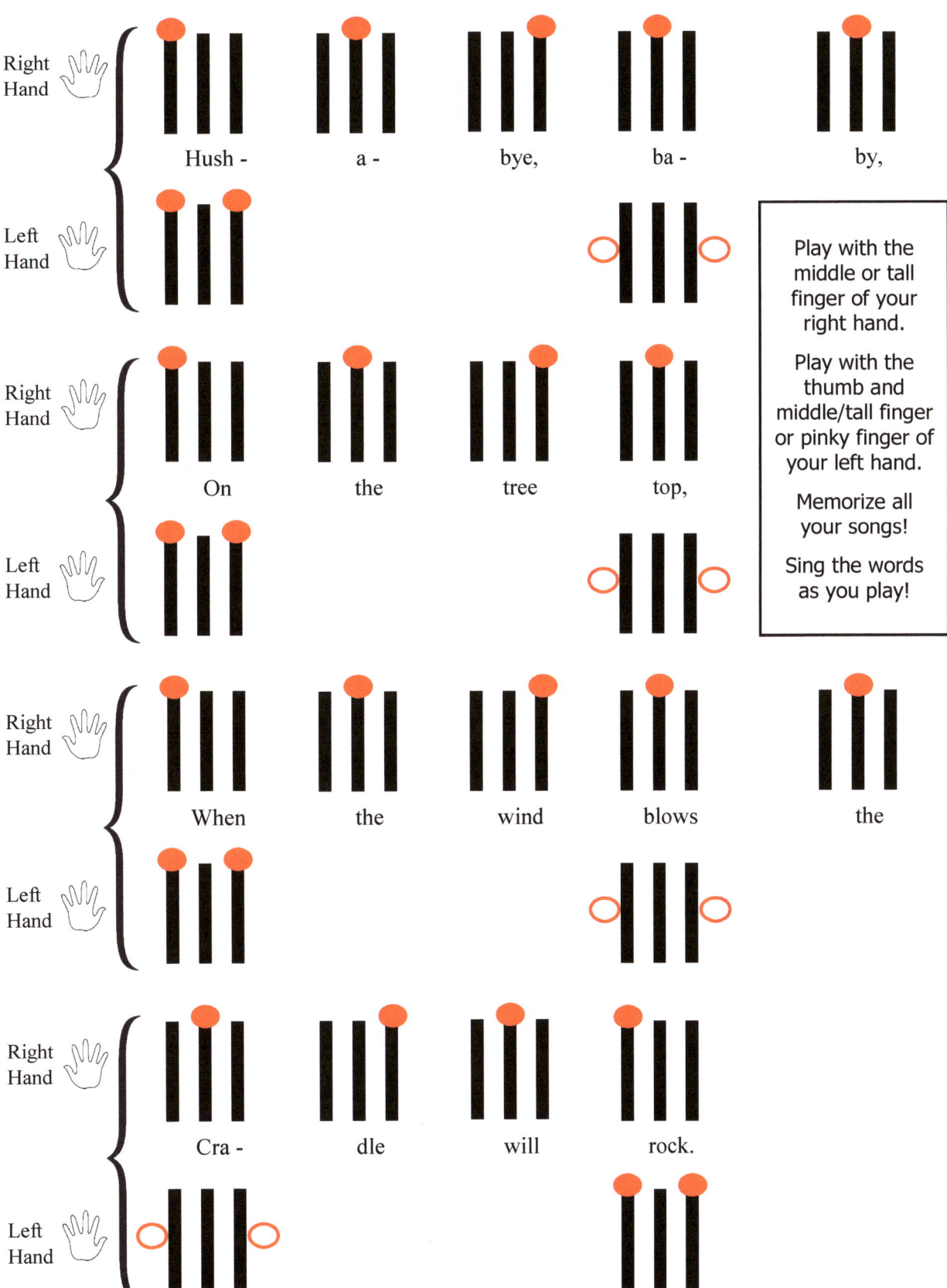

The Piano: A Brief History

Pipe Organ  Uses air blowing through pipes of different shapes and sizes to produce many different sounds and pitches.

Clavichord 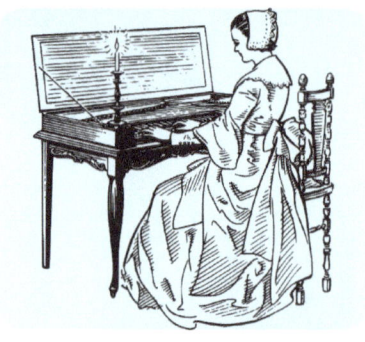 Tiny metal blades or hammers called *tangents* strike the strings. Plays very softly.

Harpsichord  Small quills pluck the strings.

Fortepiano  Hammers made out of softer material strike the strings. A soundboard increases the volume and resonance. Can play both loud and soft.

Forte means loud.   *Piano* means soft.

The Piano: A Brief History (cont.)

Piano

Modern instrument uses soft hammers to strike the strings. Uses pedals to further increase control, musicality, and resonance. Grand pianos and upright pianos of different shapes and sizes.

Electric Keyboard

Electricity produces the tone using amplification, speakers, and sometimes computer processors.

Synthesizer

Electric keyboards that can produce many sounds and special effects.

The Piano: How It Works

Keyboard
Pattern of black keys and white keys. Play these with your fingers to make sounds and patterns of sounds.

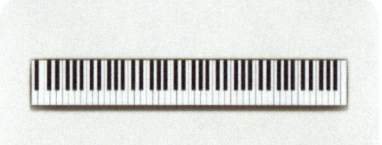
On full-size pianos there are 52 white keys and 36 black keys for a total of 88 keys (a little over seven octaves).

Hammers
Hammers strike the strings when you press the keys.

Strings
Strings produce the sound. Strings are different lengths and sizes to produce different pitches.

Dampers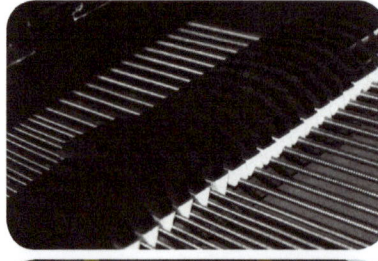
Dampers mute or stop the sound when you release the key after playing.

Soundboard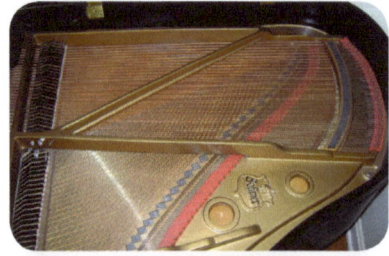
Soundboards are made of wood and increase the volume of sound and resonance.

Pedals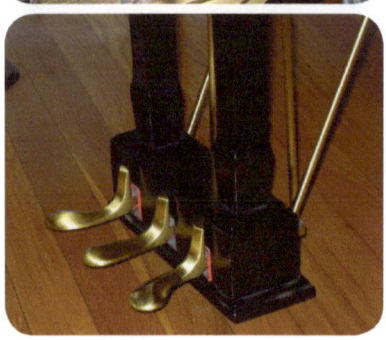
Pedals are used to sustain notes (sustain pedal, usually on the right), or to make notes softer (*una corda* or soft pedal, usually on the left).

Wow! You're Learning So Much Already!

♪ About the different kinds of pianos and keyboard instruments.

♪ How pianos evolved over time.

♪ How pianos work.

♪ Some things about good posture and piano hands.

♪ And some songs to play on the piano!

Have you looked inside a real piano?

If not, maybe your teacher or parent will help you open one up and show you what's inside! It's really cool to see!

Don't forget, memorize all your songs. One day, not too far away, you will be ready to give a piano recital for a friendly audience!

Keep up the good work!

More about Posture: Sitting at the Piano

Remember:

When we play the piano, we want our bodies, our arms and legs, our shoulders, our wrists and hands, to be *free of tension*.

Tension means tightness, which can cause discomfort, pain, and make it harder to play the piano enjoyably.

Think about good posture, sitting upright (not slouching), yet also think about remaining somewhat relaxed, loose, and tension-free.

Sit at the center of the piano. (Imagine placing your nose between the two black keys in the middle of the keyboard!)

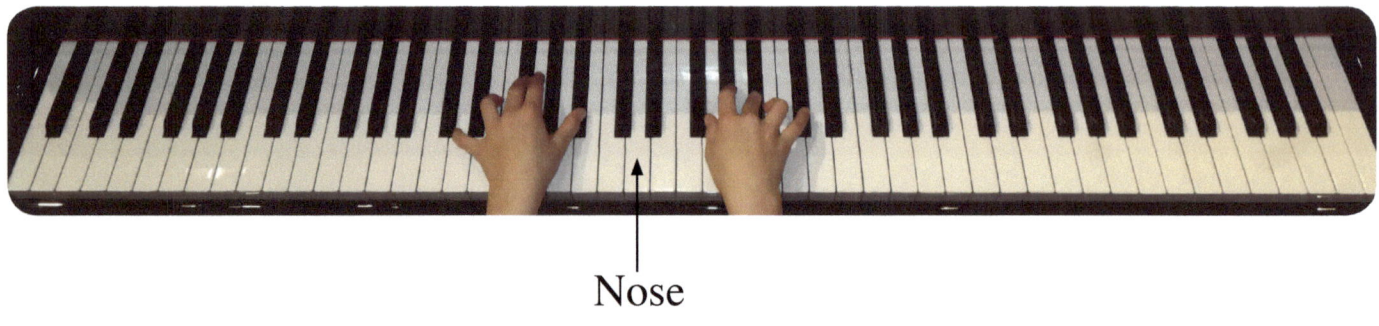

Nose

Posture: Sitting at the Piano (cont.)

Set your bench or stool at the right height so that your wrists and arms are about even with the keyboard, not too high or low.

Sit a little bit forward on your bench, toward the edge.

Keep your feet flat on the floor, or use a box, block, or bench to help you.

Hold your arms up and let your hands hang down loosely, dangling, with no tension, kind of like a ghost.

Now, when you play the piano, pivot your ghost hand wrists up just slightly as you place your fingers gently on the keys.

You are ready to play the piano, tension-free, with good sitting posture!

HANDS AND...

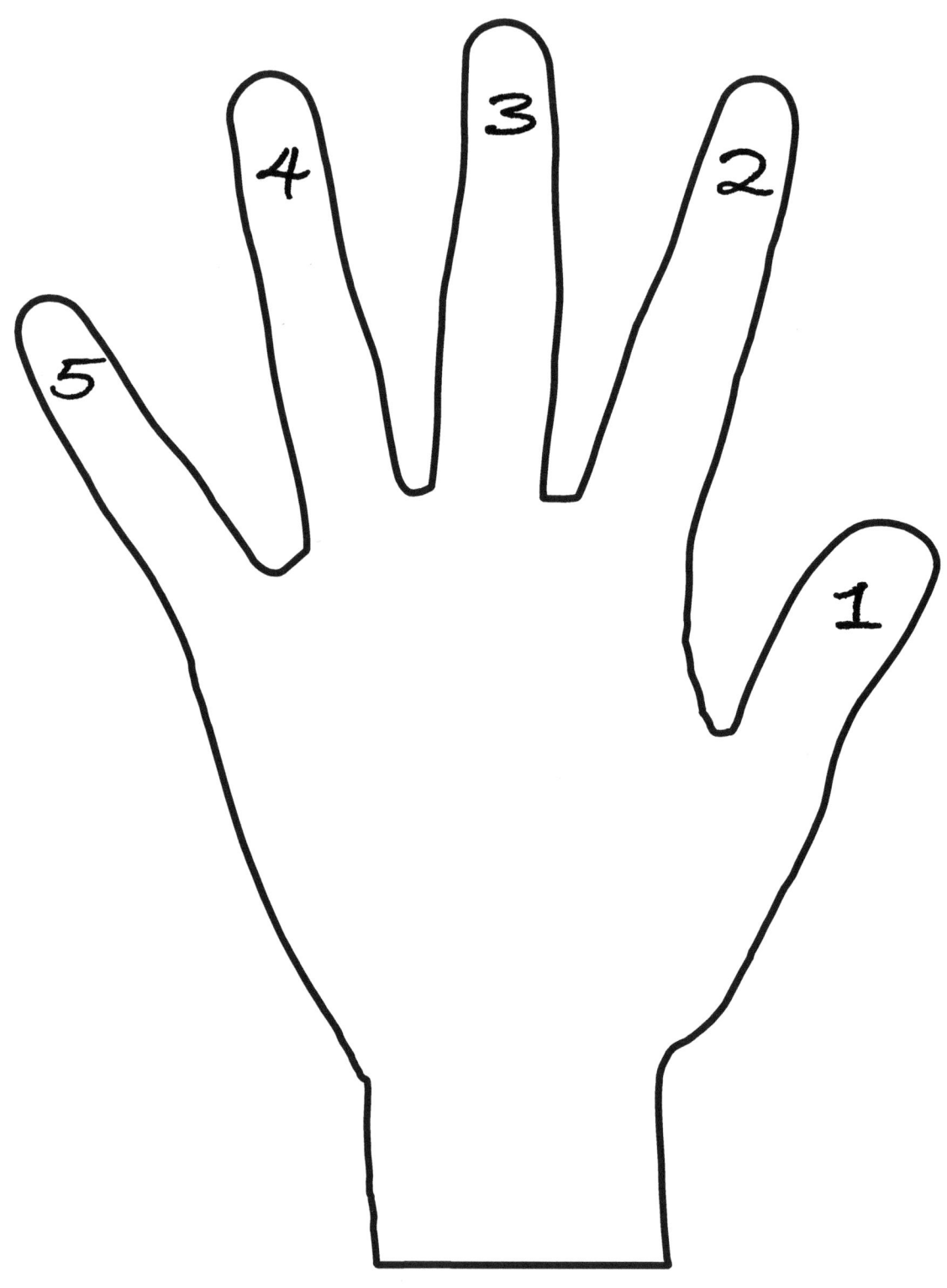

LEFT HAND (L.H.)

FINGER NUMBERS

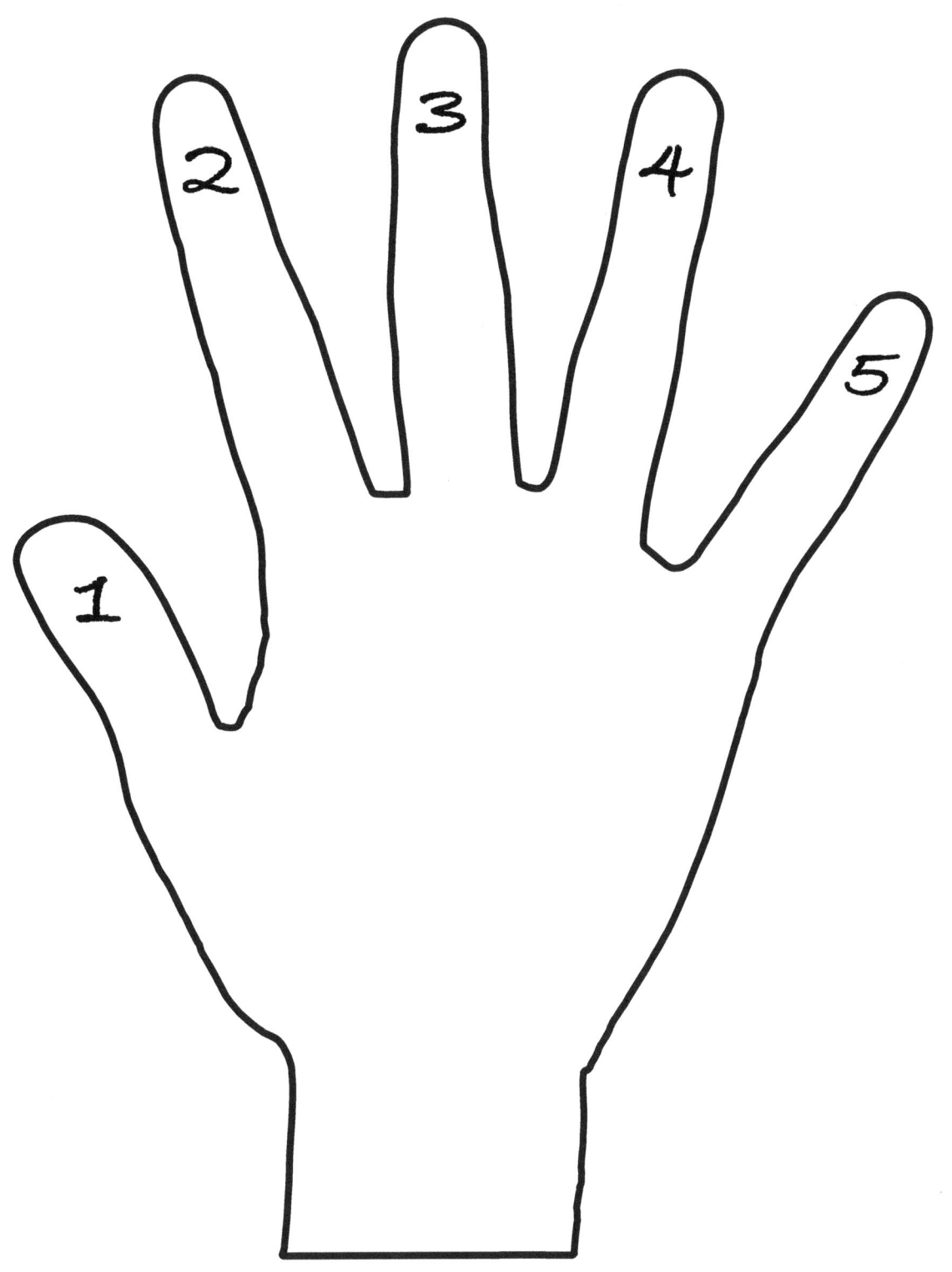

RIGHT HAND (R.H.)

DRAW YOUR HANDS, AND...

LEFT HAND (L.H.)

NUMBER YOUR FINGERS!

RIGHT HAND (R.H.)

Piano Hands and Finger Number Review

When we play the piano, we want our bodies, our arms and legs, our shoulders, our wrists and hands, to be: *(check one)*

        ___ very straight and tight

        ___ held up above our shoulders

        ___ free of tension

To have good posture at the piano means to: *(check one)*

        ___ slouch

        ___ sit upright and very stiff

        ___ sit upright, yet remain loose and tension-free

Write the finger numbers for each hand:

Now let's learn *Merrily We Roll Along*, *Mary Had a Little Lamb* (they are actually the same song with different words!), and *Go Tell Aunt Rhodie*.

For these songs, in the Right Hand, we are going to use more fingers. The finger numbers are shown on top of the note you will play.

Let's learn our next two songs: *Merrily We Roll Along* and *Mary Had a Little Lamb*

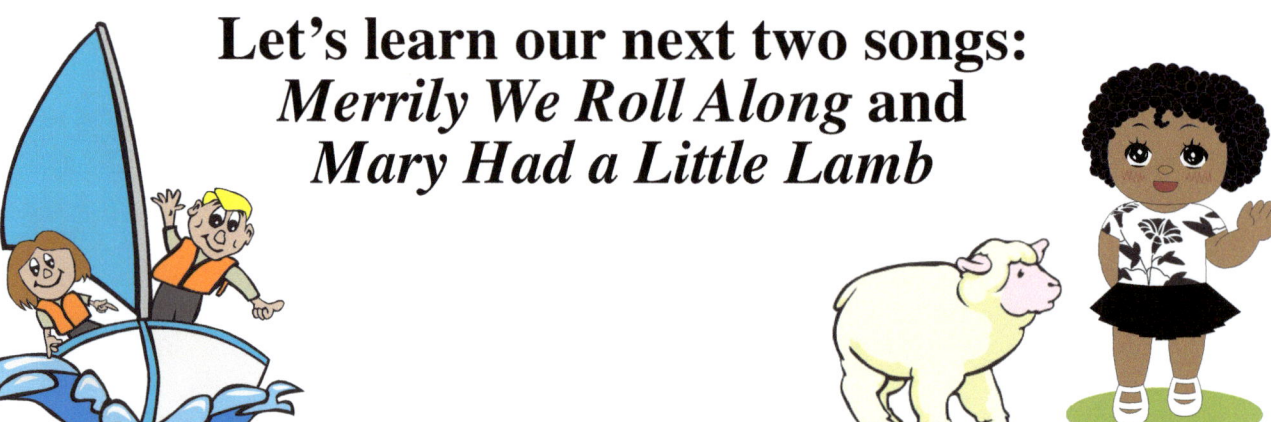

Merrily We Roll Along and *Mary Had a Little Lamb* share the same melody (pitches) but have different lyrics (words).

First, let's sing the songs:

*"Merrily we roll along, roll along, roll along,
Merrily we roll along, across the deep blue sea."*

*"Mary had a little lamb, little lamb, little lamb,
Mary had a little lamb with fleece as white as snow."*

Can you hear the same melody for both songs? Can you tell, in these songs, when the pitch goes up, when it goes down, and when it stays the same?

Next, let's clap our hands to the beat as we sing the first song:

Mer - ri - ly we	*roll a - long,*	*roll a - long,*	*roll a - long,*
Clap	Clap	Clap	Clap
1	2	3	4

Mer - ri - ly we	*roll a - long,*	*a-cross the deep*	*blue sea.*
Clap	Clap	Clap	Clap
1	2	3	4

MERRILY AND MARY (CONT.)

Now, let's clap our hands to the beat as we sing the second song:

$$\begin{cases} \textit{Ma - ry had a} & \textit{lit - tle lamb,} & \textit{lit - tle lamb,} & \textit{lit - tle lamb,} \\ \textbf{\textit{Clap}} & \textit{Clap} & \textit{Clap} & \textit{Clap} \\ \textit{1} & \textit{2} & \textit{3} & \textit{4} \end{cases}$$

$$\begin{cases} \textit{Ma - ry had a} & \textit{lit - tle lamb with,} & \textit{fleece as white as snow.} \\ \textbf{\textit{Clap}} & \textit{Clap} & \textit{Clap} & \textit{Clap} \\ \textit{1} & \textit{2} & \textit{3} & \textit{4} \end{cases}$$

Next, let's learn to play these songs on the piano!

Start with your Right Hand. This time, for these songs, we are going to use more fingers in the Right Hand. The finger numbers are shown on top of the note you will play.

For example, you will play the first note with your 3rd finger, the second note with your 2nd finger, and the third note with your 1st finger.

Curve your fingers slightly, and play on the tips of your fingers, except for your thumb. Play on the side of your thumb, near where your thumb nail meets your skin.

Remember ghost hands, and remain tension-free.

After you learn the Right Hand, then add the Left Hand and play both hands together.

Memorize all your songs, and sing the words as you play!

Merrily We Roll Along

Traditional

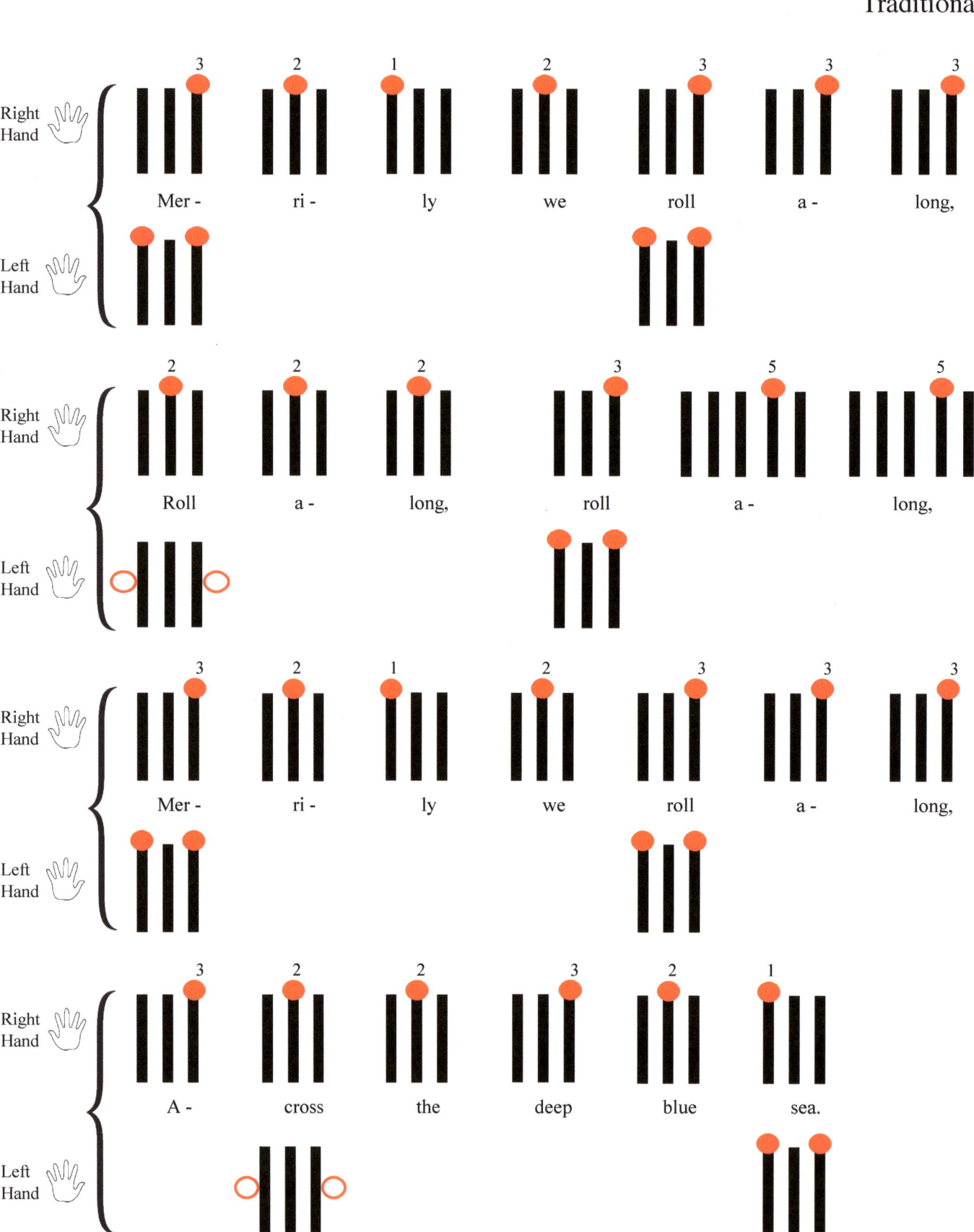

Mary Had A Little Lamb

Nursery Rhyme

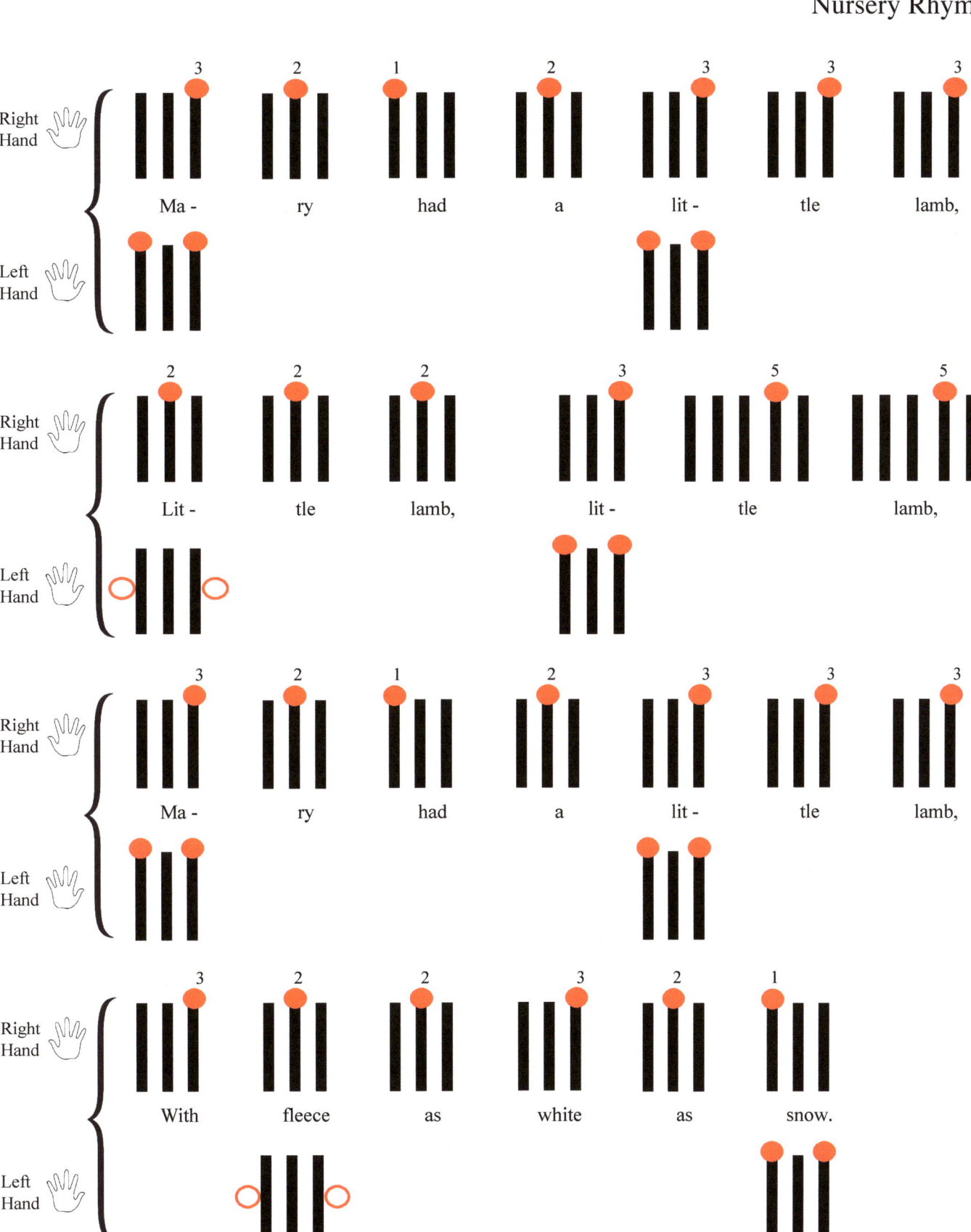

29

Let's learn our next song:
Go Tell Aunt Rhodie

First, let's sing the song:

*"Go tell Aunt Rhodie, go tell Aunt Rhodie,
Go tell Aunt Rhodie the old grey goose is gone."*

Can you tell, in this song, when the pitch goes up, when it goes down, and when it stays the same?

Next, let's clap our hands to the beat as we sing the first song:

{ *Go   tell Aunt Rho - die,   go   tell Aunt Rho - die*
Clap Clap   Clap   Clap   **Clap** Clap   Clap   Clap
1   2   3   4   *1*   2   3   4

{ *Go   tell Aunt Rho - die, the old grey goose is gone.*
Clap Clap   Clap   Clap   **Clap** Clap   Clap   Clap
1   2   3   4   *1*   2   3   4

Next, let's learn to play the song on the piano!

Start with your Right Hand. We will use all the fingers in the Right Hand. The finger numbers are shown on top of the note you will play. Remember to apply all you have been learning!

Memorize all your songs, and sing the words as you play!

Go Tell Aunt Rhodie

Traditional

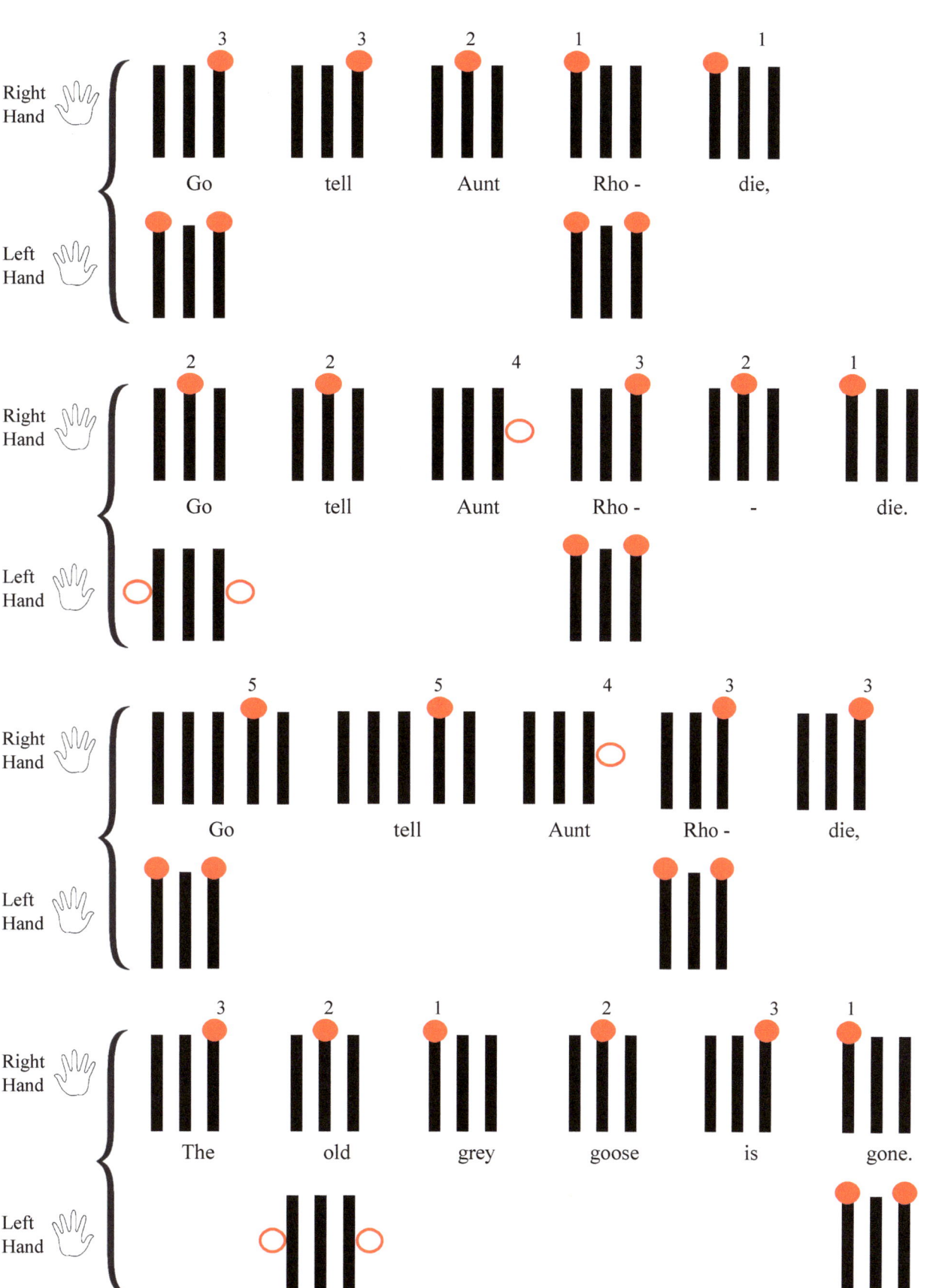

Review Part 1

*Draw an arrow going **up** the keyboard:*

*Draw an arrow going **down** the keyboard:*

Circle one:

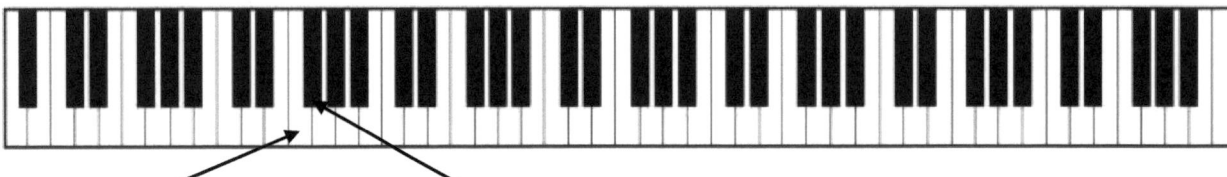

This key is **above/below** this key.

Pitch Recognition Game

Teacher: Place a soft object on the piano keyboard, and then ask the student to play any key that is higher/lower than, or above/below, the object.

Review Hands and Finger Numbers

Write the finger numbers for each hand:

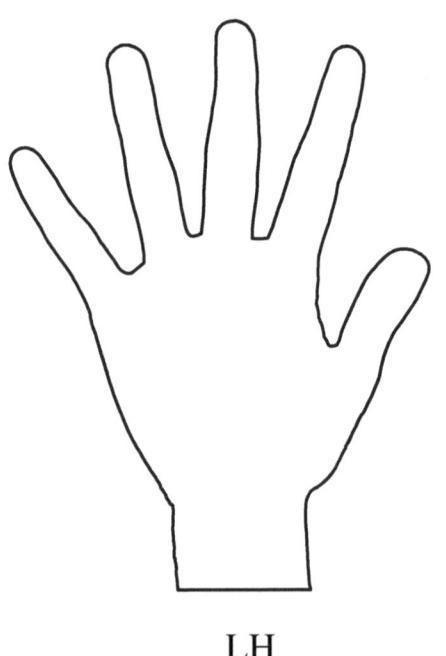
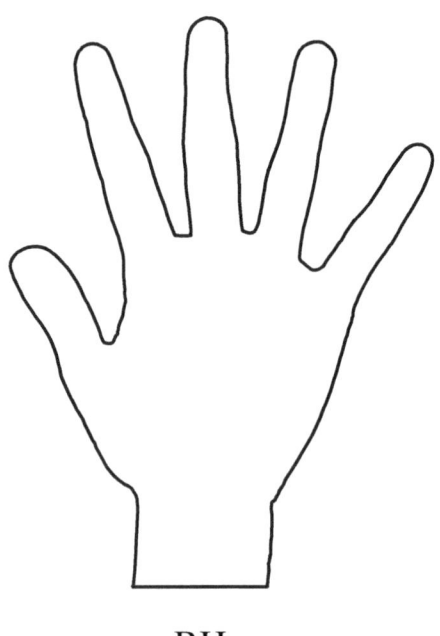

LH   RH

Good Job!

You have completed Part One

Keep Up The Good Work!

Place Sticker Here!

of your first piano lesson book!

There are three more to go...
And then you earn a prize!

THE MUSIC ALPHABET

A B C D E F G

When you reach the letter G, the music alphabet starts over again with the letter A.

A B C D E F G A B C D E F G

Can you also say it *backward*?

G F E D C B A

Going backward, when you reach the letter A, the music alphabet starts over again with the letter G.

G F E D C B A G F E D C B A

Practice forward and backward many times, until it gets easy!

MUSIC ALPHABET PRACTICE

Say the music alphabet three times going forward (or *up*):

A B C D E F G A B C D E F G A B C D E F G

(say it from memory!)

Say the music alphabet three times going backward (or *down*):

G F E D C B A G F E D C B A G F E D C B A

(say it from memory!)

Fill in the blanks (going forward or up):

A B C __ E F __

A __ __ D __ __ G

A __ C __ E __ G

__ B C __ __ F __

Fill in the blanks (going backward or down):

G F E __ C B __

G __ __ D __ __ A

G __ E __ C __ A

__ F E __ __ B __

Teacher: Ask student, "What letter comes after _____?"

Teacher: Ask student, "What letter before before _____?"

(Drill this way many times until it gets easy!)

MORE MUSIC ALPHABET PRACTICE

Fill in the blanks (going forward or up):

A __ C __ E __ G __ B __ D __ F __ A __ C __ E __ G
A __ __ D E __ __ A B __ __ E F __ __ B C __ __ F G
__ __ __ D __ __ __ A __ __ __ E __ __ __ B __ __ __ F __

Fill in the blanks (going backward or down):

G __ E __ C __ A __ F __ D __ B __ G __ E __ C __ A
G __ __ D C __ __ G F __ __ C B __ __ F E __ __ B A
__ __ __ D __ __ __ G __ __ __ C __ __ __ F __ __ __ B __

What letter comes after A? ____   What letter comes after C? ____

What letter comes after F? ____   What letter comes after G? ____

What letter comes before G? ____   What letter comes before E? ____

What letter comes before B? ____   What letter comes before A? ____

What letter comes after B? ____   What letter comes before F? ____

What letter comes after D? ____   What letter comes before C? ____

What letter comes after E? ____   What letter comes before D? ____

The Music Alphabet and the Piano Keyboard

The *black keys* and *white keys* of the piano keyboard are arranged in specific patterns and have specific shapes.

Black Keys: groups of two keys or three keys, alternating. (There is one exception at the very bottom of most piano keyboards, where there is just one black key.)

White Keys: have different shapes and positions next to the black keys and to each other.

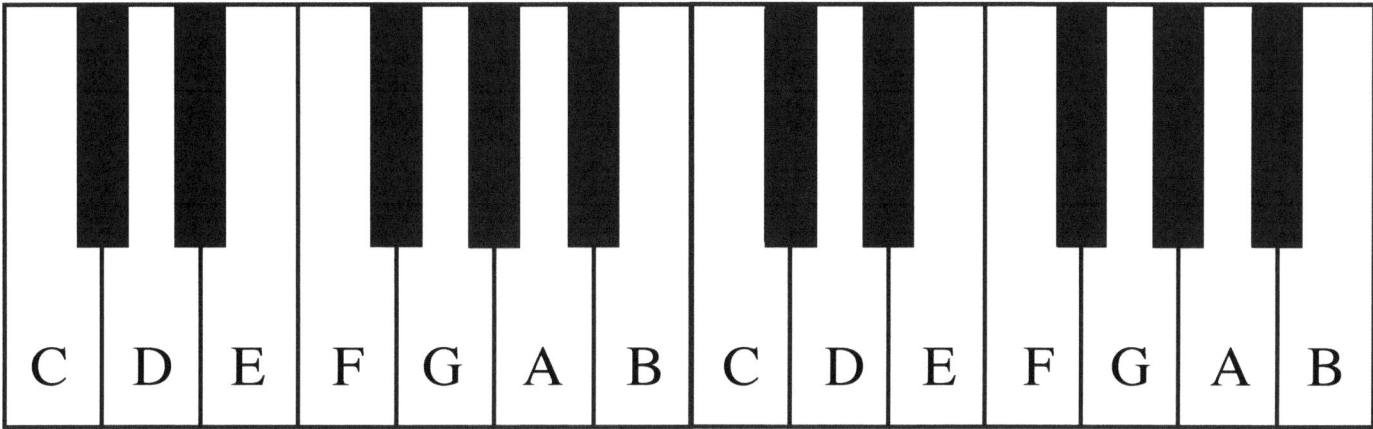

The white keys are named using the music alphabet.

White keys of the same letter name have the same shape. So, all the A's look alike, and all the B's look alike, C's, etc.

On most pianos, the lowest note on the keyboard is A. The music alphabet repeats, A B C D E F G, all the way up the white keys of the piano keyboard, usually ending with a C at the very top.

An *octave* is the distance between two of the same note. For example, A to the next A is an octave. C to the next C is an octave.

IDENTIFYING NOTES ON THE PIANO KEYBOARD

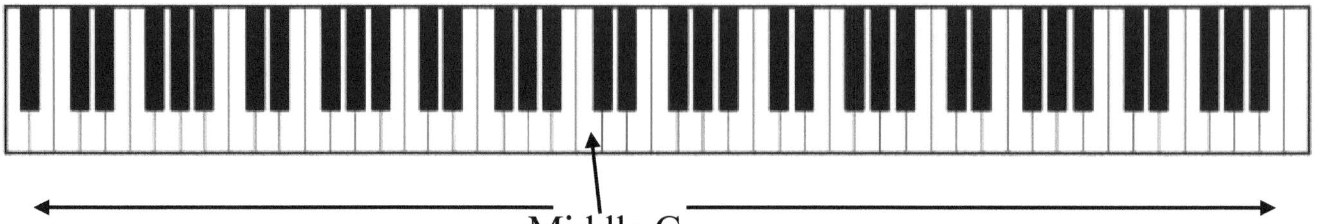

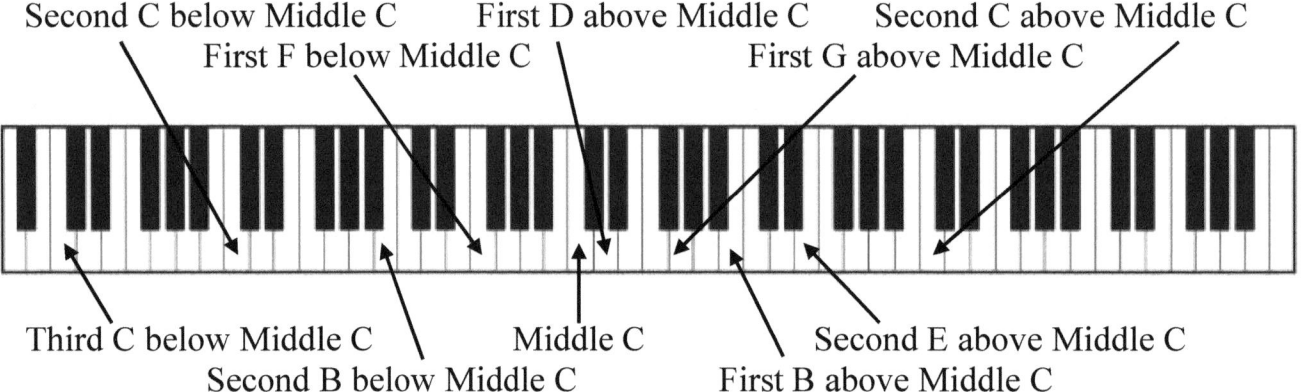

Notes lower than (or below) Middle C

Notes higher than (or above) Middle C

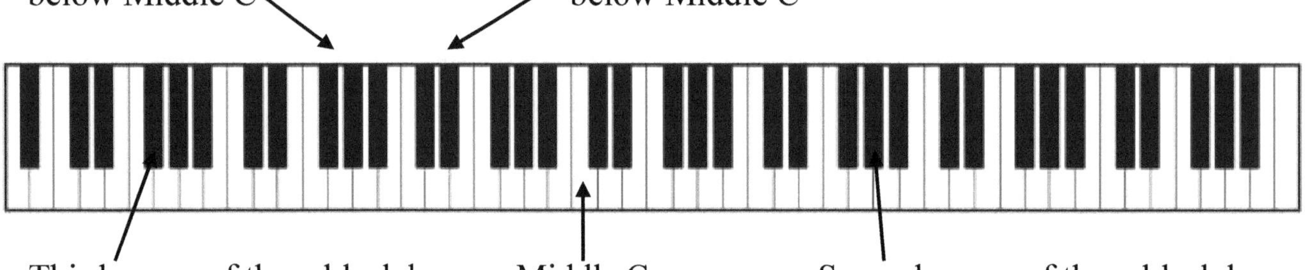

Second group of three black keys below Middle C

First group of two black keys below Middle C

Third group of three black keys below Middle C

Middle C

Second group of three black keys above Middle C

Second C below Middle C
First F below Middle C
First D above Middle C
Second C above Middle C
First G above Middle C

Third C below Middle C
Second B below Middle C
Middle C
First B above Middle C
Second E above Middle C

PRACTICE

Teacher: *Point to a set of black keys on the piano keyboard.*
Student: *Name the location of those notes, relative to Middle C (direction and distance).*

Identifying Notes on the Piano Keyboard Practice

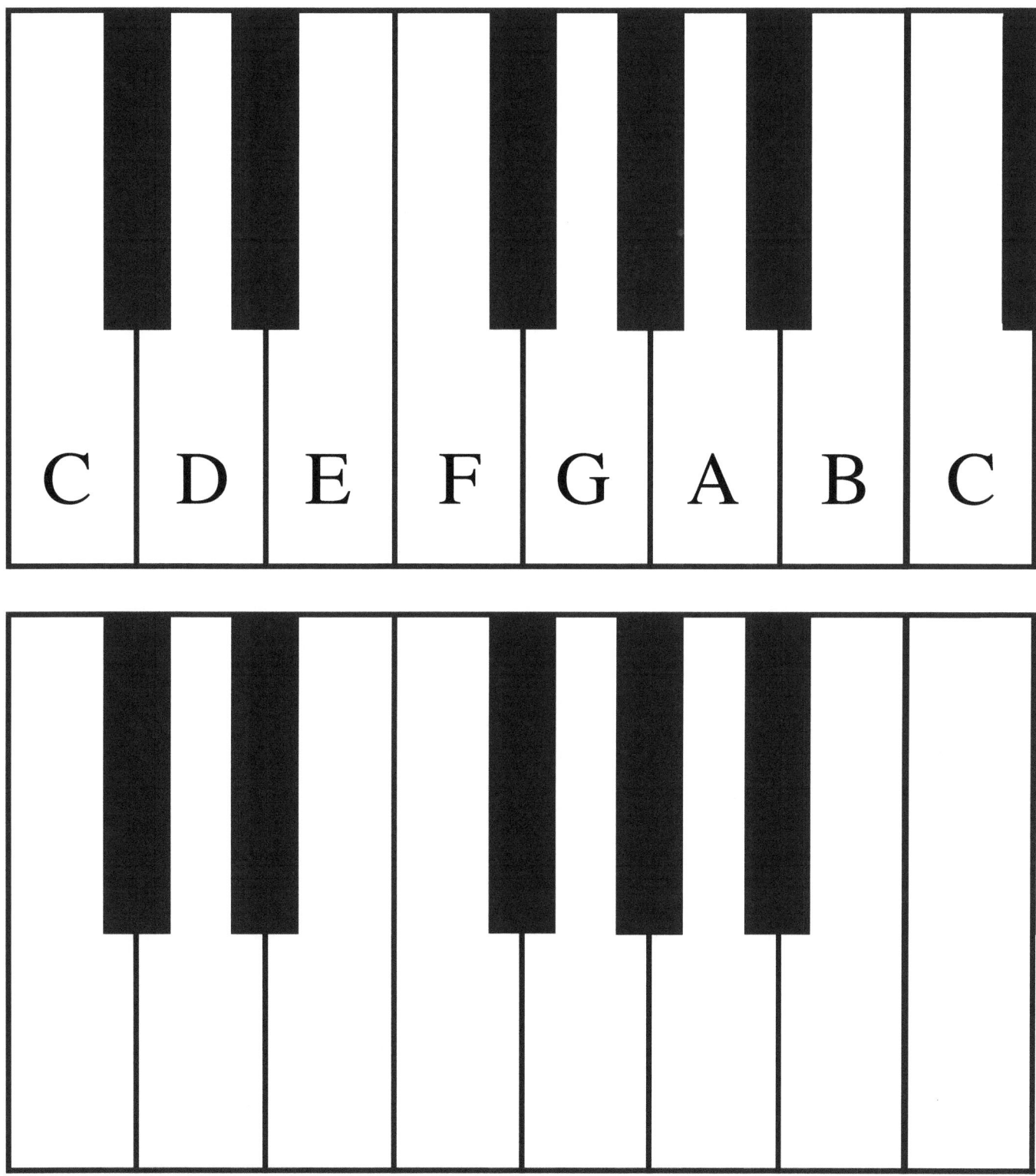

Write the letter names of the notes above.

IDENTIFYING NOTES ON THE PIANO KEYBOARD PRACTICE

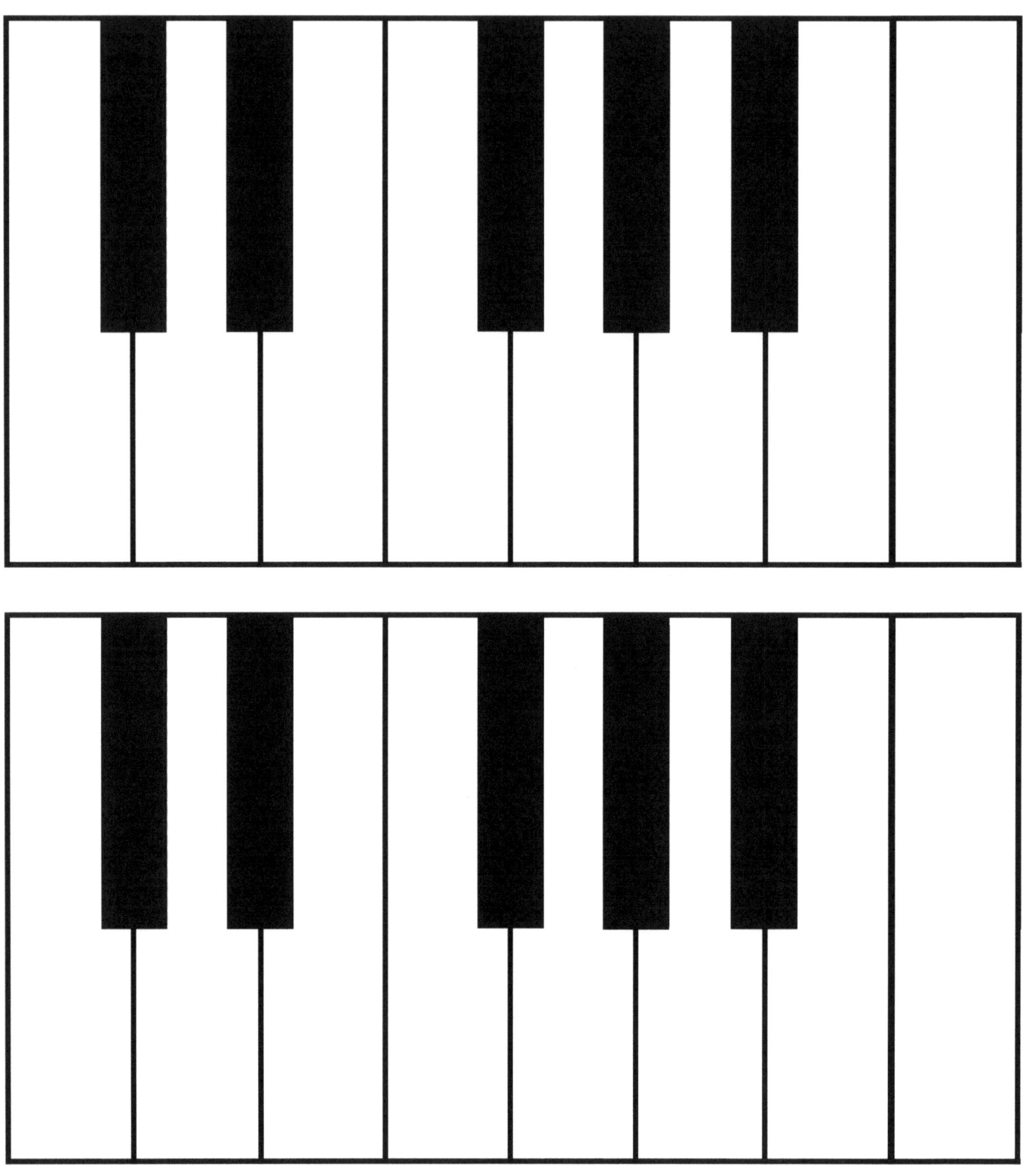

Write the letter names of the notes above.

IDENTIFYING NOTES ON THE PIANO KEYBOARD PRACTICE

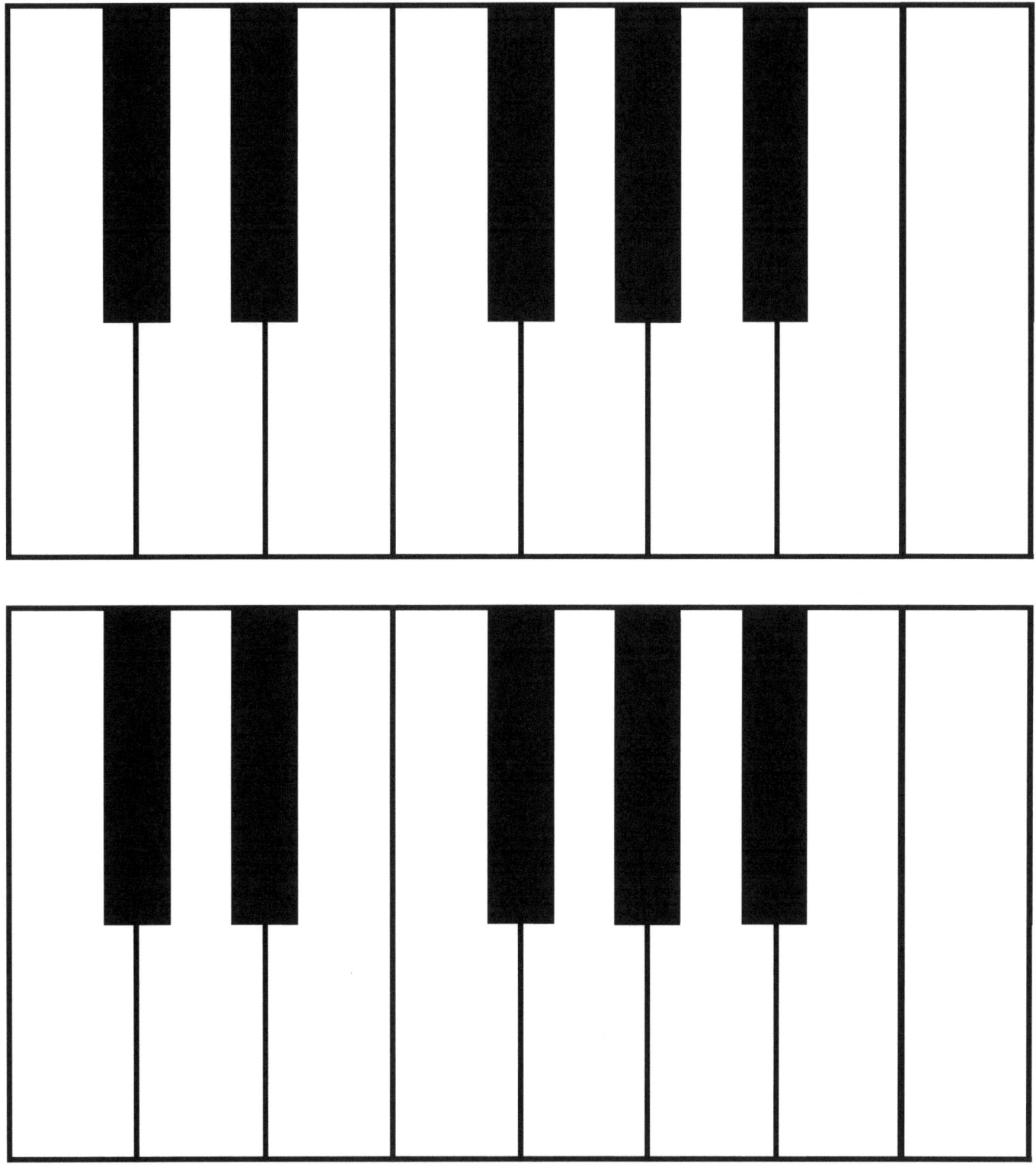

Write the letter names of the notes above.

Identifying Notes on the Piano Keyboard Practice

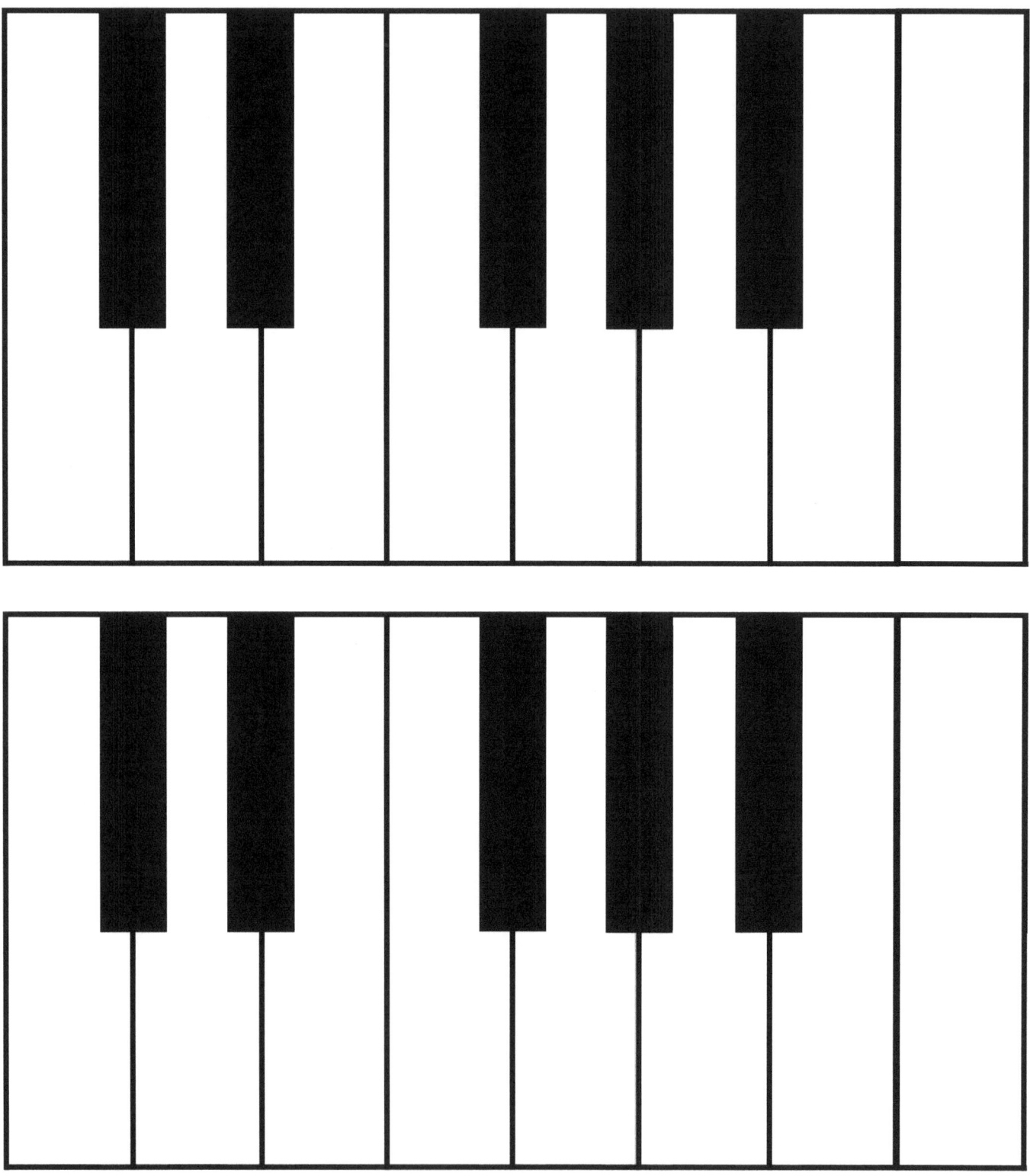

Write the letter names of the notes above.

MUSIC ALPHABET AND PIANO KEYBOARD PRACTICE

Write the music alphabet (going forward or up):

A __ __ D __ __ __ __ __ __ E __ __ __ B __ __ __ __ __

A __ __ __ __ __ __ B __ __ __ __ __ __ __ __ E __ __

Write the music alphabet (going backward or down):

G __ __ __ C __ __ __ F __ __ __ __ __ __ __ E __ __ __ __

G __ __ __ __ __ __ __ E __ __ __ __ __ __ __ C __ __

What letter comes after B? ____   What letter comes after F? ____

What letter comes before C? ____   What letter comes before A? ____

What letter comes after G? ____   What letter comes before E? ____

On your piano keyboard, play the following:

    ___ Middle C
    ___ The first C above Middle C
    ___ The first C below Middle C
    ___ The first G above Middle C
    ___ The first F below Middle C
    ___ The second E above Middle C
    ___ The second A below Middle C

The lowest note on your piano keyboard is ___.
The highest note on your piano keyboard is ___.

The distance between two of the same notes (such as F to F, or G to G), is called an _____.

Let's learn *Twinkle Twinkle Little Star!*

We'll apply the concepts you have been learning.

Here are some things to remember and keep in mind: The song will be played starting on Middle C, and then all the rest of the notes will be played in the first octave above Middle C, like this:

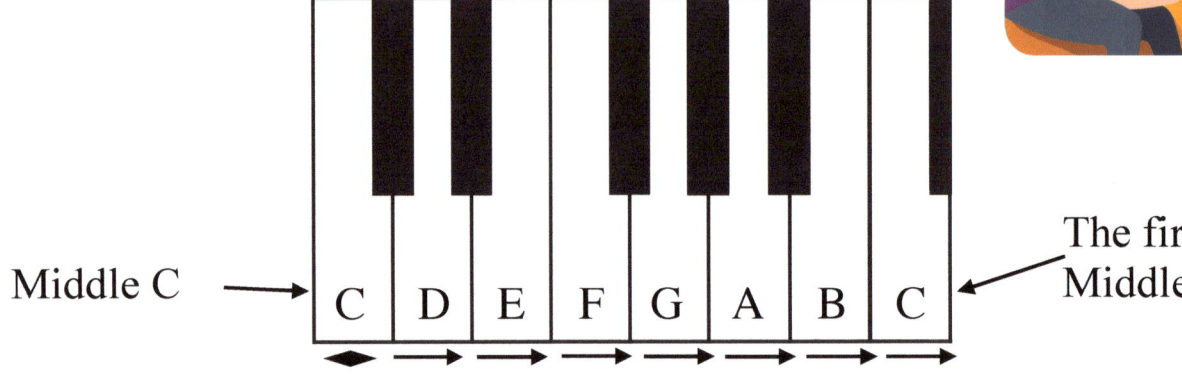

To show Middle C, we'll use a diamond shape: ◆

To show the other notes, we'll use an arrow going up (to the right), like this: ⟶ So, you'll play the first D above Middle C, the first E above Middle C, the first F above Middle C, and so forth.

Before you begin, sing and clap the song with your teacher!

When ready to play, use finger number 3 for all the notes of this song. (Remember, your 3rd finger is your middle or tall finger!)

Alternate between your Left Hand (LH) and Right Hand (RH), starting with your left hand on Middle C. Cross over your hands, gracefully, when necessary.

Don't forget ghost hands! Play on the tips of your fingers!

Memorize all your songs, and sing the words as you play!

TWINKLE TWINKLE LITTLE STAR

French Folk Tune and Children's Song

Start on Middle C with your left hand, 3rd finger.

LH 3		RH 3		*(cross over)* LH 3		*(cross over)* RH 3
C Twin-	**C** kle,	**G** twin-	**G** kle,	**A** lit-	**A** tle	**G** star,

LH 3		RH 3		LH 3		RH 3
F How	**F** I	**E** won-	**E** der	**D** what	**D** you	**C** are.

LH 3		RH 3		LH 3		RH 3
G Up	**G** a-	**F** bove	**F** the	**E** world	**E** so	**D** high,

LH 3		RH 3		LH 3		RH 3
G Like	**G** a	**F** dia-	**F** mond	**E** in	**E** the	**D** sky.

LH 3		RH 3		LH 3		RH 3
C Twin-	**C** kle,	**G** twin-	**G** kle,	**A** lit-	**A** tle	**G** star,

LH 3		RH 3		LH 3		RH 3
F How	**F** I	**E** won-	**E** der	**D** what	**D** you	**C** are.

Did You Know?

The melody of *Twinkle Twinkle Little Star* is also the melody of several other songs!

Baa Baa Black Sheep
Pease Porridge Hot
The ABC Song

See if you can play the melody you learned for *Twinkle Twinkle Little Star* while singing the words to these other songs. Adapt the number of notes in the song, as necessary, to match the words and syllables of the new songs.

BAA BAA BLACK SHEEP

Baa, Baa, black sheep, have you any wool? Yes, sir! Yes, sir! Three bags full.
One for my master, and one for my dame, and One for the little boy who lives in the lane.
Baa, Baa, black sheep, have you any wool? Yes, sir! Yes, sir! Three bags full.

PEASE PORRIDGE HOT

Pease porridge hot, pease porridge cold,
Pease porridge in the pot, nine days old.

THE ABC SONG

A B C D E F G   H I J K L M N O P   Q R S   T U V   W, X, Y and Z.
Now I know my A B C's, next time won't you sing with me!

For more fun, see if you can play and sing *The ABC Song*, <u>backward</u>!

THE ABC SONG – BACKWARD

Z Y X W V U T   S R Q P O N M   L K J   I H G   F E D   C B A.
Me with sing you won't time next, C's B A my know I now!

WOLFGANG AMADEUS MOZART

In 1782, Wolfgang Amadeus Mozart wrote a composition for piano based on this same melody. In fact, the melody originated in France, and came from a popular folk song called, *Ah, vous dirai-je Maman*.

Mozart called his piano piece, *12 Variations on the Theme, 'Ah, vous dirai-je Maman.'*

Listen to a recording of this piece. It is something you may wish to play on the piano someday!

Introduction to Music Notation

Music Notation are the words, symbols, numbers, and diagrams we use to write music down on paper, or in a computer software program, so that other musicians can sing or play it.

Music Notation Vocabulary

Composer – the person who invents a song or piece of music and writes it down so that other people can sing the song or play the piece of music on an instrument.

Composition – the music that a composer writes.

Publisher – the person or company who prints the music the composer has written down (composition) so that it can be reproduced many times for performers, students and teachers to purchase, use, learn, sing, and play.

Sheet Music or Music Score – the paper on which the publisher prints the music, which is sometimes an individual song or piece, and sometimes a book of songs or pieces.

Music Notation – the words, symbols and diagrams used by the composer to write the music down on paper.

Lyrics – the words of a song.

(Lyrics are often written on the music score along with the music notation. In piano music, lyrics are often positioned in the middle, with the right hand on the top line, above the lyrics, and the left hand on the bottom line, below the lyrics.)

The next few pages contain examples of different types of music notation and music scores, including notation from traditional Western culture, past and present, contemporary music, avant garde, and other styles, cultures, and historical periods, such as Greek, Indian, and Indonesian.

We have been using some pictorial types of music notation in this lesson book to help you learn how to play the piano. We are working toward understanding standard Western music notation.

MUSIC NOTATION EXAMPLES

Traditional Western music notation.

Early beginnings of Western music: Gregorian chant.

Music Notation Examples (cont.)

Ancient Sumer hymn drawings.

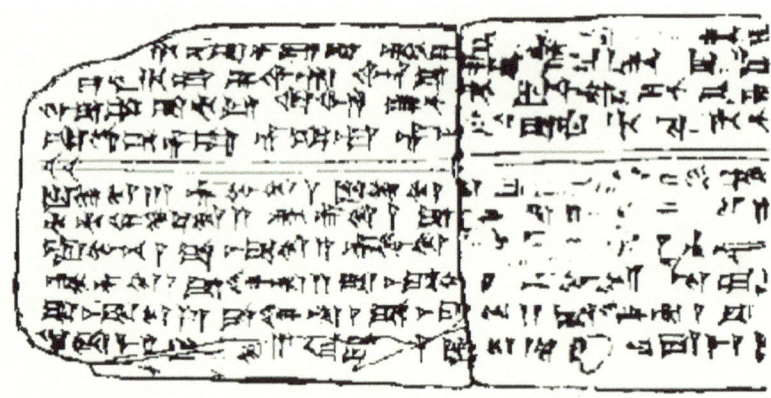

Ancient Byzantine

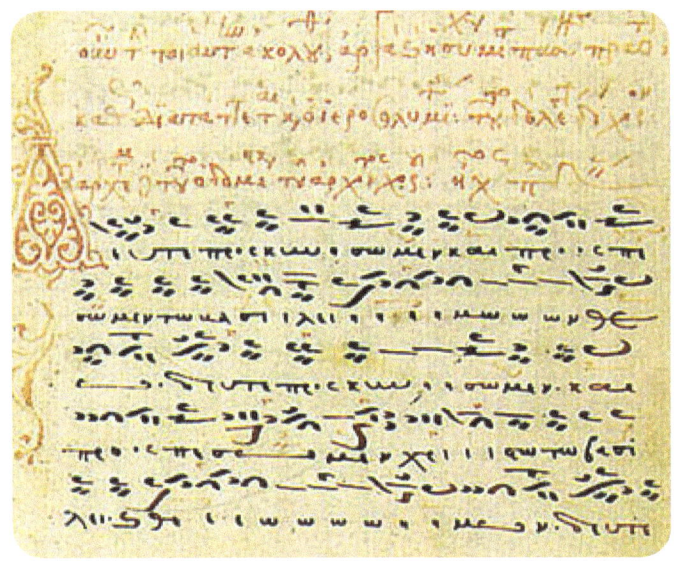

Ancient Greek

Indian

MUSIC NOTATION EXAMPLES (CONT.)

Examples of Avant Garde and Graphic Scores:

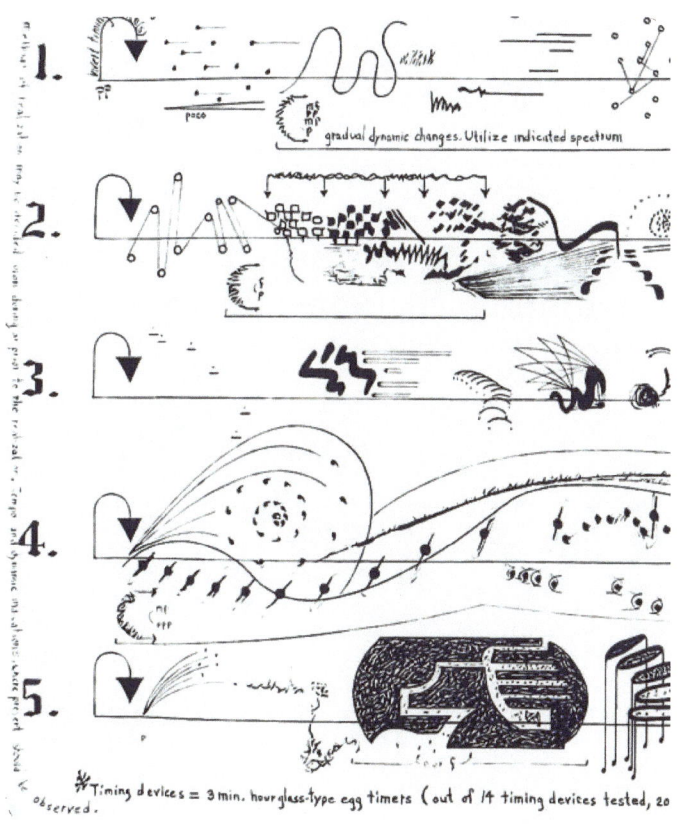

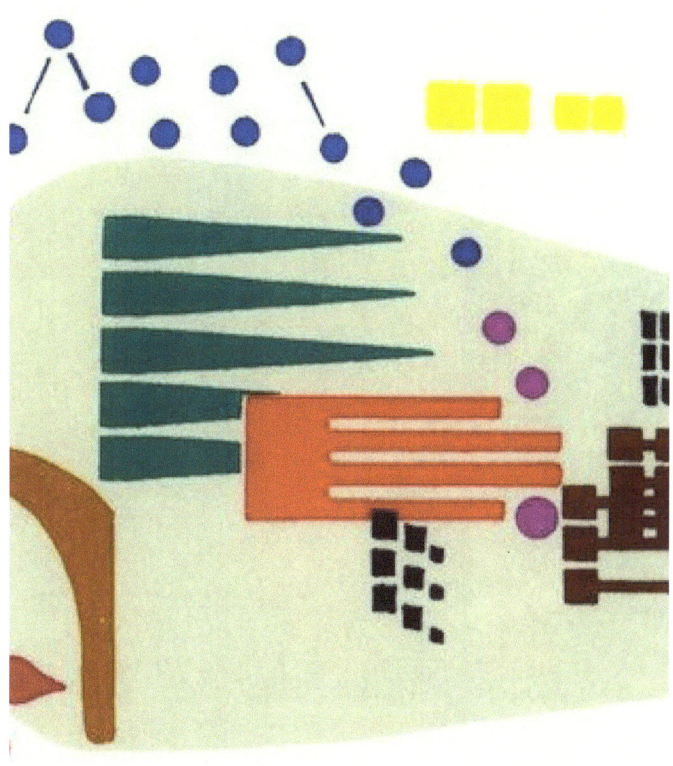

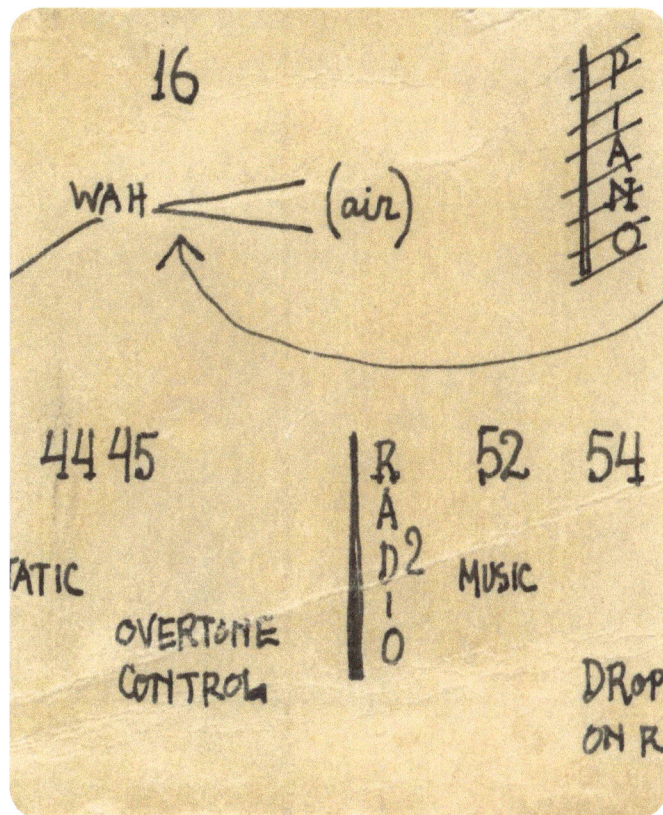

Let's learn the *Cuckoo Song!*

We'll apply the concepts you have been learning.

Here are some things to remember and keep in mind:

The song will be played all up and down the piano, using notes below Middle C and notes above Middle C. Some of the notes will be very high on the keyboard! Like this:

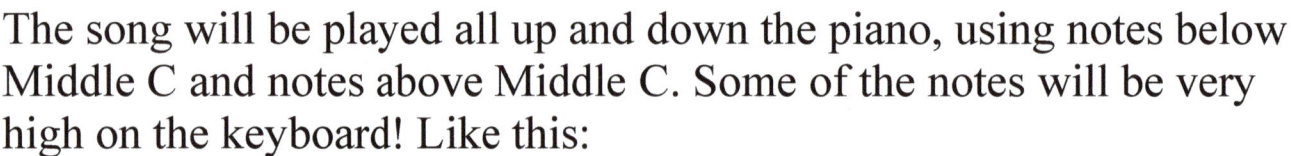

To show Middle C, we'll use a diamond shape: ◆

To show the other notes, we'll use arrows going up (to the right), or down (to the left), like this:

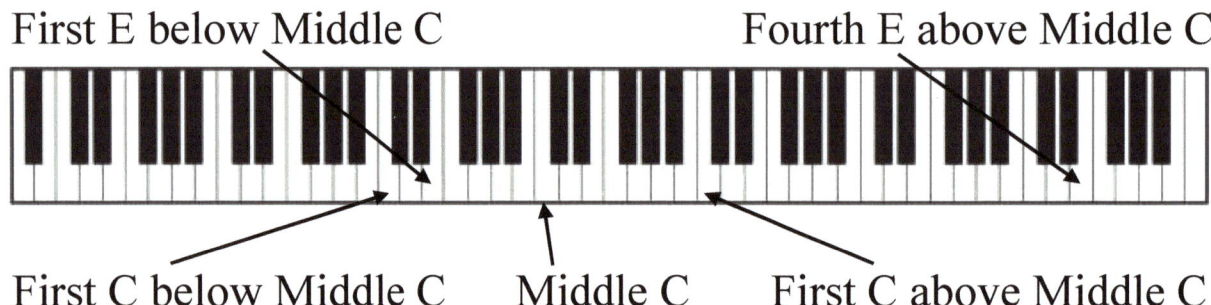

Use the hand and finger numbers that are written above each note. The song starts with the Right Hand on the first E below Middle C, and then the Left Hand plays the first C below Middle C. And then you work your way up the piano keyboard!

Don't forget ghost hands!

Memorize all your songs, and sing the words as you play!

THE CUCKOO SONG

Ruth Stevenson Alling

RH	LH	RH	LH	RH	LH	RH	LH
3	3	3	3	3	3	3	3
E	C	E	C	E	C	E	C
Cuc -	koo!	Cuc -	koo!	Cuc -	koo!	Cuc -	koo!

RH (only)

1	2	3	4	5
C	D	E	F	G
Sings	the	bird	all	day.

RH	LH	RH	LH	RH	LH	RH	LH
3	3	3	3	3	3	3	3
E	C	E	C	E	C	E	C
Cuc -	koo!	Cuc -	koo!	Cuc -	koo!	Cuc -	koo!

RH (only)

1	2	3	2	1
C	D	E	D	C
Hear	it	far	a -	way.

RH	LH
3	3
E	C
Cuc -	koo!

Let's learn *Hooray!*

We'll apply the concepts you have been learning.

Here are some things to remember and keep in mind:

The song will be played all over the piano, using notes below Middle C and notes above Middle C. Some of the notes will be very high on the keyboard! Like this:

First D below Middle C   Third D above Middle C

Second G below Middle C   Middle C   First D above Middle C

To show Middle C, we'll use a diamond shape: ◆

To show the other notes, we'll use arrows going up (to the right), or down (to the left), like this:

First above Middle C →
First below Middle C ←
Second above Middle C ⇒
Third above Middle C ≡▶
Third below Middle C ≡▶

Use the hand and finger numbers that are written above each note. The song starts with the Left Hand on the second G below Middle C, and then the Right Hand plays the first D below Middle C. And then you work your way up the piano keyboard!

Don't forget ghost hands!

Memorize all your songs, and sing the words as you play!

HOORAY!

Dennis Frayne

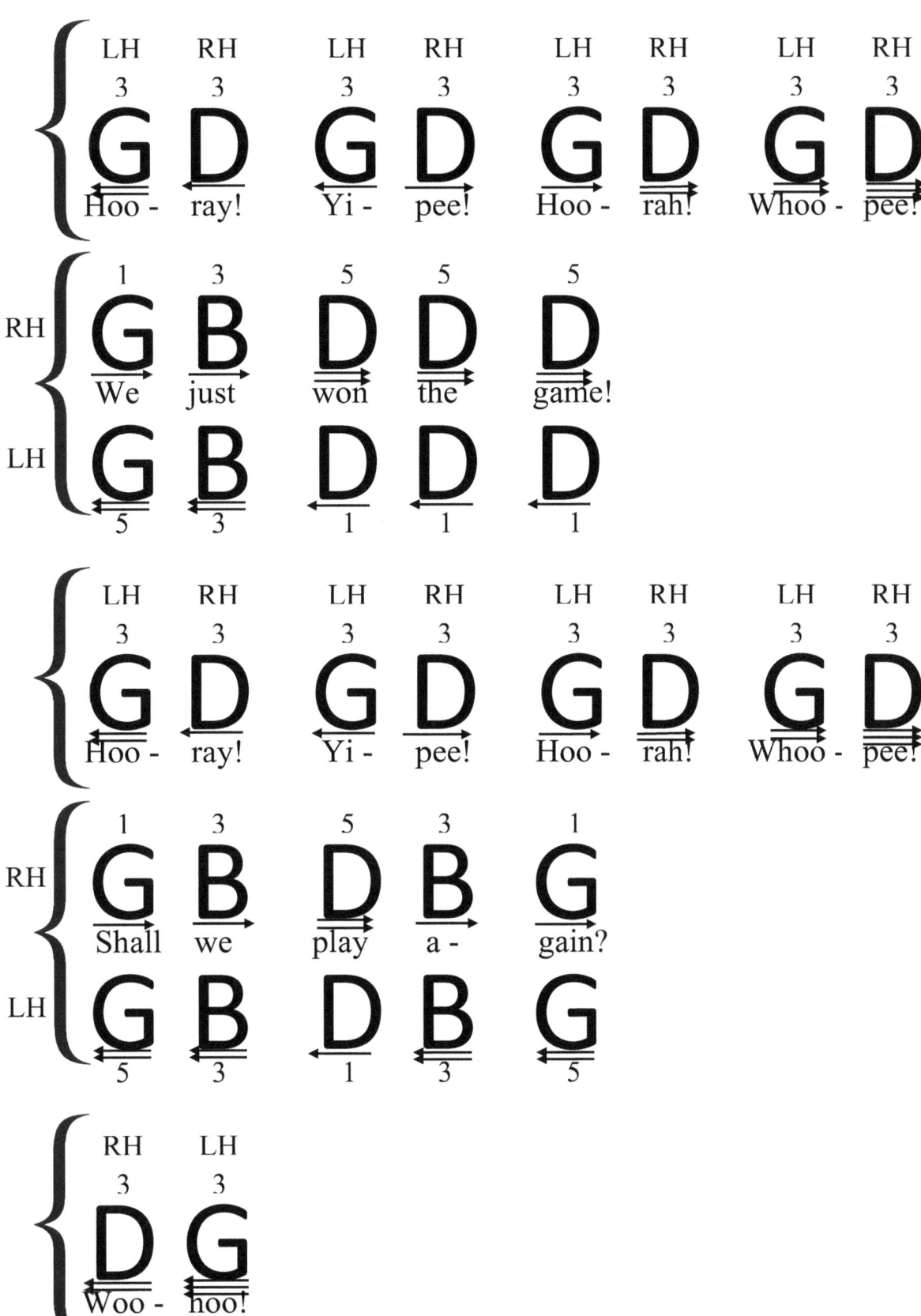

PIANO KEYBOARD AND IDENTIFYING NOTES PRACTICE

Write in the letter names for the white keys:

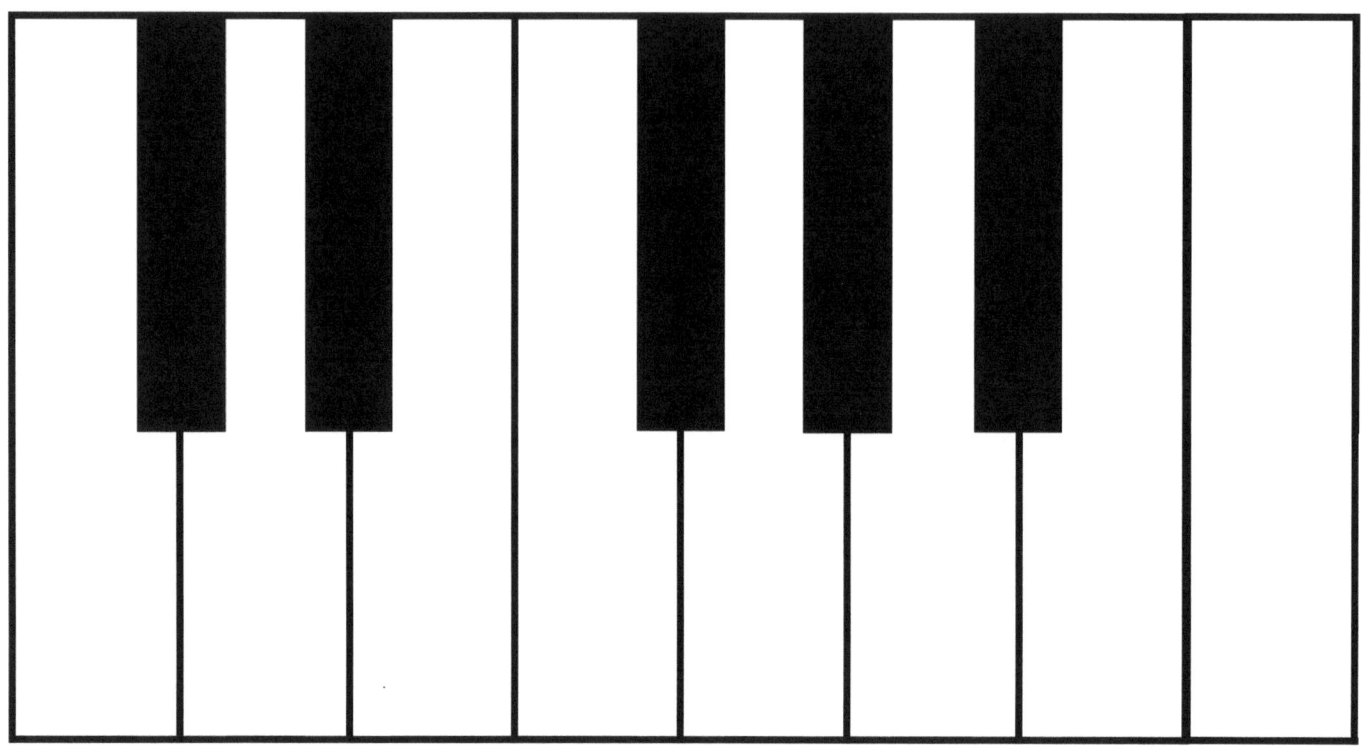

Draw an arrow to the following keys:

The first F below Middle C   The first G above Middle C

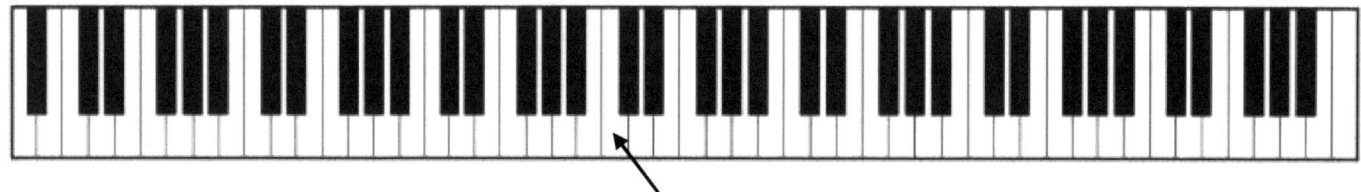

Middle C

The second G below Middle C   The third C above Middle C

Play each A on your piano keyboard, going from the bottom, up.
Play each C on your piano keyboard, going from the top, down.

PIANO KEYBOARD AND IDENTIFYING NOTES PRACTICE (CONT.)

Write in the letter names for the white keys:

Draw an arrow to the following keys:

The first D below Middle C The first B above Middle C

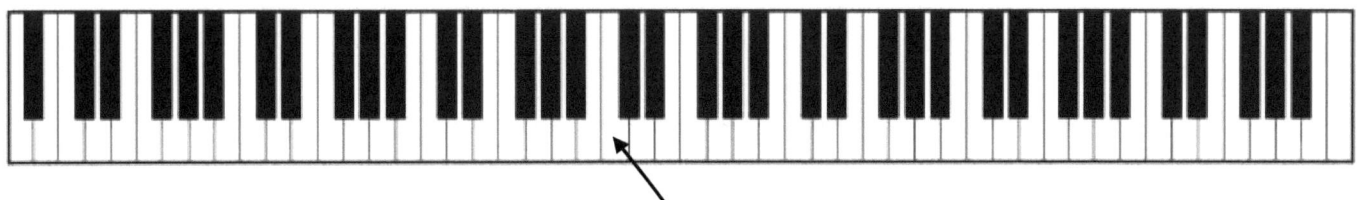

Middle C

The third C below Middle C The fourth A above Middle C

Play each F on your piano keyboard, going from the bottom, up.
Play each G on your piano keyboard, going from the top, down.

SCALES, KEYS, AND MODES

In music, we have different *scales* so we can compose and perform music in different *modes* and in different *keys*.

We compose music in different *modes* because we want the music to sound a certain way, and in different *keys* because we want the music to go up and down over a certain range (how high is the highest note, and how low is the lowest note).

Here are some examples of several scales or modes:

Do, Re, Mi, and so forth, is called **Solfege**, or **Solfeggio**.

Play and sing the scales, going forward and backward! (See the following page for correct finger numbers.) As you learn your scales, it will be beneficial to your ear training progress if you practice playing the scales while singing, both using the letter names and the solfege syllables.

Listen to the *Do Re Mi* song in the memorable scene from Rodgers and Hammerstein's *The Sound of Music*.

SCALES, KEYS, AND MODES (CONT.)

Play the *C Major* and *A Minor* scales on the piano, using the fingerings indicated. Start with the Right Hand on Middle C for C Major, and on the first A below middle C for A Minor, and the Left Hand one octave below.

Remember, an *octave* is the distance between two of the same note name. For example, C to C is an octave, and A to A is an octave. It is called an octave because the distance represents 8 notes! Each scale covers one octave.

When you play the scales, you will start out playing up and down one octave. (Later, you will learn to play up and down two octaves, then three and four octaves!) Practice the Right Hand and Left Hand separately, and then put them together.

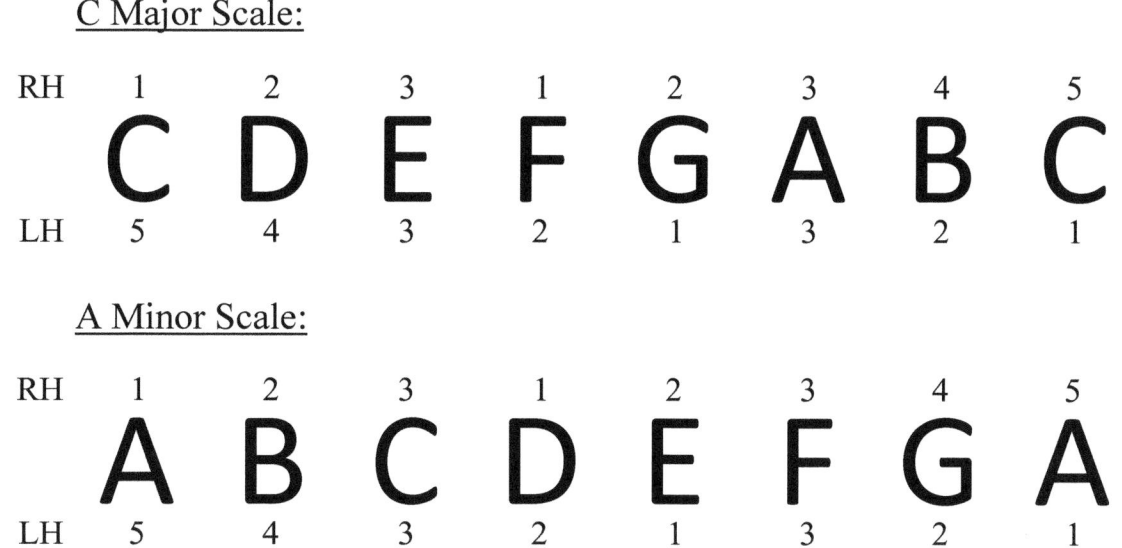

Play forward, and then backward (up and then down). Follow the finger numbers written, both directions (simply read from right to left when you go down).

Sing the solfege syllables and letter names as you play!

Practice your scales every day as you progress through this lesson book, and memorize them!

Let's learn *Three Blind Mice!*

Three Blind Mice is a song written using notes of the C Major Scale. As we learn this song, we are going to sing it both with the lyrics and with solfege syllables. Musicians often refer to singing a melody with the solfege syllables as *singing on solfege*.

First, let's clap and sing the song:

Three	*blind*	*mice,*		*Three*	*blind*	*mice,*	
Clap	Clap	Clap	Clap	**Clap**	Clap	Clap	Clap
1	*2*	*3*	*4*	*1*	*2*	*3*	*4*

See	*how they run,*			*See*	*how they run,*		
Clap	Clap	Clap	Clap	**Clap**	Clap	Clap	Clap
1	*2*	*3*	*4*	*1*	*2*	*3*	*4*

They all ran af-ter the far-mer's wife,
    Clap   Clap   Clap   Clap
    1   *2*   *3*   *4*

Who cut off their tails with a car-ving knife.
    Clap   Clap   Clap   Clap
    1   *2*   *3*   *4*

Did you e - ver see such a sight in your life
    Clap   Clap   Clap   Clap
    1   *2*   *3*   *4*

As three	*blind*	*mice?*		*Three*	*blind*	*mice!*	
Clap	Clap	Clap	Clap	**Clap**	Clap	Clap	Clap
1	*2*	*3*	*4*	*1*	*2*	*3*	*4*

Three Blind Mice (cont.)

Next, let's sing it on solfege! If we can continue to clap while we sing, that would be best!

Mi	Re	Do		Mi	Re	Do	
Clap	Clap	Clap	Clap	**Clap**	Clap	Clap	Clap
1	*2*	*3*	*4*	*1*	*2*	*3*	*4*

So	Fa Fa Mi			So	Fa Fa Mi		
Clap	Clap	Clap	Clap	**Clap**	Clap	Clap	Clap
1	*2*	*3*	*4*	*1*	*2*	*3*	*4*

So Do Do Ti La Ti Do   So So
Clap   Clap   Clap   Clap
1   *2*   *3*   *4*

    So Do Do Do Ti La Ti Do   So So
    Clap   Clap   Clap   Clap
    1   *2*   *3*   *4*

        So So Do Do Ti La Ti Do   So So
        Clap   Clap   Clap   Clap
        1   *2*   *3*   *4*

Fa Mi	Re	Do		Mi	Re	Do	
Clap	Clap	Clap	Clap	**Clap**	Clap	Clap	Clap
1	*2*	*3*	*4*	*1*	*2*	*3*	*4*

For more singing and ear training practice, sing the song also on the note letter names. Give it a try!

Finally, let's learn to play the song on the piano. Sing the song as you play, with the lyrics, on solfege, and on letter names.

Memorize all your songs!

Three Blind Mice

Using notes from the C Major Scale   English Nursery Rhyme and Round

	3	2	1				
RH	E	D	C	E	D	C
	Three	blind	mice.	Three	blind	mice.
	Mi	Re	Do	Mi	Re	Do
LH	E	F	E	E	F	E
	C	B	C	C	B	C
	1	1				
	3	4 (or 5)				

	5	4		3				
RH	G	F	F	E	G	F	F	E
	See	how	they	run.	See	how	they	run.
	So	Fa	Fa	Mi	So	Fa	Fa	Mi
LH	E	F		E	E	F		E
	C	B		C	C	B		C

	2	5	4	3	4	5	2	
RH	G	C	C	B	A	B	C	G	G
	They	all	ran	af-	ter	the	far-	mer's	wife
	So	Do	Do	Ti	La	Ti	Do	So	So
LH		E					E		B
		C		G			C		
		1		5			1		4
		3					3		

Three Blind Mice (cont.)

RH	G	C	C	C	B	A	B	C	G	G
finger	2	5			4	3	4	5	2	
lyric	Who	cut	off	their	tails	with	a	car-	ving	knife!
solfège	So	Do	Do	Do	Ti	La	Ti	Do	So	So
LH		E / C (1,3)			G (5)			E / C (1,3)		B (4)

RH	G	G	C	C	B	A	B	C	G	G	G
finger	2	5			4	3	4	5	2		
lyric	Did	you	e-	ver	see	such	a	sight	in	your	life
solfège	So	So	Do	Do	Ti	La	Ti	Do	So	So	So
LH			E / C (1,3)		G (5)			E / C (1,3)			B (4)

RH	F	E	D	C		E	D	C
finger	1	3	2	1				
lyric	As	three	blind	mice?		Three	blind	mice!
solfège	Fa	Mi	Re	Do		Mi	Re	Do
LH		E / C (1, 3)	F / B (1, 4 or 5)	E / C		E / C (1)	G	C (5)

Let's learn *Un elefante*

Un elefante is a Mexican children's counting song about elephants swinging on a spider web! The song uses notes from the C Major scale.

First, let's clap and sing the song. If you are not familiar with this song or the lyrics, listen to several recordings to help you learn the melody, rhythm, and pronunciation.

$\Big\{$ Un   e - le -   fan -   te   se ba - lan - ce - a -   ba
   Clap   Clap   **Clap**   Clap
   1   2   *1*   2

$\Big\{$ So -   bre   la   te - la de u-na a-ra   -   ña
   Clap   Clap   **Clap**   Clap
   1   2   *1*   2

$\Big\{$ Co -   mo veí -   a   que   no   se ca - í   a
   Clap   Clap   **Clap**   Clap
   1   2   *1*   2

$\Big\{$ Fue-ron a bus - car   ot - ro e -le -fan   -   te.
   Clap   Clap   **Clap**   Clap
   1   2   *1*   2

Next, let's learn to play the song on the piano.

Sing the song as you play, both with the lyrics and on solfege. (Like *Three Blind Mice,* the solfege is written below the lyrics.)

Continue to memorize all your songs!

Un Elefante

Using notes from the C Major Scale   Mexican Children's Counting Song

RH: G(4) G(4) F(3) E(2) E(2)   G(4) G(4) G(4) F(3) E(2) E(2)
    Un e- le- fan- te   se ba- lan- ce- a- ba
    So So Fa Mi   Mi   So So So   Fa   Mi Mi

LH: ←E / ←C (1,3)   ←E / ←C

RH: G(4) G G A(5) G(4) F(3) E(2) F(3) E(2) D(1)
    So- bre la te- la de u- na a- ra- a- na
    So   So So La So Fa   Mi Fa Mi Re

LH: ←E / ←C   ←G (5)

RH: F(3) F E(2) D(1) D   F(3) F E(2) D(1) D
    Co- mo vei- a   que   no   se ca- i   a
    Fa   Fa Mi   Re Re   Fa   Fa Mi   Re   Re

LH: ←G   ←G

RH: G(4) G G A(5) G(4) F(3) E(2) D(1) E(3) D(2) C(1)
    Fue- ron a bus- car ot- ro   ele- fan- -   te.
    So   So So La So   Fa   Mi   Re   Mi   Re Do

LH: ←G   ←E / ←C   ←C

Let's learn *Balonku*

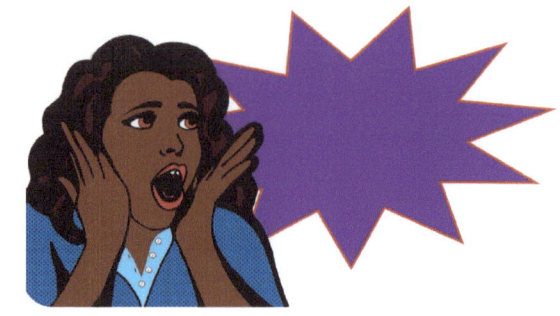

Balonku is an Indonesian children's counting song about balloons being popped! The song uses notes from the C Major scale.

First, let's clap and sing the song. If you are not familiar with this song or the lyrics, listen to several recordings to help you learn the melody, rhythm, and pronunciation.

$$\begin{cases} \textit{Ba-lon-ku} \quad\quad a\ -\ da \quad\quad li\ -\ ma \\ \textit{Clap} \quad \textbf{Clap} \quad \textit{Clap} \quad \textit{Clap} \quad \textit{Clap} \quad \textbf{Clap} \quad \textit{Clap} \quad \textit{Clap} \\ 4 \quad\quad \boldsymbol{1} \quad\quad 2 \quad\quad 3 \quad\quad 4 \quad\quad \boldsymbol{1} \quad\quad 2 \quad\quad 3 \end{cases}$$

$$\begin{cases} \textit{Ru-pa ru}\ -\ pa\ -\ wa\ -\ ma\ -\ nya \\ \textit{Clap} \quad \textbf{Clap} \quad \textit{Clap} \quad \textit{Clap} \quad \textit{Clap} \quad \textbf{Clap} \quad \textit{Clap} \quad \textit{Clap} \\ 4 \quad\quad \boldsymbol{1} \quad\quad 2 \quad\quad 3 \quad\quad 4 \quad\quad \boldsymbol{1} \quad\quad 2 \quad\quad 3 \end{cases}$$

$$\begin{cases} \textit{Hi-jau ku}\ -\ \textit{ning} \quad ke\ -\ la\ -\ bu \\ \textit{Clap} \quad \textbf{Clap} \quad \textit{Clap} \quad \textit{Clap} \quad \textit{Clap} \quad \textbf{Clap} \quad \textit{Clap} \quad \textit{Clap} \\ 4 \quad\quad \boldsymbol{1} \quad\quad 2 \quad\quad 3 \quad\quad 4 \quad\quad \boldsymbol{1} \quad\quad 2 \quad\quad 3 \end{cases}$$

$$\begin{cases} \textit{Me-rah mu}\ -\ da \quad\quad dan \quad bi\ -\ ru. \\ \textit{Clap} \quad \textbf{Clap} \quad \textit{Clap} \quad \textit{Clap} \quad \textit{Clap} \quad \textbf{Clap} \quad \textit{Clap} \quad \textit{Clap} \\ 4 \quad\quad \boldsymbol{1} \quad\quad 2 \quad\quad 3 \quad\quad 4 \quad\quad \boldsymbol{1} \quad\quad 2 \quad\quad 3 \end{cases}$$

Next, let's learn to play the song on the piano. In this arrangement, some of the melody is played with the Left Hand.

Sing the song as you play, both with the lyrics and on solfege. (The solfege is written below the lyrics.)

Memorize all your songs!

BALONKU

Using notes from the C Major Scale   Indonesian Children's Counting Song

Hand							
RH			*(cross over)* 3 E ←ku		3 E →da		3 E ⇒ma
	Ba- Mi	lon- Fa	So	a- Do	So	li- Mi	So
LH	E 5→	F 4→	G 3→	C 1→	G 3→	E 5→	G 3→

Hand							
RH	2 D	3 E	4 F	2 D	5 G	4 F	3 E
	Ru- Re	pa- Mi	ru Fa	pa Re	wa- So	ma- Fa	nya Mi
LH			G ←1		G ←5		C ←3 (or 1)

Hand							
RH			*(cross over)* 3 F ←ku-		3 G →ke-		3 E ⇒bu
	Hi- Do	jau Do	La	ning La	Ti	la- Do	So
LH	C 5◇	C ◇	A 1→	A →	B 2→	C 1→	G 4→

Hand							
RH	3 E →	4 F →	5 G →	4 F →	3 E →	2 D →	1 C ◇
	Me- Mi	rah Fa	mu- So	da Fa	dan Mi	bi- Re	ru. Do
LH			G ←1		G ←5		C ←3 (or 5)

67

Let's learn *Wayfaring Stranger*

Wayfaring Stranger is a Southern American folk hymn or gospel song about a sorrowful person on the journey through life.

The song is in Minor mode, using notes of the A Minor scale.

Let's clap and sing the song:

$\Big\{$ *I'm just a poor   way - far - ing stran-ger*
Clap   Clap   **Clap**   Clap   Clap   Clap   **Clap**   Clap
3   4   **1**   2   3   4   **1**   2

$\Big\{$ *While trav'ling through   the world of woe.*
Clap   Clap   **Clap**   Clap   Clap   Clap   **Clap**   Clap
3   4   **1**   2   3   4   **1**   2

$\Big\{$ *Yet there's no sick - ness, toil, nor danger,*
Clap   Clap   **Clap**   Clap   Clap   Clap   **Clap**   Clap
3   4   **1**   2   3   4   **1**   2

$\Big\{$ *In that bright world   to which I go.*
Clap   Clap   **Clap**   Clap   Clap   Clap   **Clap**   Clap
3   4   **1**   2   3   4   **1**   2

WAYFARING STRANGER (CONT.)

I'm	go - ing	there		to	see my	Fa -	ther!
Clap	Clap	**Clap**	Clap	Clap	Clap	**Clap**	Clap
3	*4*	***1***	*2*	*3*	*4*	***1***	*2*

I'm	go - ing	there		no	more to	roam.	
Clap	Clap	**Clap**	Clap	Clap	Clap	**Clap**	Clap
3	*4*	***1***	*2*	*3*	*4*	***1***	*2*

I'm	on - ly	go	-	ing	o - ver	Jor -	dan,
Clap	Clap	**Clap**	Clap	Clap	Clap	**Clap**	Clap
3	*4*	***1***	*2*	*3*	*4*	***1***	*2*

I'm	on - ly	go	-	ing	o - ver	home.	
Clap	Clap	**Clap**	Clap	Clap	Clap	**Clap**	Clap
3	*4*	***1***	*2*	*3*	*4*	***1***	*2*

Minor mode has two possible methods of solfege. *Do-based minor* and *La-based minor*. Do-based minor goes from Do to Do, and La- based minor goes from La to La.

DO-BASED MINOR

*Do Re **Me** Fa So **Le Te** Do*

LA-BASED MINOR

La Ti Do Re Mi Fa So La

In Do-based minor, the 3rd, 6th, and 7th syllables change – from Mi to Me, from La to Le, and from Ti to Te. La-based minor does not require these changes.

Both methods are useful in training our ears, so let's sing the song using both solfege scales.

Sing the song as you play it on the piano, both with the lyrics and on solfege. (The solfege is written below the lyrics.)

Memorize all your songs!

WAYFARING STRANGER

Using notes from the A Minor Scale — Southern American Folk Hymn

RH	1 A I'm Do La	1 A just Do La	5 E a So Mi	5 E poor So Mi	4 D way- Fa Re	5 E far- So Mi	4 D ing Fa Re	3 C stran- Me Do	1 A ger, Do La
LH				C / A (1/3)					C / A

RH	1 A While Do La	1 A trav'- Do La	5 E ling So Mi	4 D through Fa Re	1 A the Do La	3 C world Me Do	4 D of Fa Re	5 E woe. So Mi
LH				F / D				C / A

RH	1 A Yet Do La	1 A there's Do La	5 E no So Mi	5 E sick- So Mi	4 D ness, Fa Re	5 E toil, So Mi	4 D nor Fa Re	3 C dan- Me Do	1 A ger, Do La
LH				C / A					C / A

RH	1 A In Do La	1 A that Do La	5 E bright So Mi	4 D world Fa Re	3 C to Me Do	1 A which Do La	2 G I Te So	3 A go. Do La
LH				F / D				C / A

WAYFARING STRANGER (CONT.)

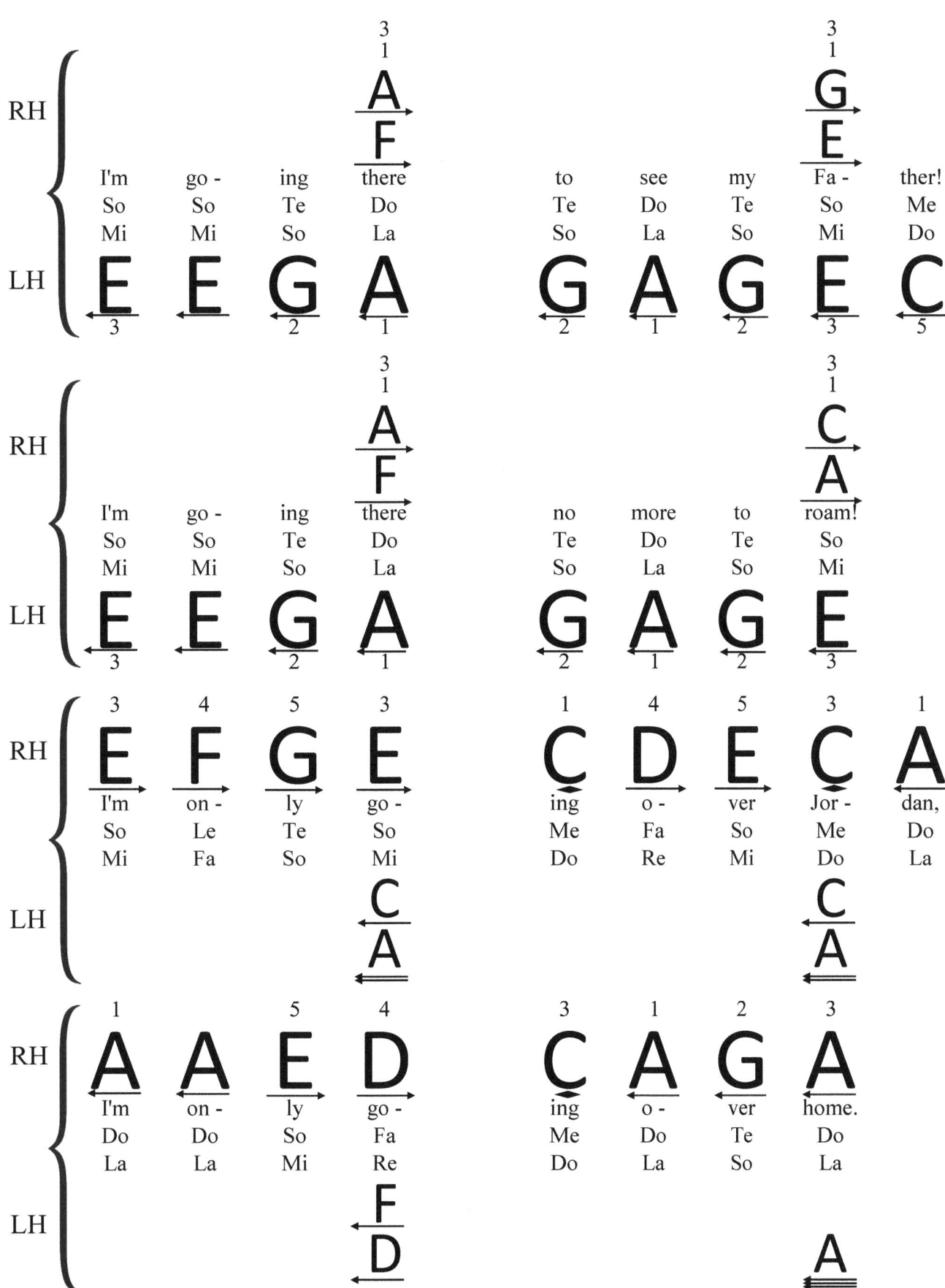

Review Part 2

Write the music alphabet going up (forward): _____

Write the music alphabet going down (backward): _____

What letter comes after B? ____   What letter comes after G? ____

What letter comes before F? ____   What letter comes before A? ____

What letter comes after C? ____   What letter comes after D? ____

What letter comes before B? ____   What letter comes before E? ____

What letter comes before G? ____   What letter comes before D? ____

Play each A on the piano keyboard going up. How many are there? _____

Play each B on the piano keyboard going up. How many are there? _____

Play each C on the piano keyboard going down. How many are there? _____

Play each D on the piano keyboard going down. How many are there? _____

Play each E on the piano keyboard going up. How many are there? _____

Play each F on the piano keyboard going down. How many are there? _____

Play each G on the piano keyboard going up. How many are there? _____

Fill in the letter names on this keyboard:

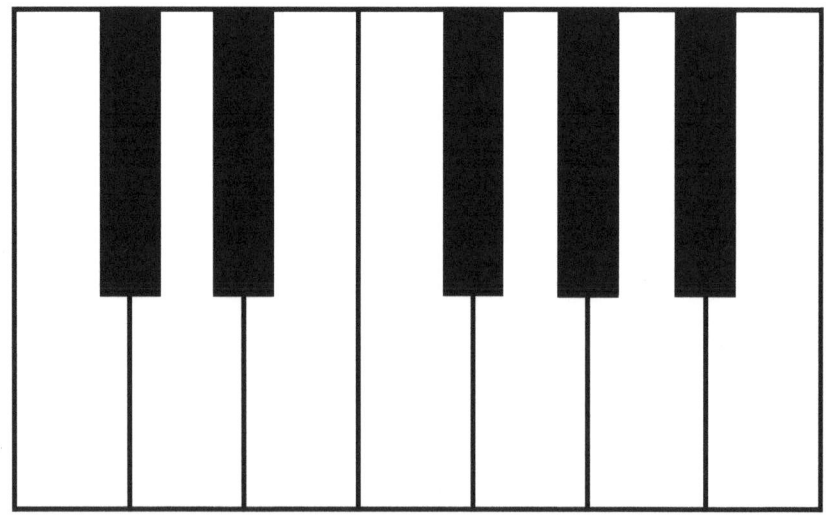

REVIEW PART 2 (CONT.)

__ *Play Middle C*
__ *Play the first C above Middle C*
__ *Play the second C above Middle C*
__ *Play the first C below Middle C*
__ *Play the second C below Middle C*
__ *Play the first G above Middle C*
__ *Play the first F below Middle C*
__ *Play the first D above Middle C*
__ *Play the second A below Middle C*

__ *Play Middle C*
__ *Play the third C above Middle C*
__ *Play the second A above Middle C*
__ *Play the first B below Middle C*
__ *Play the second E below Middle C*
__ *Play the fourth B above Middle C*
__ *Play the first D below Middle C*
__ *Play the third F above Middle C*
__ *Play the third G below Middle C*

WORD MATCH

Composer — A company who prints and sells music.

Publisher — The words of a song.

Sheet Music — Syllables like Do Re Mi Fa So La Ti Do.

Music Notation — A person who invents and writes music.

Lyrics — The music printed on paper.

Octave — The distance of 8 between two notes.

Solfege — Words, symbols, diagrams the composer uses to write down the music.

Fill in the letter names on this keyboard:

REVIEW PART 2 (CONT.)

Fill in the blanks to complete the scale on solfege syllables (forward or up):

Do _____ Mi _____ _____ La Ti _____

Fill in the blanks to complete the scale on solfege syllables (backward or down):

Do _____ La _____ _____ Mi Re _____

Write the C Major Scale: C _____ _____ _____ _____ _____ _____ _____

Write the A Minor Scale: A _____ _____ _____ _____ _____ _____ _____

What letter comes after C? _____   What letter comes after A? _____

What letter comes before G? _____   What letter comes before B? _____

What key (note) is in between the two black keys? _____

What two keys (notes) are in between the three black keys? _____ and _____

What key (note) is just above the two black keys? _____

What key (note) is just below the two black keys? _____

What key (note) is just above the three black keys? _____

What key (note) is just below the three black keys? _____

How many sets of two black keys are on the piano keyboard you are playing? _____

How many sets of three black keys are on the piano keyboard you are playing? _____

What is the lowest note on the piano keyboard you are playing? _____

What is the highest note on the piano keyboard you are playing? _____

Fill in the letter names on this keyboard:

WELL DONE!

You have completed Part Two

Keep Up The Good Work!

Place Sticker Here!

of your first piano lesson book!

There are two more to go...
And then you earn a prize!

Accidentals

Sharps, flats, and naturals

We name the black keys by the names of the white keys that they are situated right next to.

Sharp: means go *up* (⟶), or *raise* the note.

Flat: means go *down* (⟵), or *lower* the note.

Sharped and flatted notes are called *altered* notes. Examples:

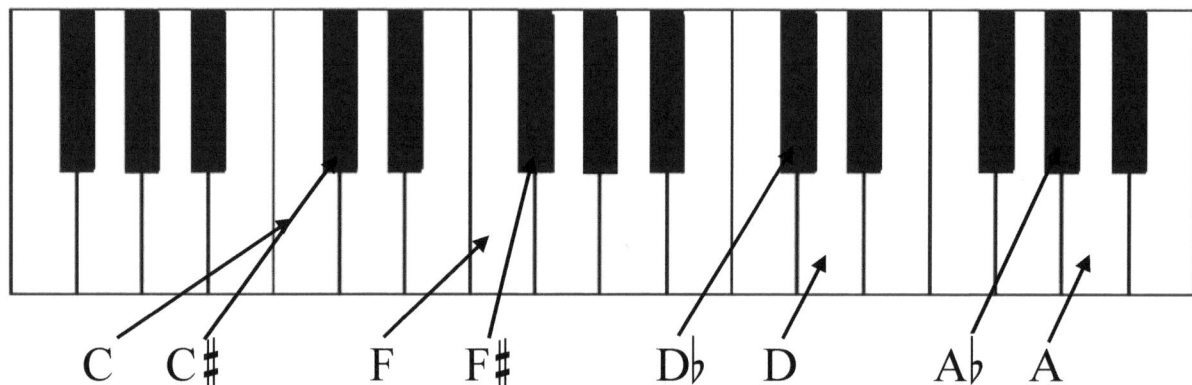

Natural: means *stay the same* (don't go up or down).
For example, a C natural is just a C (an *unaltered* C).

Sometimes, in music, a note is to be played sharped or flatted (altered), and then that note is to be played again, but *not* sharped or flatted (unaltered). If a note was sharped or flatted, a natural would undo that, and make the note unaltered again.

In our next piece, *The Wind*, you are going to play many notes with accidentals (sharps and flats). Follow the Right Hand (RH) and Left Hand (LH) indicators, and the finger numbers written.

Continue to memorize all your pieces!

THE WIND

Ruth Stevenson Alling and Dennis Frayne

RH: 1 C 3 C# 1 D 3 D# 1 E | 1 C 3 C# 1 D 3 D# 1 E
LH: C C# D D# E | C C# D D# E
    1 3 1 3 1 | 1 3 1 3 1

RH: 1 C 3 C# 1 D 3 D# 1 E 3 E♭ 1 D 3 D♭ 1 C 2 D 3 E♭
LH: C C# D D# E E♭ D D♭ C D E♭
    1 3 1 3 1 3 1 3 1 3 2

RH: 1 G 3 G# 1 A 3 A# 1 B | 1 G 3 G# 1 A 3 A# 1 B
LH: G G# A A# B | G G# A A# B
    1 3 1 3 1 | 1 3 1 3 1

RH: 1 G 3 G# 1 A 3 A# 1 B 3 B♭ 1 A 3 A♭ 1 G 2 B 3 C
LH: G G# A A# B B♭ A A♭ G G C
    1 3 1 3 1 3 1 3 1 1 5

HALF STEPS AND WHOLE STEPS

A half step goes from one pitch to the very next pitch. Examples *(play each of these on the piano, paying attention to the sound of a half step)*:

C to C♯	G to G♯	A to B♭	B♭ to B♮	A♯ to A♮
E to F	F to F♯	B to C	G♭ to G♮	D to D♭
D♯ to D♮	F to E	D♭ to C	A to A♯	C to B

A whole step goes from one pitch to another pitch, skipping over one pitch. Examples *(play each of these on the piano, paying attention to the sound of a whole step)*:

C to D	F to G	A to B	B to C♯	D to E
E to F♯	A♭ to B♭	F♯ to G♯	E to D	G to F
A to G	E♭ to D♭	A♭ to G♭	G to A	B to A

Half steps and whole steps are called ***intervals***. An *interval* is the distance between two notes.

An octave is also an example of an interval. An octave is an interval of 8. Half steps and whole steps are intervals of 2.

Play many different half steps and whole steps on the piano keyboard. Listen carefully as you play, noticing the difference in sound between a half step and a whole step. Play both going up and down.

Teacher: Play various half step and whole step intervals on the piano.
Student: Watch and identify the intervals.

Now try it without looking!

HALF STEPS AND WHOLE STEPS PRACTICE

Play the following intervals on the piano and indicate whether they are half steps (HS) or whole steps (WS):

F to F♯ _____   G to G♭ _____

A to B _____   C to D _____

A♭ to B♭ _____   D♯ to C♯ _____

E to F _____   F to G _____

C to B _____   F♯ to G _____

E♭ to D _____   A to G♯ _____

Continue this type of practice.

Teacher: Play some half step and whole step intervals on the piano.
Student: Without looking, use your ear to determine whether each is a half step or a whole step.

Challenge question! Look carefully at the piano keyboard below. Is it possible to have a half step between two black keys? Yes/No *(circle one)*

A whole step is an interval of ___. A half step is an interval of ___. An octave is an interval of ___.

Now, let's learn some more songs using accidentals!

Let's learn *Hush! Little Baby*

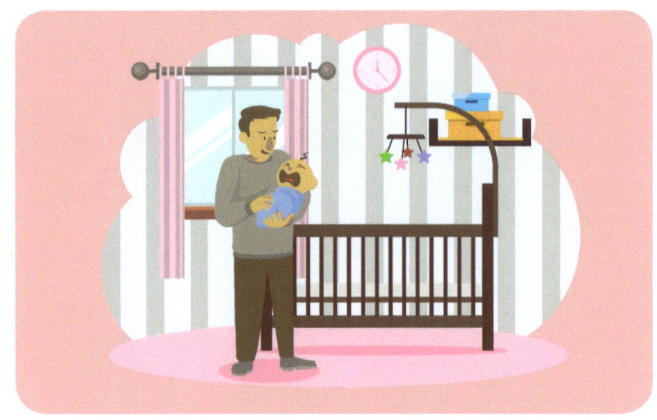

Hush Little Baby is a children's lullaby. It uses notes from the G Major Scale.

First, let's clap and sing the song:

Hush!	*lit - tle*	*ba -*	*by,*	*don't*	*say*	*a*	*word,*
Clap	Clap	Clap	Clap	**Clap**	Clap	Clap	Clap
1	2	3	4	*1*	2	3	4

Pa-pa's	*gon-na buy*	*you*	*a*	*mock -*	*ing*	*bird.*	*And*
Clap	Clap	Clap	Clap	**Clap**	Clap	Clap	Clap
1	2	3	4	*1*	2	3	4

If	*that*	*mock -*	*ing*	*bird*	*won't*	*sing,*	
Clap	Clap	Clap	Clap	**Clap**	Clap	Clap	Clap
1	2	3	4	*1*	2	3	4

Pa-pa's	*gon-na buy*	*you*	*a*	*dia -*	*mond*	*ring.*	
Clap	Clap	Clap	Clap	**Clap**	Clap	Clap	Clap
1	2	3	4	*1*	2	3	4

Next, let's learn to play the song on the piano!

Sing the song as you play, both with the lyrics and on solfege. (The solfege is written below the lyrics.)

Memorize all your songs!

Hush! Little Baby

Using notes from the G Major Scale   Traditional American Lullaby

Line 1

RH: D B B B C B A A A
Lyrics: Hush! lit- tle ba- by, don't say a word,
Solfège: So Mi Mi Mi Fa Mi Re Re Re
Fingering: 1 4 4 4 5 4 3 3 3

LH: B/G (fingers 1/3), then C/F# (fingers 1/4)

Line 2

RH: D D A A A A B A G G
Lyrics: Pa- pa's gon- na buy you a mock- ing bird.
Solfège: So So Re Re Re Re Mi Re Do Do
Fingering: 1 4 5 4 3

LH: C/F#, then B/G

Line 3

RH: D D B B C B A A
Lyrics: And if that mock- ing bird don't sing,
Solfège: So So Mi Mi Fa Mi Re Re
Fingering: 1 4 4 5 4 3

LH: B/G, then C/F#

Line 4

RH: D D A A A A B A G G
Lyrics: Pa- pa's gon- na buy you a dia- mond ring.
Solfège: So So Re Re Re Re Mi Re Do Do
Fingering: 1 4 5 4 3

LH: C/F#, then B/G

81

Let's learn *Happy Birthday*

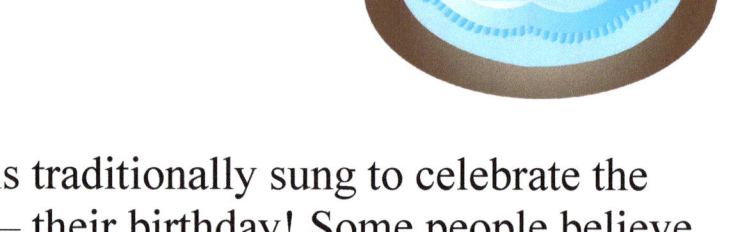

Happy Birthday is a song that is traditionally sung to celebrate the anniversary of a person's birth – their birthday! Some people believe *Happy Birthday* is the most recognized song in the English language.

First, let's clap and sing the song:

$$\begin{cases} \textit{Hap-py birth - day} & \textit{to} & \textit{you.} & \\ \textit{Clap} \quad \textbf{\textit{Clap}} \quad \textit{Clap} & \textit{Clap} & \textbf{\textit{Clap}} & \textit{Clap} \\ \textit{3} \quad\quad \textit{\textbf{1}} \quad\quad\quad \textit{2} & \textit{3} & \textit{\textbf{1}} & \textit{2} \end{cases}$$

$$\begin{cases} \textit{Hap-py birth - day} & \textit{to} & \textit{you.} & \\ \textit{Clap} \quad \textbf{\textit{Clap}} \quad \textit{Clap} & \textit{Clap} & \textbf{\textit{Clap}} & \textit{Clap} \\ \textit{3} \quad\quad \textit{\textbf{1}} \quad\quad\quad \textit{2} & \textit{3} & \textit{\textbf{1}} & \textit{2} \end{cases}$$

$$\begin{cases} \textit{Hap-py birth - day} & \textit{dear} & \underline{\quad\quad\quad} & \\ \textit{Clap} \quad \textbf{\textit{Clap}} \quad \textit{Clap} & \textit{Clap} & \textbf{\textit{Clap}} & \textit{Clap} \\ \textit{3} \quad\quad \textit{\textbf{1}} \quad\quad\quad \textit{2} & \textit{3} & \textit{\textbf{1}} & \textit{2} \end{cases}$$

$$\begin{cases} \textit{Hap-py birth - day} & \textit{to} & \textit{you.} & \\ \textit{Clap} \quad \textbf{\textit{Clap}} \quad \textit{Clap} & \textit{Clap} & \textbf{\textit{Clap}} & \textit{Clap} \\ \textit{3} \quad\quad \textit{\textbf{1}} \quad\quad\quad \textit{2} & \textit{3} & \textit{\textbf{1}} & \textit{2} \end{cases}$$

Next, let's learn to play the song on the piano!

Happy Birthday uses the notes of the F Major Scale.
Sing the song as you play, both with the lyrics and on solfege. (The solfege is written below the lyrics.)

Memorize all your songs! (*Happy Birthday* is a terrific song to keep memorized always, since you may have many opportunities to play and sing it over your lifetime!)

HAPPY BIRTHDAY

Using notes from the F Major Scale   Traditional American Birthday Song

RH: C(1) C(2) D(1) C(4) F(3) E
    Hap- py birth- day to   you.
    So   So La   So   Do   Ti

LH: A   Bb
            F   E
            3   1,4

RH: C(1) C(2) D(1) C(5) G(4) F
    Hap- py birth- day to   you.
    So   So La   So   Re   Do

LH: Bb   A
            E   F

RH: C(1) C(5) C(3) A(1) F(3) E(2) D
    Hap- py birth- day, dear   Ti La
    So   So So   Mi   Do

LH: A   Bb
            F

RH: Bb(4) Bb(3) A(1) F(2) G(1) F
    Hap- py   birth- day to   you.
    Fa   Fa   Mi   Do   Re   Do

LH: C   C   F
            1   5   1 (or 3)

83

Accidentals, Half Steps, and Whole Steps Review

Student: Play the following intervals on the piano and determine, by sight, whether they are half steps (HS) or whole steps (WS):

F to F♯ _____   A to B _____

B to C _____   C♯ to D♯ _____

A♭ to B♭ _____   D to C♯ _____

E to F♯ _____   G♭ to A♭ _____

E to E♯ _____   B to B♯ _____

F to F♭ _____   C to C♭ _____

Teacher: Play the following intervals on the piano.
Student: Determine, by ear, whether they are half steps (HS) or whole steps (WS):

F to G _____   E to E♭ _____

A♯ to B _____   C♯ to D _____

A to B _____   D♯ to C♯ _____

E to F♯ _____   F to G _____

C to B _____   F♯ to G _____

E♭ to D♭ _____   A to A♭ _____

Accidentals, Half Steps, and Whole Steps Review (cont.)

The symbol that raises a note by a half step is called a _____. *Draw one:* ____

The symbol that lowers a note by a half step is called a _____. *Draw one:* ____

The symbol that cancels an altered note is called a _____. *Draw one:* ____

Look at the song, *Hush Little Baby*. Circle the correct answer:

- The interval between the first lyric, "ba-by," is a half step/whole step.
- The interval between the lyrics of the second line, "you a," is a half step whole step.
- The interval between the lyrics of the last line, "dia-mond," is a half step whole step.

Look at the song, *Happy Birthday*. Circle the correct answer:

- The interval between the first lyric, "birth-day," is a half step/whole step.
- The interval between the lyrics of the second line, "to you," is a half step/whole step.
- The interval between the lyrics of the last line, "-py birth-," is a half step/whole step.

Look at the next song, *America*. Circle the correct answer:

- The interval between the first lyric, "count-ry," is a half step/whole step.
- The interval between the lyrics of the second line, "land of," is a half step/whole step.
- The interval between the lyrics of the fourth line (top of the second page), "fa- thers," is a half step/whole step.

On the keyboard above, circle the key of the note that is a half step above D.
What is that note called? _____

On the keyboard above, circle the key of the note that is a half step below G.
What is that note called? _____

On the keyboard above, circle the key of the note that is a whole step below B.
What is that note called? _____

AMERICA

Using notes from the F Major Scale   Traditional Patriotic Hymn

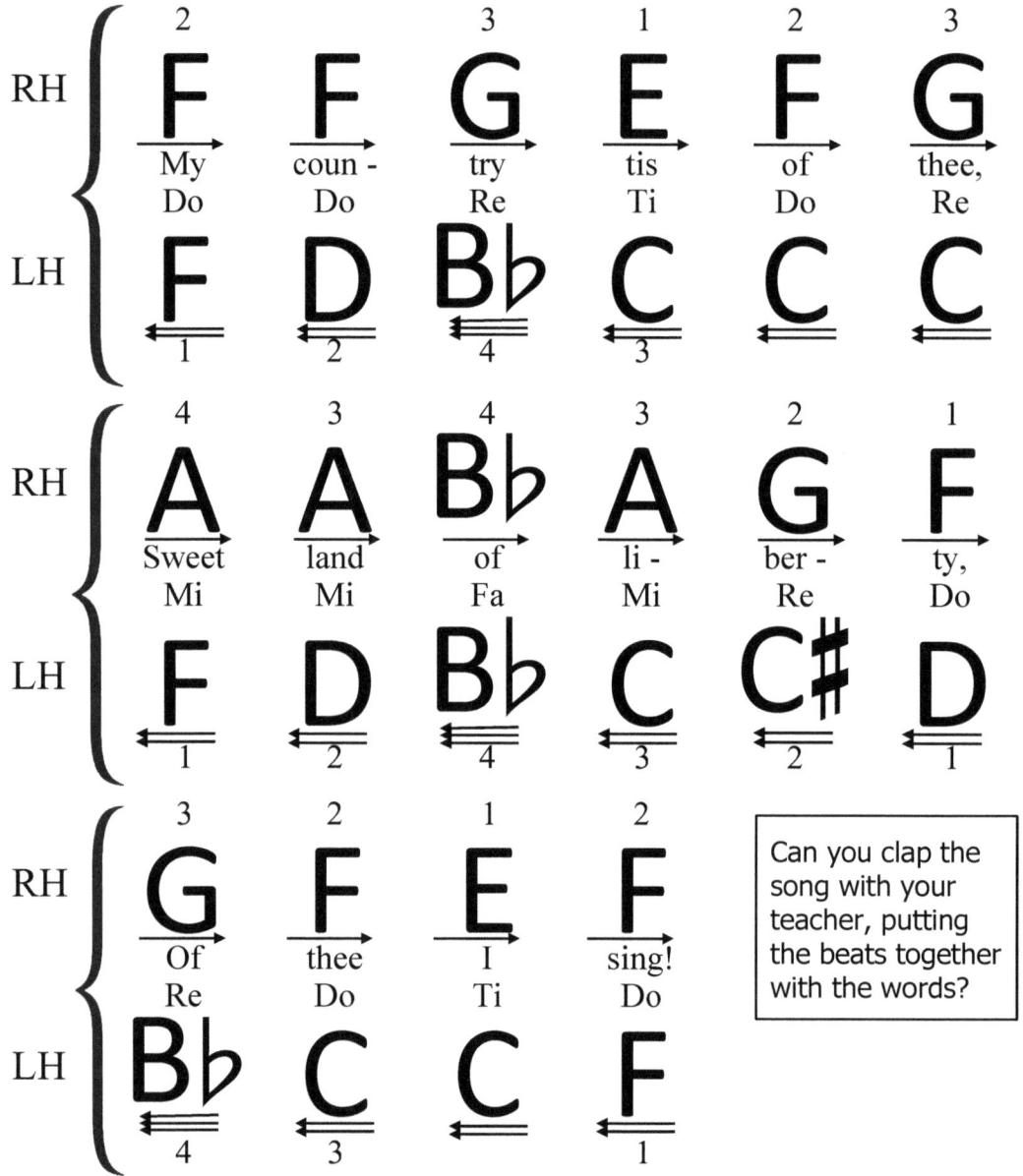

86

America (cont.)

RH	5 C Land / So	C where / So	C my / So	C fa- / So	4 B♭ thers / Fa	3 A died, / Mi		
LH	F / 5	A / 3	C / 1	F / 5	F	F		

RH	4 B♭ Land / Fa	B♭ of / Fa	B♭ the / Fa	B♭ Pil- / Fa	3 A grim's / Mi	2 G pride, / Re		
LH	C / 5	E / 3	G / 1	C / 5	C	C		

RH	3 A From / Mi	4 B♭ ev- / Fa	3 A - / Mi	2 G ry / Re	1 F - / Do	2 A moun- / Mi	3 B♭ tain / Fa	4 C side, / So
LH	F / 5	F	F	F	F	F	G / 4	A / 3

RH	5 D Let / La	3 B♭ - / Fa	2 A free- / Mi	1 G dom / Re	2 F ring! / Do
LH	B♭ / 2		C / 1	C / 5	F / 3 (or 1)

First 5 Major Scales on the Piano Keyboard

All major scales have the same pattern of half steps and whole steps:

Whole Step, Whole Step, Half Step, Whole Step, Whole Step, Whole Step, Half Step. (WS, WS, HS, WS, WS, WS, HS.)

If we start on any key, and follow this pattern, we will produce a major scale.

C Major

The C Major scale has no sharps or flats.

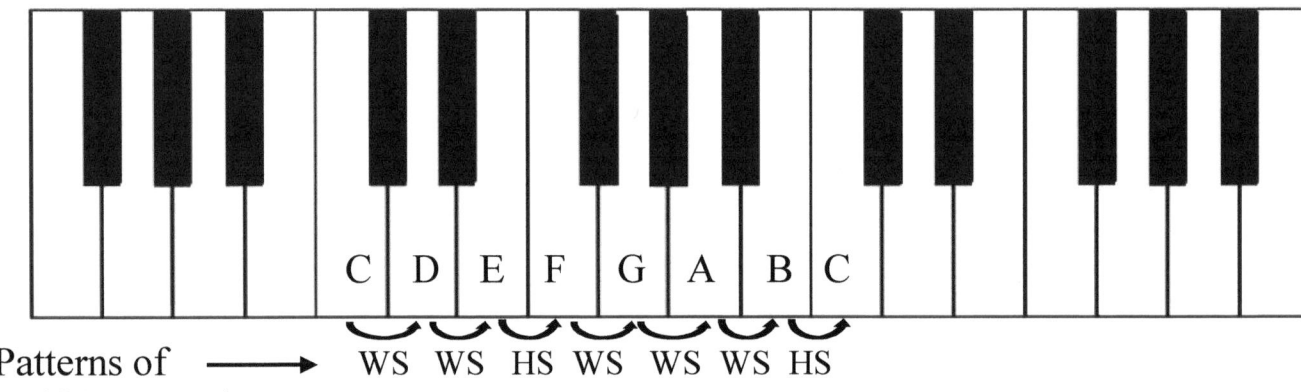

Patterns of Half Steps and Whole Steps →

G Major

The G Major scale has one sharp, F♯.

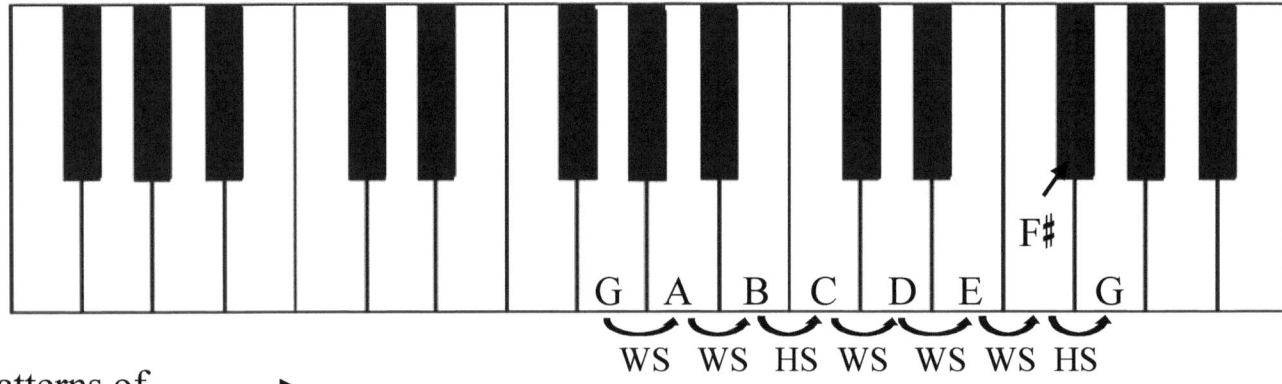

Patterns of Half Steps and Whole Steps →

First 5 Major Scales on the Piano Keyboard (cont.)

D Major

The D Major scale has two sharps, F♯ and C♯.

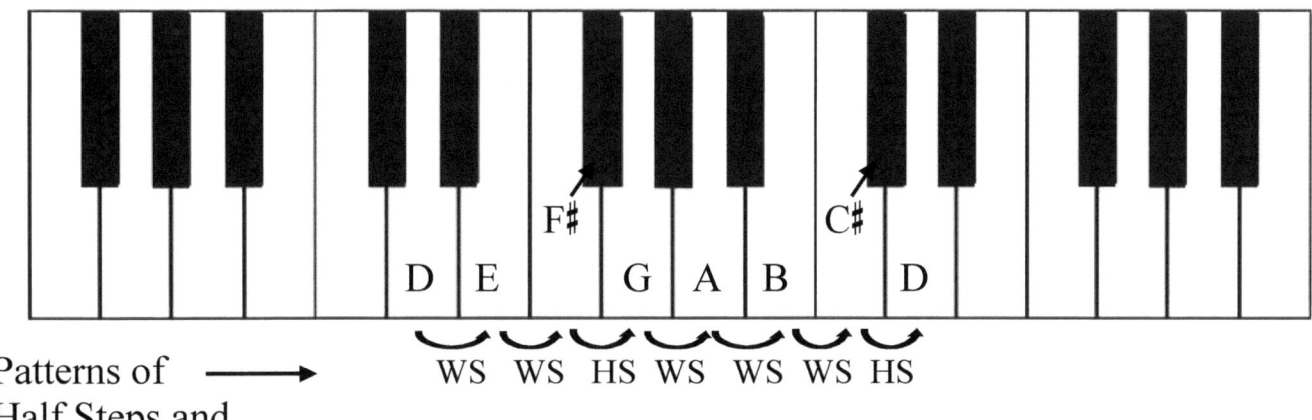

Patterns of Half Steps and Whole Steps →

A Major

The A Major scale has three sharps, F♯, C♯, and G♯.

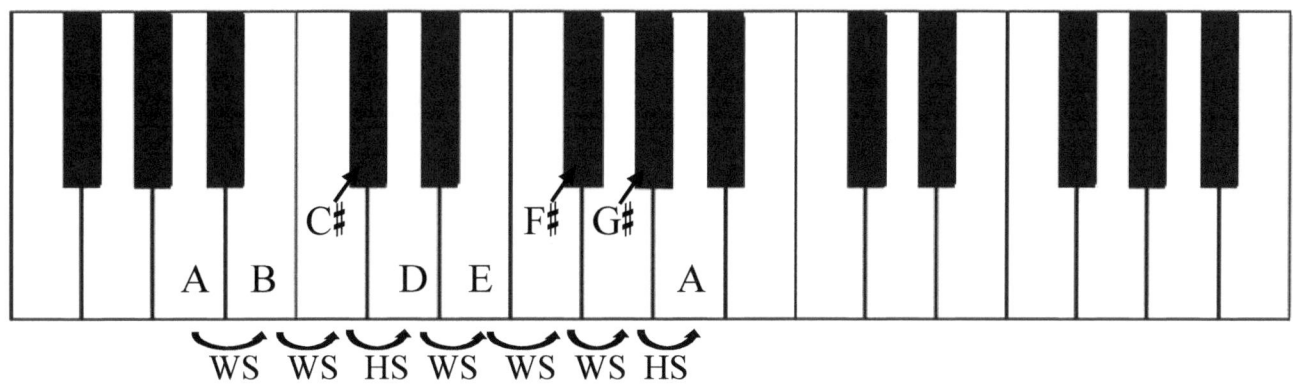

E Major

The E Major scale has four sharps, F♯, C♯, G♯, and D♯.

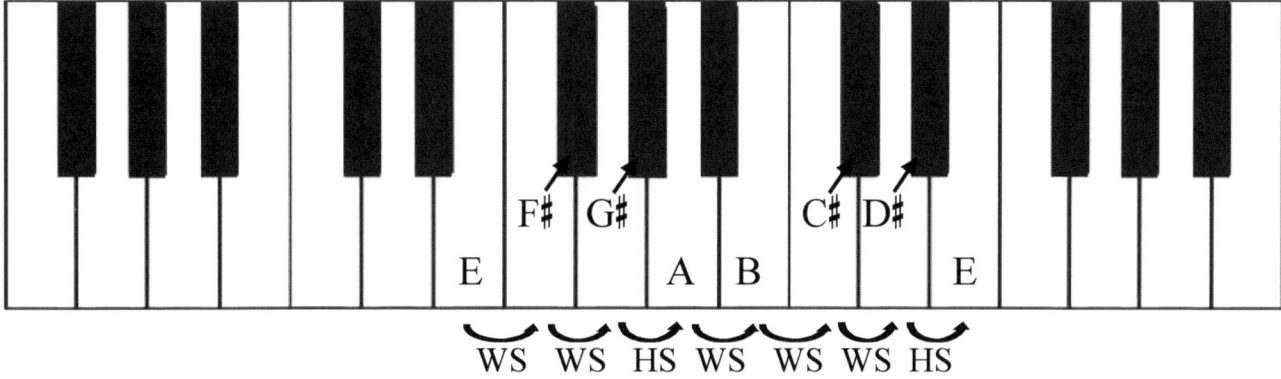

First 5 Major Scales

The fingering is the same for each of these first five major scales!

	RH	1	2	3	1	2	3	4	5
C Major		C	D	E	F	G	A	B	C
	LH	5	4	3	2	1	3	2	1

	RH	1	2	3	1	2	3	4	5
G Major		G	A	B	C	D	E	F#	G
	LH	5	4	3	2	1	3	2	1

	RH	1	2	3	1	2	3	4	5
D Major		D	E	F#	G	A	B	C#	D
	LH	5	4	3	2	1	3	2	1

	RH	1	2	3	1	2	3	4	5
A Major		A	B	C#	D	E	F#	G#	A
	LH	5	4	3	2	1	3	2	1

	RH	1	2	3	1	2	3	4	5
E Major		E	F#	G#	A	B	C#	D#	E
	LH	5	4	3	2	1	3	2	1

Learn to play each of these scales, one octave, going up and down, from memory!
Sing the solfege syllables as you play the scales. *(Do, Re, Mi, Fa, So, La, Ti, Do.)*

First 5 Major Scales (cont.)

Write out the first 5 major scales, going forward (up), using the appropriate accidentals:

C Major C _ _ _ _ _ _ _

G Major G _ _ _ _ _ _ _

D Major D _ _ _ _ _ _ _

A Major A _ _ _ _ _ _ _

E Major E _ _ _ _ _ _ _

Write out the first 5 major scales, going backward (down), using the appropriate accidentals:

C Major C _ _ _ _ _ _ _

G Major G _ _ _ _ _ _ _

D Major D _ _ _ _ _ _ _

A Major A _ _ _ _ _ _ _

E Major E _ _ _ _ _ _ _

Let's learn *La Raspa*

La Raspa is a dance that originated in the state of Veracruz in Mexico.

Since it is a dance, and doesn't have words (lyrics), let's clap and sing the song on solfege:

So Do	*So Do*	*So Do*		*So Do Re Do*	*Ti*	*Do Re*	
Clap	*Clap*	*Clap*	*Clap*	**Clap**	*Clap*	*Clap*	*Clap*
1	*2*	*3*	*4*	***1***	*2*	*3*	*4*

So Ti	*So Ti*	*So Ti*		*So Ti Do Ti*	*La*	*Ti Do*	*So Do*
Clap	*Clap*	*Clap*	*Clap*	**Clap**	*Clap*	*Clap*	*Clap*
1	*2*	*3*	*4*	***1***	*2*	*3*	*4*

La Raspa uses notes from the C Major scale.

Look at the music on the next page. Notice that the Right Hand starts on the first G above Middle C, then after playing E and C together, moves up to the second G above Middle C, and then after playing E and C together again moves up to the third G above Middle C.

And at the end of the dance, notice that the Right Hand moves up to the second G above Middle C, and the Left Hand moves down to the second G below Middle C.

Sing the solfege as you play. (Sing in a singing range that is comfortable for you).

Memorize all your songs!

La Raspa

Using notes from the C Major Scale   Dance from Verzcruz, Mexico

RH: (2) G → / (5,1) C E → / (2) G ⇒ / (5,1) C E ⇒ / (2) G ⇒ / (5,1) C E ⇒
LH: E / C (1,3) ← / E / C ← / E / C ←

RH: (1) G → (4) C → (5) D → (4) C → (3) B → (4) C → (5) D →
LH: C (5) ← / E (3) ← / (1) G F (2) ←

RH: (2) G → (4,1) B F → / (2) G ⇒ (4,1) B F ⇒ / (2) G ⇒ (4,1) B F ⇒
LH: G F (1,2) ← / G F ← / G F ←

RH: (1) G → (3) B → (4) C → (3) B → (2) A → (3) B → (4) C → (2) G → (5,1) C E ⇒
LH: G F (1,2) ← / G F ← / E C (1,3) ← / G (2 or 1) ← C (5) ←

Let's learn *La Cucaracha*

La Cucaracha is a traditional Latin American folk song about a cockroach who cannot walk.

First, let's clap and sing the lyrics:

La cu - ca - ra - cha, la cu - ca - ra - cha,
        Clap   *Clap*
        1   2

        Ya no pue-de ca-mi- nar.
        Clap   *Clap*
        1   2

Por que no tie - ne, por que le fal - ta,
        Clap   *Clap*
        1   2

        Las dos pa-ti-tas de a-trás.
        Clap   *Clap*
        1   2

La Cucaracha uses notes from the G Major scale. Notice the F sharps!

Sing the song as you play, both with the lyrics and on solfege. (The solfege is written below the lyrics.)

Memorize all your songs!

La Cucaracha

Using notes from the G Major Scale — Traditional Latin American Folk Song

RH	D (3)	D (2)	D (1)	G (3)	B (5)	D (3)	D (2)	D (1)	G (3)	B (5)
	La/So	cu-/So	ca-/So	ra-/Do	cha,/Mi	la/So	cu-/So	ca-/So	ra-/Do	cha,/Mi
LH				B/G (1/3)					B/G	

RH	G (4)	G	F# (3)	F#	E (2)	E	D (1)			
	Ya/Do	no/Do	pue-/Ti	de/Ti	ca-/La	mi/La	nar./So			
LH	B (1)	B (2)	A (3)	A	G	G	F# (4)	D (5)		

RH	D (3)	D (2)	D (1)	F# (3)	A (5)	D (3)	D (2)	D (1)	F# (3)	A (5)
	Por/So	que/So	no/So	tie-/Ti	ne,/Re	por/So	que/So	le/So	fal-/Ti	ta,/Re
LH				C/F# (1/4)					C/F#	

RH	D (4)	D	E (5)	D (4)	C (3)	B (2)	A (1)	G (3)
	Las/So	dos/So	pa-/La	ti-/So	tas/Fa	de/Mi	a-/Re	trás./Do
LH	F# (2)	F#	G (1)	F# (2)	E (3)	D (1)	C (2)	B (3)	G (5)

95

Let's learn *Michael, Row the Boat Ashore*

Michael, Row the Boat Ashore is an African-American Spiritual, written by slaves when they were fighting for and winning their freedom from slavery during the American Civil War.

This song has been written here three times, each with the same melody, but each using notes from a different scale. Musicians refer to songs using different scales as being in different *keys*.

First, the song is written using notes from the C Major Scale.

Second, the song is written using notes from the D Major Scale.

Third, the song is written using notes from the E Major Scale.

When we write the same song using notes from different scales, or in different keys, we call that *transposing* the music.

When a song transitions from one key to another key, we call that a *key change*, or a *modulation*.

As you learn this song on the piano in the different keys, sing the melody with the lyrics and on solfege. (The solfege is written in below the lyrics.)

Once you learn and memorize this song, you will have completed Part Three of your piano lesson book!

Keep up the good work!

Michael, Row the Boat Ashore

Using notes from the C Major Scale

African-American Spiritual

	1	3	5	1	3	4	3		1	3	4	3
RH	C	E	G	E	G	A	G		E	G	A	G
	Mi-	chael,	row	the	boat	a-	shore,		Hal-	le-	lu-	jah!
	Do	Mi	So	Mi	So	La	So		Mi	So	La	So
LH			E / C (1/3)				E / C			A / F		E / C

	1	3	1	4	3	2		1	2	3	2	1
RH	E	G	G	E	F	E	D	C	D	E	D	C
	Mi-	chael,	row	the	boat	a-	shore,	Hal-	le-	lu-	-	jah!
	Mi	So	So	Mi	Fa	Mi	Re	Do	Re	Mi	Re	Do
LH		E / C (1/3)		A / F	G / E	F / D		G / E	A / F	B / F		E / C (lower F/G)

	1	3	5	1	3	4	3		1	3	4	3
RH	C	E	G	E	G	A	G		E	G	A	G
	Sis-	ter	help	to	trim	the	sail,		Hal-	le-	lu-	jah!
	Do	Mi	So	Mi	So	La	So		Mi	So	La	So
LH			E / C (1/3)				E / C			A / F		E / C

	1	3	1	4	3	2		1	2	3	2	1
RH	E	G	G	E	F	E	D	C	D	E	D	C
	Sis-	ter	help	to	trim	the	sail,	Hal-	le-	lu-	-	jah!
	Mi	So	So	Mi	Fa	Mi	Re	Do	Re	Mi	Re	Do
LH		E / C (1/3)		A / F	G / E	F / D		G / E	A / F	B / F		E / C

MICHAEL, ROW THE BOAT ASHORE

Using notes from the D Major Scale — African-American Spiritual

Line 1:
RH: D (1) F♯ (3) A (5) F♯ (2) A (4) B (5) A (4) — F♯ (2) A (4) B (5) A (4)
Lyrics: Mi-chael, row the boat a-shore, Hal-le-lu-jah!
Solfège: Do Mi So Mi So La So — Mi So La So
LH: F♯/D (3/5) under "row"; F♯/D under "shore"; B/G (1/2) under "lu"; F♯/D (3/5) under "jah"

Line 2:
RH: F♯ (3) A (5) A (3) F♯ (4) G (3) F♯ (2) E — D (1) E (2) F♯ (3) E (2) D (1)
Lyrics: Mi-chael, row the boat a-shore, Hal-le-lu - jah!
Solfège: Mi So So Mi Fa Mi Re — Do Re Mi Re Do
LH: F♯/D under "row"; B/G (1/2) under "boat"; A/F♯ (1/3) under "a-"; G/E (2/4) under "shore"; A/F♯ (2) under "Hal"; B/G (1/3) under "le"; C♯/G/A (1/2) under "lu"; F♯/D (3/5) under "jah"

Line 3:
RH: D (1) F♯ (3) A (5) F♯ (2) A (4) B (5) A (4) — F♯ (2) A (4) B (5) A (4)
Lyrics: Sis-ter help to trim the sail, Hal-le-lu-jah!
Solfège: Do Mi So Mi So La So — Mi So La So
LH: F♯/D under "help"; F♯/D under "sail"; B/G under "lu"; F♯/D under "jah"

Line 4:
RH: F♯ (3) A (5) A (3) F♯ (4) G (3) F♯ (2) E — D (1) E (2) F♯ (3) E (2) D (1)
Lyrics: Sis-ter help to trim the sail, Hal-le-lu - jah!
Solfège: Mi So So Mi Fa Mi Re — Do Re Mi Re Do
LH: F♯/D under "help"; B/G under "trim"; A/G/F♯ under "the"; G/E under "sail"; A/F♯ under "Hal"; B/G under "le"; C♯/G/A under "lu"; F♯/D under "jah"

98

Michael, Row the Boat Ashore

Using notes from the E Major Scale
African-American Spiritual

[Piano arrangement using letter-name notation with finger numbers. Notes from the E Major Scale.]

Line 1 (RH): E(1) G#(3) B(5) G#(1) B(3) C#(4) B(3) | G#(1) B(3) C#(4) B(3)
Lyrics: Mi - chael, row the boat a - shore, Hal - le - lu - jah!
Solfège: Do Mi So Mi So La So Mi So La So

Line 1 (LH): G#/E (1,3) ... G#/E ... C#/A (1,2) E (1,3)

Line 2 (RH): G#(1) B(3) B(1) G#(4) A(3) G#(2) F#(1) | E(1) F#(2) G#(3) F#(2) E(1)
Lyrics: Mi - chael, row the boat a - shore, Hal - le - lu - jah!
Solfège: Mi So So Mi Fa Mi Re Do Re Mi Re Do

Line 2 (LH): G#/E C#/A B/G# A/F# B/G# (2) C#/A (1,2) D#/B (1,2) G#/E (1,3)

Line 3 (RH): E(1) G#(3) B(5) G#(1) B(3) C#(4) B(3) | G#(1) B(3) C#(4) B(3)
Lyrics: Sis - ter help to trim the sail, Hal - le - lu - jah!
Solfège: Do Mi So Mi So La So Mi So La So

Line 3 (LH): G#/E (1,3) ... G#/E ... C#/A E

Line 4 (RH): G#(1) B(3) B(1) G#(4) A(3) G#(2) F#(1) | E(1) F#(2) G#(3) F#(2) E(1)
Lyrics: Sis - ter help to trim the sail, Hal - le - lu - jah!
Solfège: Mi So So Mi Fa Mi Re Do Re Mi Re Do

Line 4 (LH): G#/E C#/A B/G# A/F# B/G# C#/A D#/B G#/E

Wow! By now you have learned and memorized at least 18 songs!

How many are you continuing to play from memory? **Strive for ten!**

Which are your favorites?

Have you given your first piano recital for a friendly audience?

You know a good practice tip?

Record yourself playing your songs on a recording device such as a cell phone or tablet computer. Listen to yourself playing your songs, and you will learn a few things from this experience!

Keep up the good work!

REVIEW PART 3

Write the music alphabet going up (forward): _____
Write the music alphabet going down (backward): _____
Write the solfege scale going up (forward): _____
Write the solfege scale going down (backward): _____

What letter comes after C? _____   What letter comes after G? _____
What letter comes before G? _____   What letter comes before A? _____
What letter comes after D? _____   What letter comes after B? _____
What letter comes before F? _____   What letter comes before E? _____

Play each A on the piano keyboard going up. How many are there? _____
Play each B on the piano keyboard going up. How many are there? _____
Play each C on the piano keyboard going down. How many are there? _____
Play each D on the piano keyboard going down. How many are there? _____
Play each E on the piano keyboard going up. How many are there? _____
Play each F on the piano keyboard going down. How many are there? _____
Play each G on the piano keyboard going up. How many are there? _____

Fill in the letter names on this keyboard:

Review Part 3 (cont.)

__ *Play Middle C*
__ *Play the first C above Middle C*
__ *Play the second C above Middle C*
__ *Play the first C below Middle C*
__ *Play the second C below Middle C*
__ *Play the first G above Middle C*
__ *Play the first F below Middle C*
__ *Play the first E above Middle C*
__ *Play the second B below Middle C*

__ *Play the third C above Middle C*
__ *Play the fourth C above Middle C*
__ *Play the second B above Middle C*
__ *Play the first D below Middle C*
__ *Play the second F below Middle C*
__ *Play the fourth D above Middle C*
__ *Play the first E below Middle C*
__ *Play the third G above Middle C*
__ *Play the third A below Middle C*

Music Vocabulary Match

Half Step	Altering a note by lowering its pitch.
Lyrics	An interval of eight (8).
Interval	Removing or clearing the sharp or flat from a note.
Natural	Going from one note to the very next note.
Octave	The distance between two notes.
Whole Step	Sharps, flats, and naturals.
Sharp	Syllables like Do Re Mi Fa So La Ti Do.
Solfege	The words of a song.
Accidentals	Altering a note by raising its pitch.
Flat	Going from one note to another note, skipping over one note.

Fill in the letter names on this keyboard:

102

REVIEW PART 3 (CONT.)

Fill in the blanks for the solfege syllables, going from La to La:

   La ____ ____ ____ ____ ____ ____ ____

Write the C Major Scale: C ____ ____ ____ ____ ____ ____ ____
Write the A Minor Scale: A ____ ____ ____ ____ ____ ____ ____
Write the G Major Scale: G ____ ____ ____ ____ ____ ____ ____
Write the D Major Scale: D ____ ____ ____ ____ ____ ____ ____
Write the A Major Scale: A ____ ____ ____ ____ ____ ____ ____
Write the E Major Scale: E ____ ____ ____ ____ ____ ____ ____

What key (note) is in between the two black keys? ____

What two keys (notes) are in between the three black keys? ____ and ____

What key (note) is just above the two black keys? ____

What key (note) is just below the two black keys? ____

What key (note) is just above the three black keys? ____

What key (note) is just below the three black keys? ____

What is the lowest note on the piano keyboard you are playing? ____

What is the highest note on the piano keyboard you are playing? ____

Fill in the letter names on this keyboard:

Review Part 3 (cont.)

Student: Play the following intervals on the piano and determine, by sight, whether they are half steps (HS) or whole steps (WS):

G to G♯ _____   G to F _____

B to C _____   C♯ to D _____

A♭ to B♭ _____   D♯ to C♯ _____

E to F _____   G to A _____

D to C _____   F♯ to G♯ _____

E♭ to D♭ _____   A to G _____

Teacher: Play the following intervals on the piano.
Student: Determine, by ear, whether they are half steps (HS) or whole steps (WS):

F to G _____   E to E♭ _____

A♯ to B _____   C♯ to D _____

A to B _____   D♯ to C♯ _____

E to F♯ _____   F to G _____

C to B _____   F♯ to G _____

E♭ to D♭ _____   A to A♭ _____

An octave is an interval of ____.

Half steps and whole steps are intervals of ____.

STRONG WORK!

You have completed Part Three

Keep Up The Good Work!

Place Sticker Here!

of your first piano lesson book!

There is just one more to go...
And then you earn a prize!

Music Notation

The Staff

We put notes on a staff to show how high or low the pitch is. Notes on the staff will represent keys on the piano.

When composers first invented this type of music notation, they started with just one line. A note on the line meant a specific pitch, and notes higher or lower meant notes higher or lower in pitch. For example:

To make the notation more accurate, composers added more lines. They experimented with three lines, seven lines, and ultimately decided that five lines was best. They called these five lines a *staff*.

Staff

Count the lines. There are 5 lines. Can you count the spaces in between the lines? There are four spaces in between the lines. We can put notes on the lines, and on the spaces in between the lines:

MUSIC NOTATION: THE STAFF (CONT.)

Here's a song written using notes relative to one line. Let's say the line represents the note E, specifically, the first E above Middle C. Can you play the song on the piano keyboard?

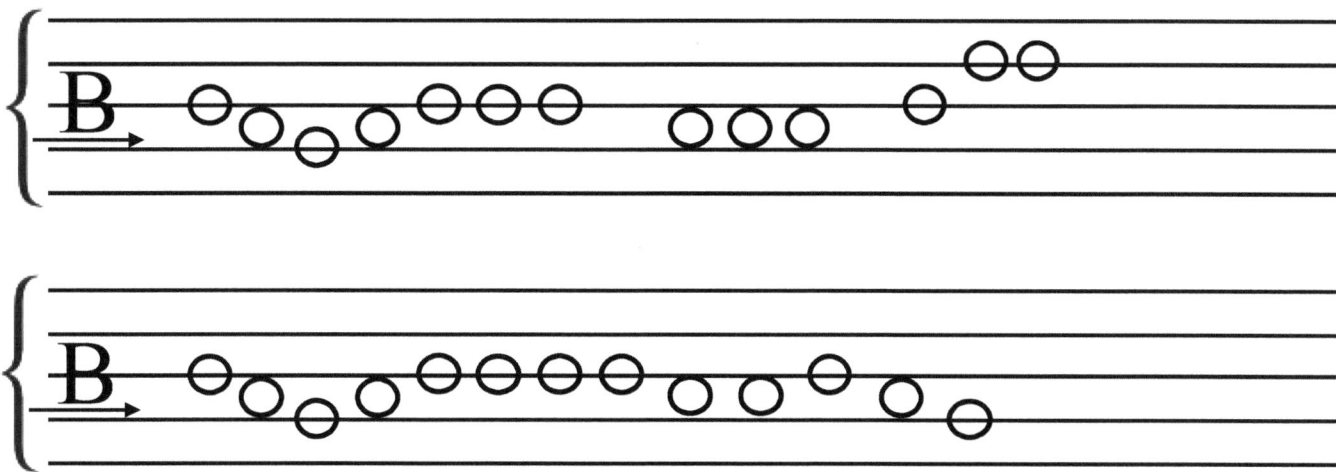

This is how musicians first started reading and writing music hundreds of years ago in Western Europe, where our present system of common practice Western music notation began to be developed.

Let's read and play the song again using a staff of five lines. This time, we are going to start on the note B, specifically, the first B above Middle C. We'll specify this B as the middle line of the staff.

The letter at the beginning of the staff shows us the location of one note. Then, we can go up and down to determine the other notes.

Music Notation

Clefs

When we identify the location of one note on a staff, so that by knowing that one note we can go up and down to determine the other notes, we call that guide note on the staff a *clef*.

For example, the clef on the staff below tells us that the second line from the bottom of the staff is a G, specifically, the first G above Middle C.

We can refer to this clef as a *"G clef."*

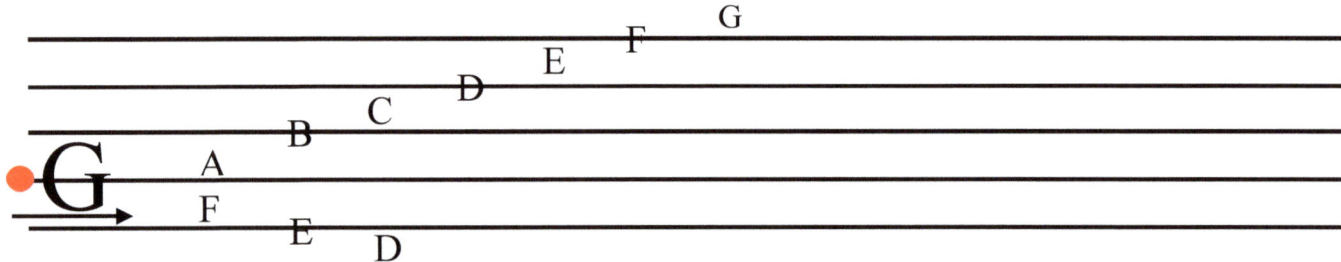

For another example, the clef on the staff below tells us that the second line from the top of the staff is an F, specifically, the first F below Middle C.

We can refer to this clef as an *"F clef."*

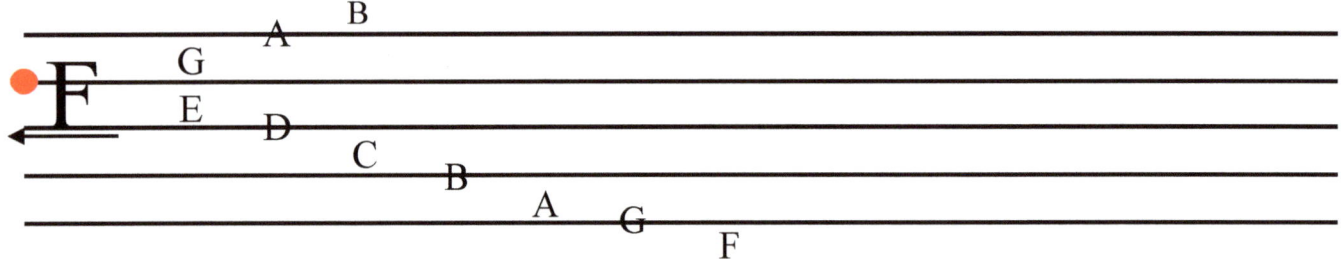

The G clef and the F clef have become two of the important clefs we use in music today. The G clef is also called the *treble clef*, and the F clef is also called the *bass clef*.

The treble clef staff generally contains notes above Middle C, and the bass clef staff generally contains notes below Middle C.

STAFF AND CLEF PRACTICE

Draw ten different notes on various lines of the staff below:

Draw ten different notes on various spaces of the staff below:

Write in the missing notes on the G clef staff below:

Write in the missing notes on the F clef staff below:

Going *up* the staff means going to the right / left *(circle one)* on the piano keyboard?

Going *down* the staff means going to the right / left *(circle one)* on the piano keyboard?

Paw-Paw Patch

Appalachian Folk Song

Play the notes on the G clef with your Right Hand, and the notes on the F clef with your Left Hand. Clap the beat while you sing the song before beginning to play it on the piano. The claps and beats are written below the lyrics and solfege. Then, sing as you play the song on the piano!

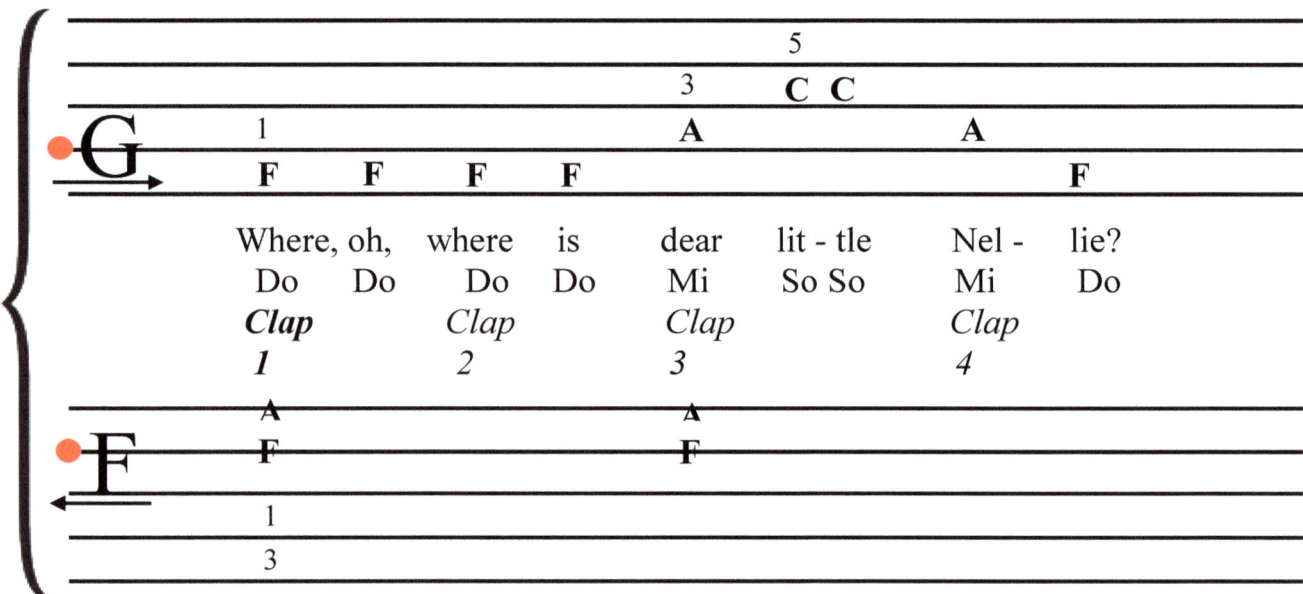

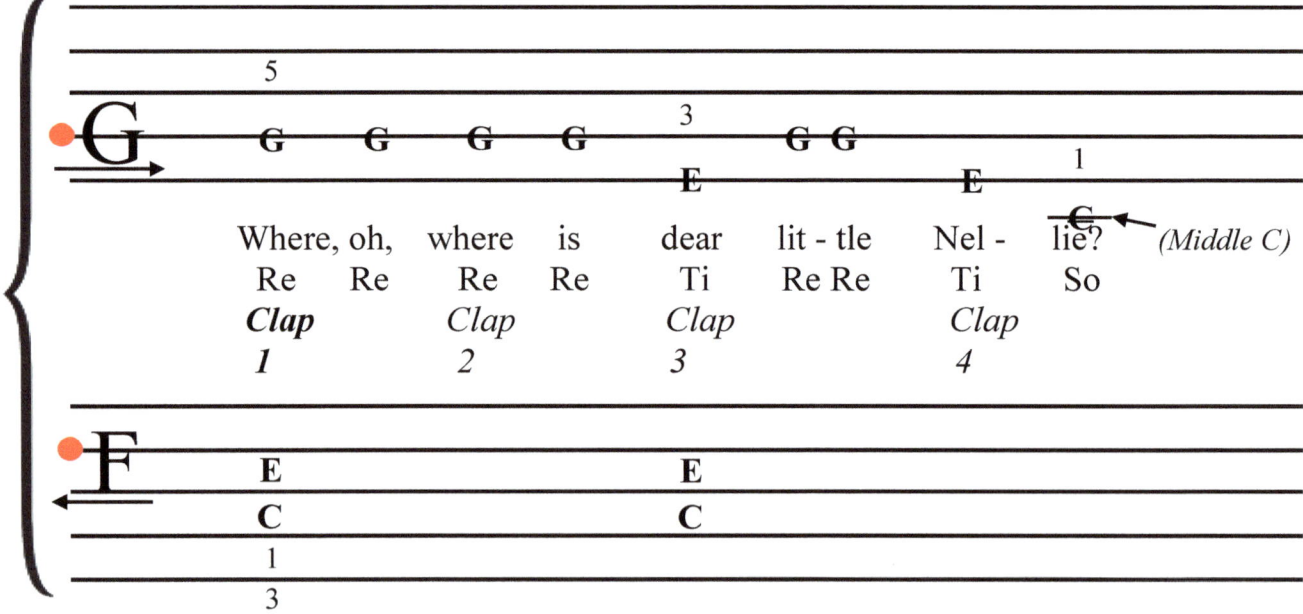

PAW-PAW PATCH (CONT.)

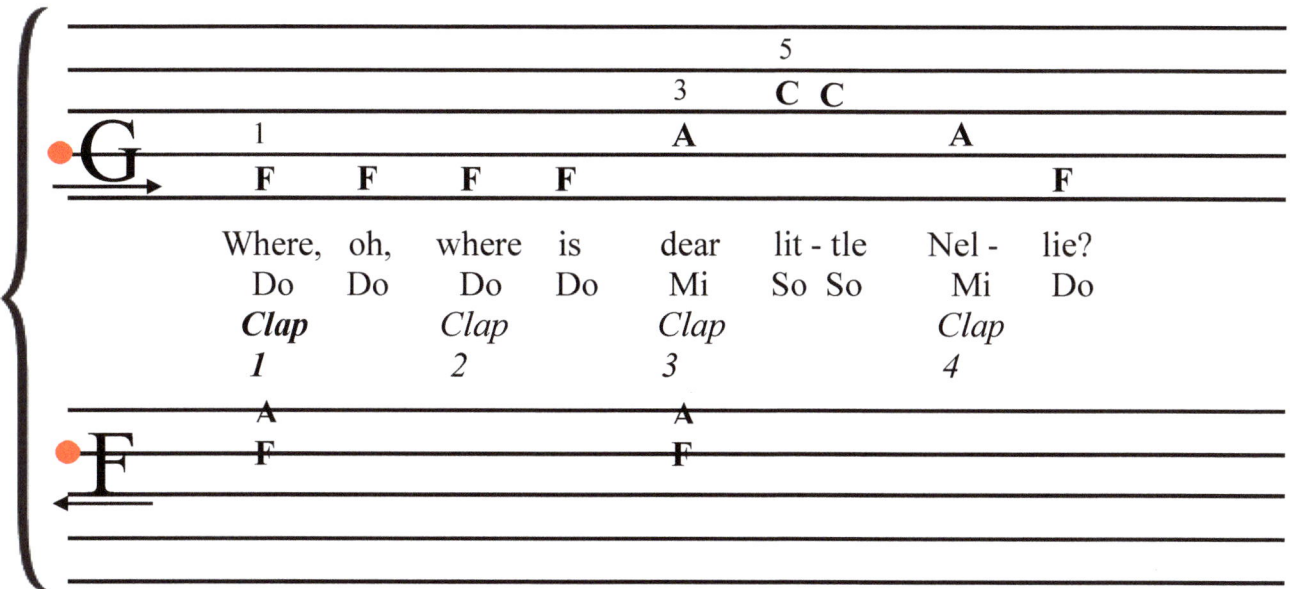

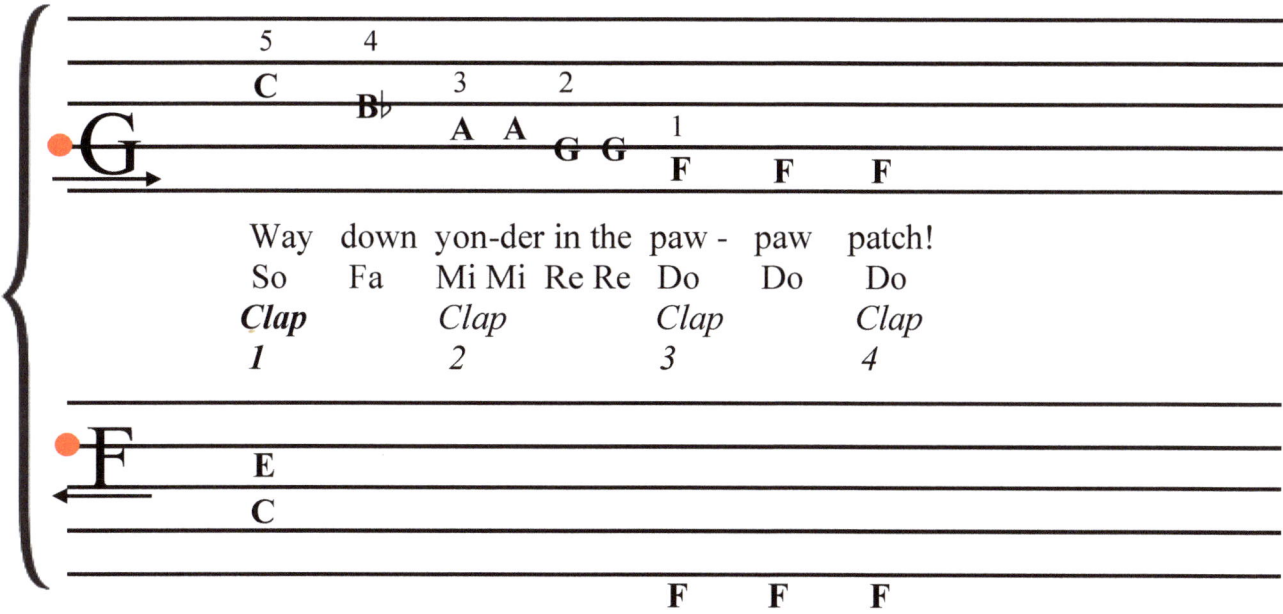

Remember, memorize all of your songs, sing the words as you play, and sing the melody on solfege.

Always sit with good posture, and continue to play free of tension (ghost hands)!

TREBLE CLEF

(G Clef)

The G clef is called the *treble clef*. The treble clef sign tells us that the second line from the bottom of the staff is a G, specifically, the first G above Middle C.

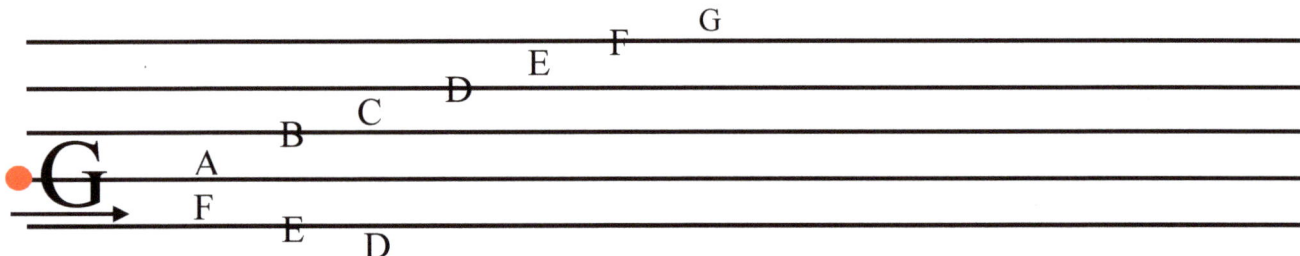

The treble clef sign is a big, fancy G. It doesn't look exactly like a G any more, but it started out that way!

The treble clef sign circles around the second line from the bottom of the staff, which is the G (first G above Middle C). This is how it "points" to the G:

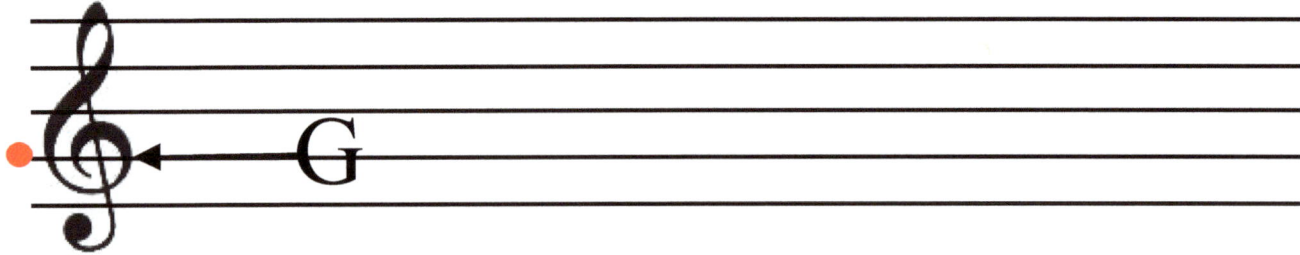

Bass Clef

(F Clef)

The F clef is called the ***bass clef***. The bass clef sign tells us that the second line from the top of the staff is an F, specifically, the first F below Middle C.

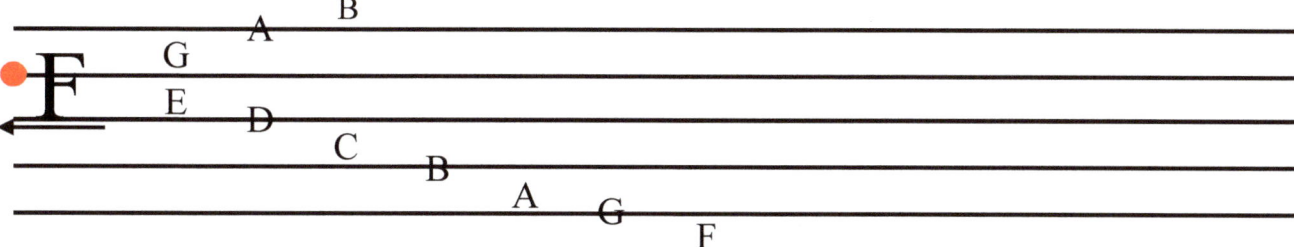

The bass clef sign is a big, fancy F. It doesn't look exactly like an F any more, but it started out that way!

The bass clef sign's two dots are placed above and below the second line from the top of the staff, which is the F (first F below Middle C). This is how it "points" to the F:

TREBLE AND BASS CLEF PRACTICE

Draw ten notes on the treble clef G line of the staff below:

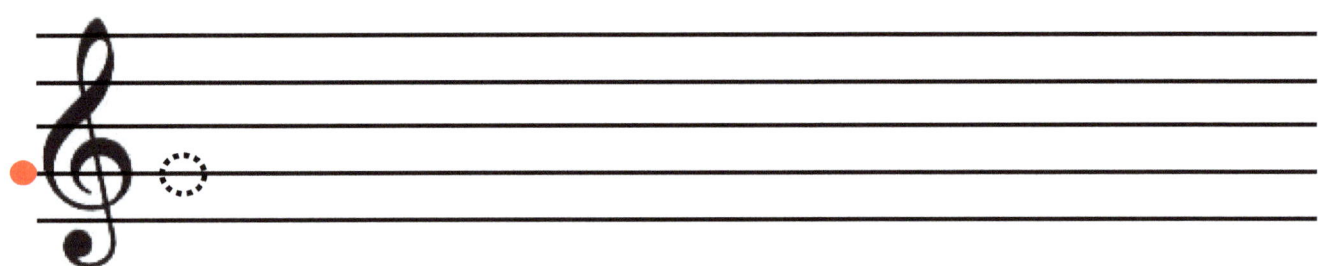

Draw ten notes on the bass clef F line of the staff below:

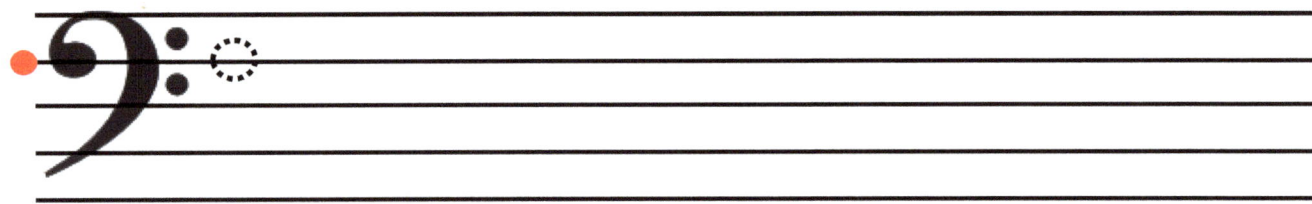

Draw five treble clef signs below. Be sure to have the curl wrap around the second-line G.

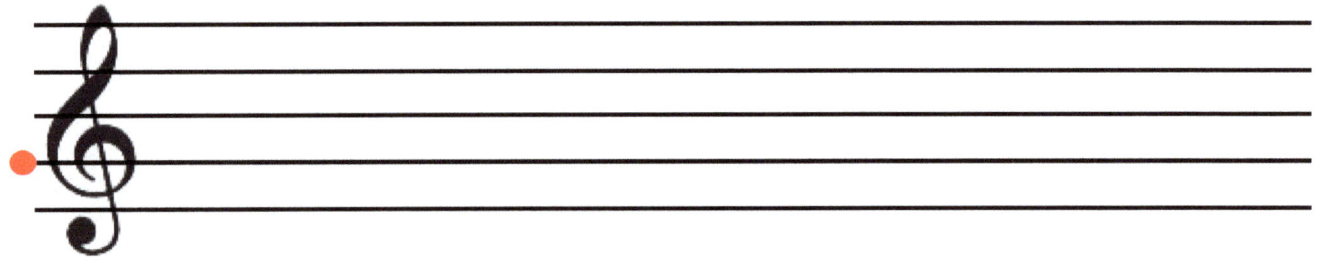

Draw five bass clef signs below. Be sure to place the two dots above and below the second-line F.

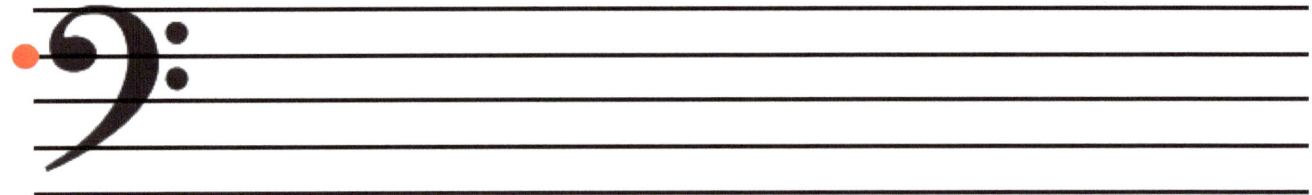

Treble and Bass Clef Practice (cont.)

The space just above the treble clef line G is A (going up the music alphabet).

Draw five notes on the treble clef G line, and then five notes on the treble clef A space, on the staff below:

The space just above the bass clef line F is G (going up the music alphabet).

Draw five notes on the bass clef F line, and then five notes on the bass clef G space, on the staff below:

The space just below the treble clef line G is F (going down the music alphabet).

Draw five notes on the treble clef G line, and then five notes on the treble clef F space, on the staff below:

The space just below the bass clef line F is E (going down the music alphabet).

Draw five notes on the bass clef F line, and then five notes on the bass clef E space, on the staff below:

I'm super proud of you!

You're beginning to read music on the *grand staff*!

This is a huge accomplishment!

You are making outstanding progress!

Have fun learning *London Bridge*!

And...

Keep up the good work!

Let's learn *London Bridge*

London Bridge is an English Nursery Rhyme. The London Bridge spans the River Thames in London, England. Once, when the new London Bridge was being rebuilt and modernized, the old London Bridge was sold to a builder in the United States, and transported there, brick by brick, and piece by piece. It was rebuilt in Arizona and now spans a channel of water between Lake Havasu and Thompson Bay, off the Colorado River.

The song is written using notes from the C Major Scale.

The music is written using notes placed on the G clef, or treble clef, and on the F clef, or bass clef.

Play the notes on the G clef with your Right Hand, and the notes on the F clef with your Left Hand.

Clap the beat while you sing the song before beginning to play it on the piano. The claps and beats are written below the lyrics and solfege. Then, sing as you play the song on the piano!

Continue to memorize all your songs!

LONDON BRIDGE

Using notes from the C Major Scale

English Nursery Rhyme

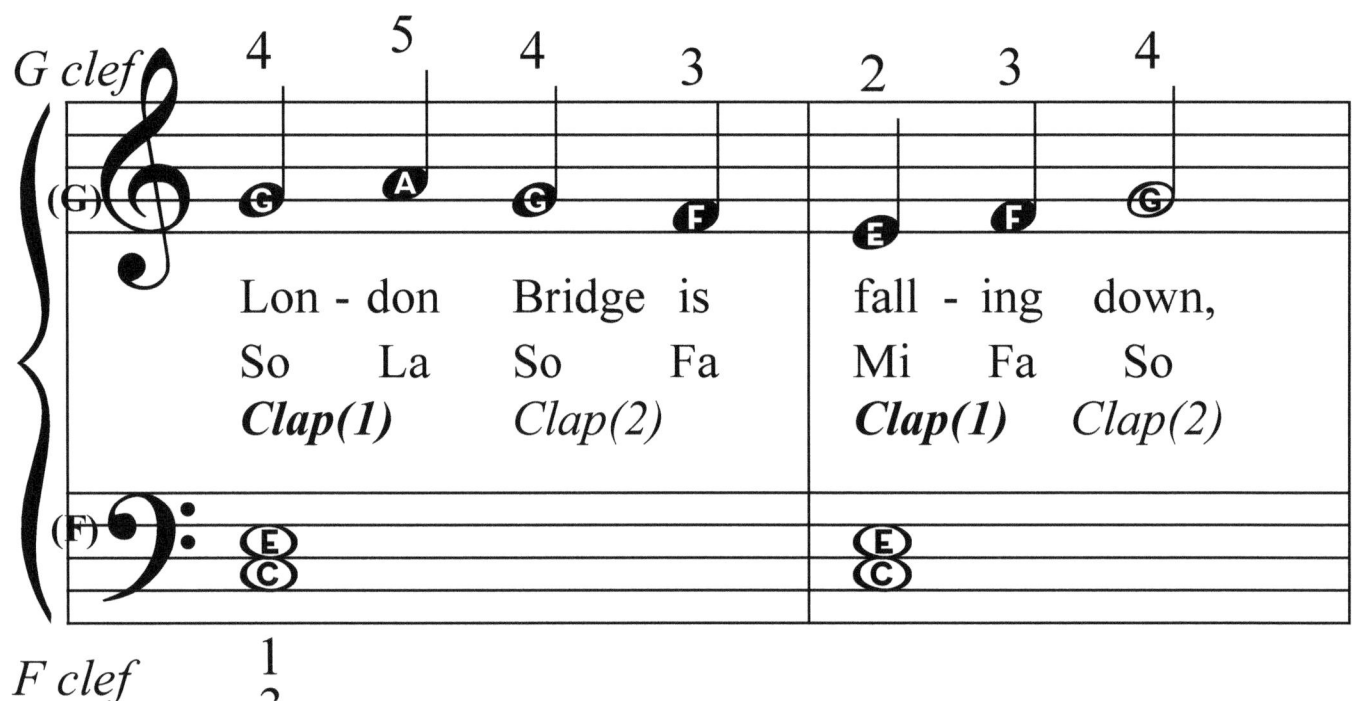

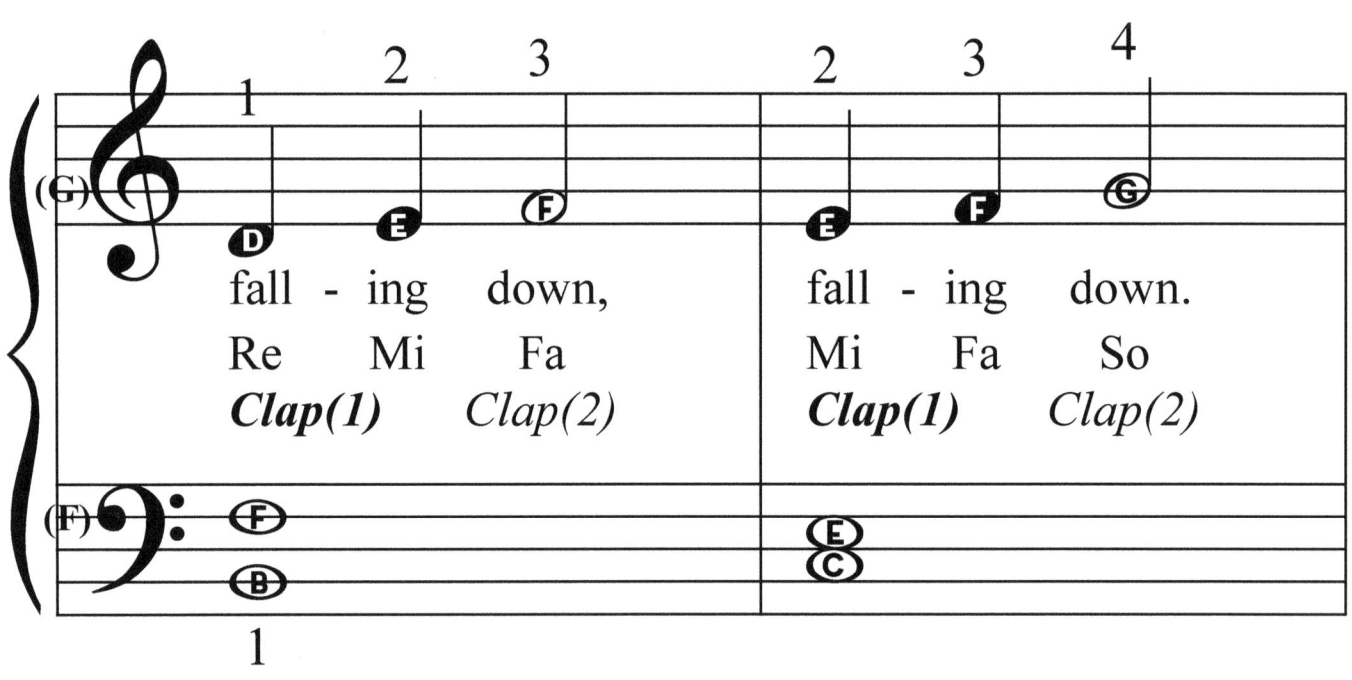

London Bridge (cont.)

Using notes from the C Major Scale English Nursery Rhyme

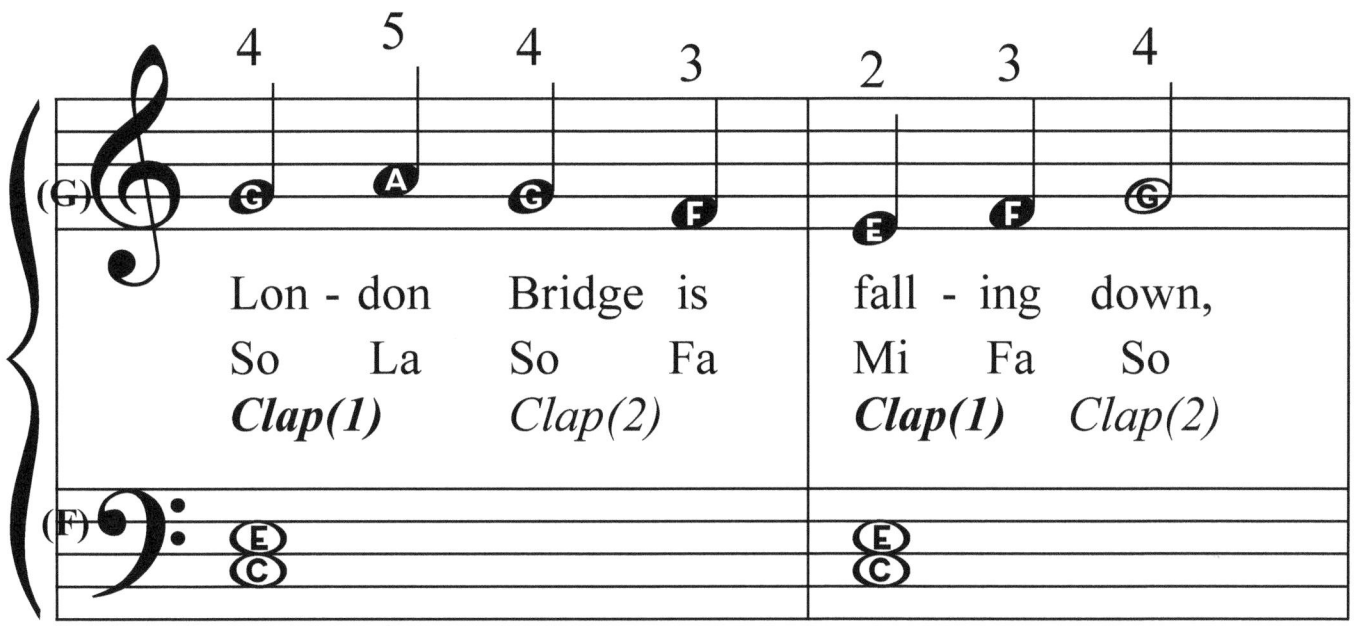

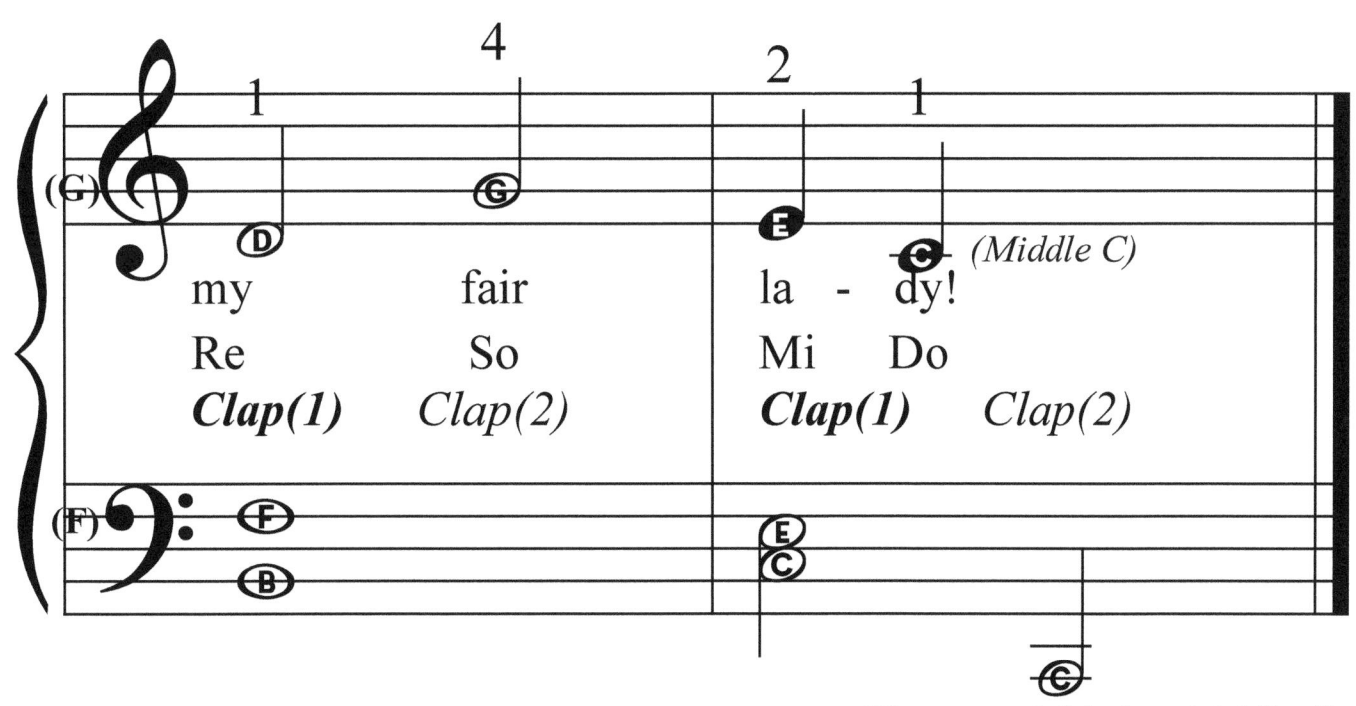

(The second C below Middle C)

MORE TREBLE AND BASS CLEF PRACTICE

*Draw ten notes on the **treble clef G** line of the staff below:*

*Draw ten notes on the **bass clef F** line of the staff below:*

Draw five treble clef signs below. Be sure to have the curl wrap around the second-line G.

Draw five bass clef signs below. Be sure to place the two dots above and below the second-line F.

MORE TREBLE AND BASS CLEF PRACTICE (CONT.)

The space right *below* G on the treble clef is ___. (Remember, it's the letter that comes right before G in the music alphabet!)

The space right *above* G on the treble clef is ___. (Remember, it's the letter that comes right after G in the music alphabet!)

Draw ten notes on the F space that is just below the G line of the treble clef staff below:

Draw ten notes on the A space that is just above the G line of the treble clef staff below:

Draw the notes indicated below on the correct lines or spaces:

G   A   F   G   F   G   A   A   F   G

MORE TREBLE AND BASS CLEF PRACTICE (CONT.)

The space right *below* F on the bass clef is ___. (Remember, it's the letter that comes right before F in the music alphabet!)

The space right *above* F on the bass clef is ___. (Remember, it's the letter that comes right after F in the music alphabet!)

Draw ten notes on the E space that is just below the F line of the bass clef staff below:

Draw ten notes on the G space that is just above the F line of the bass clef staff below:

Draw the notes indicated below on the correct lines or spaces:

F   G   E   F   E   F   G   G   E   F

MORE TREBLE AND BASS CLEF PRACTICE (CONT.)

Draw the notes indicated below on the correct lines or spaces:

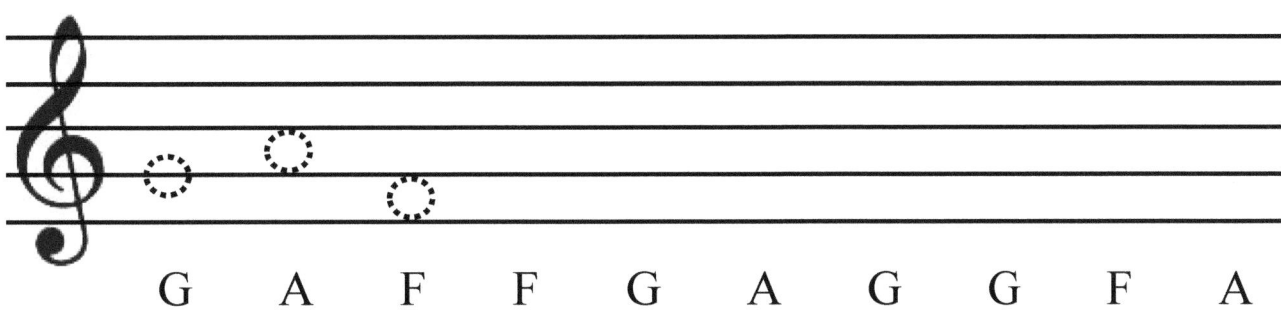

G A F F G A G G F A

Draw the notes indicated below on the correct lines or spaces:

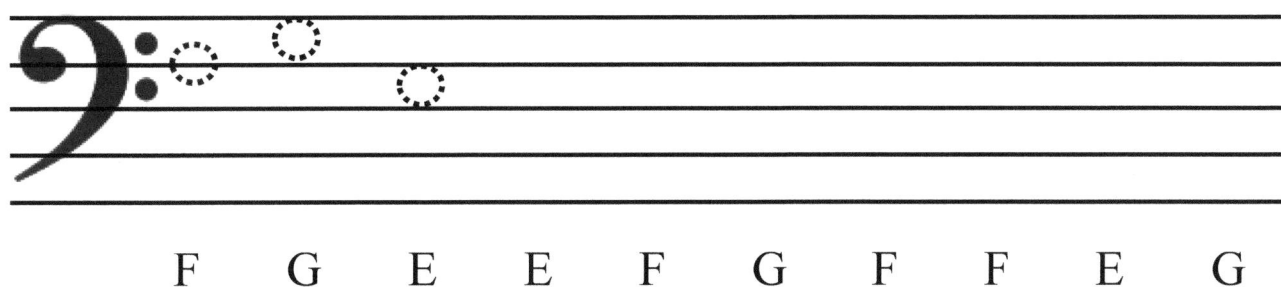

F G E E F G F F E G

Draw the notes indicated below on the correct lines or spaces:

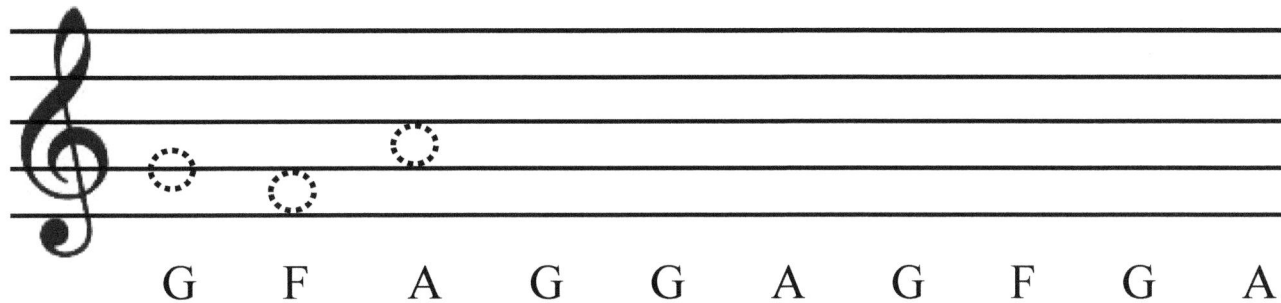

G F A G G A G F G A

Draw the notes indicated below on the correct lines or spaces:

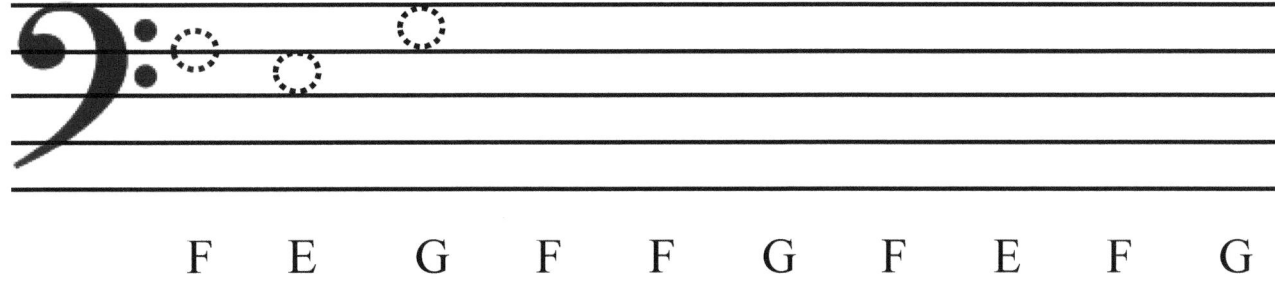

F E G F F G F E F G

Los Pollitos

Using notes from the G Major Scale   Cuban Children's Song and Game

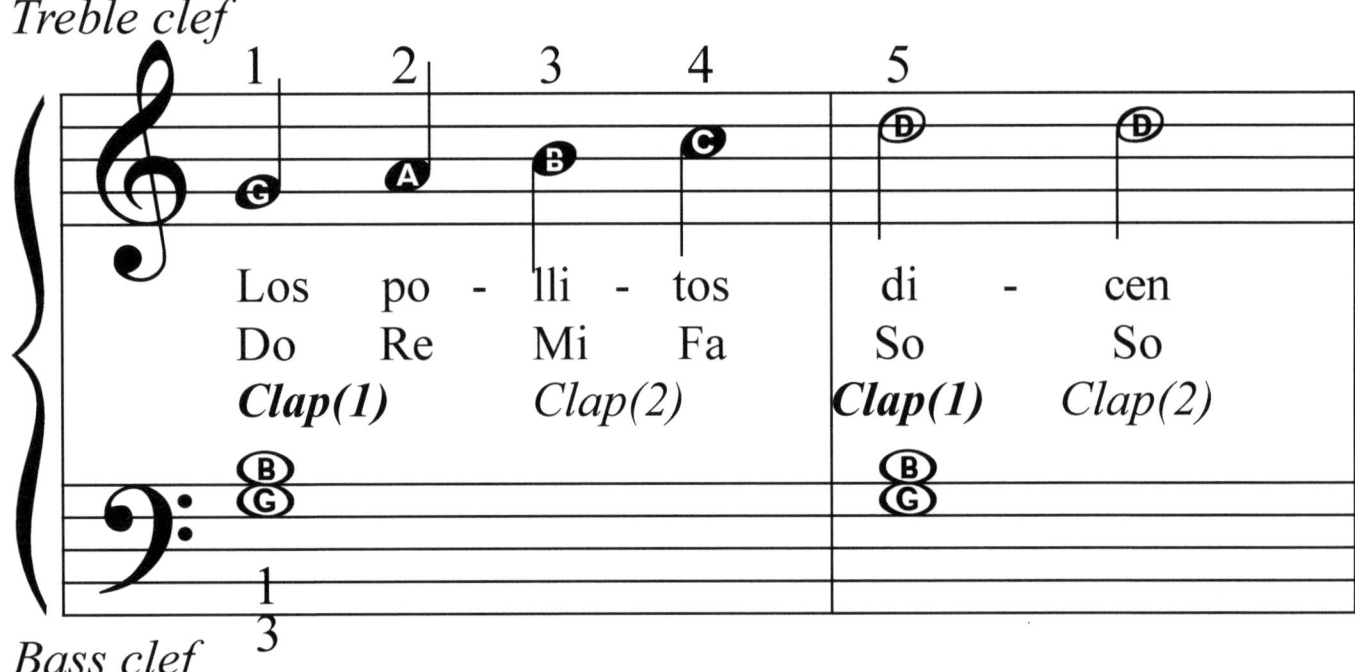
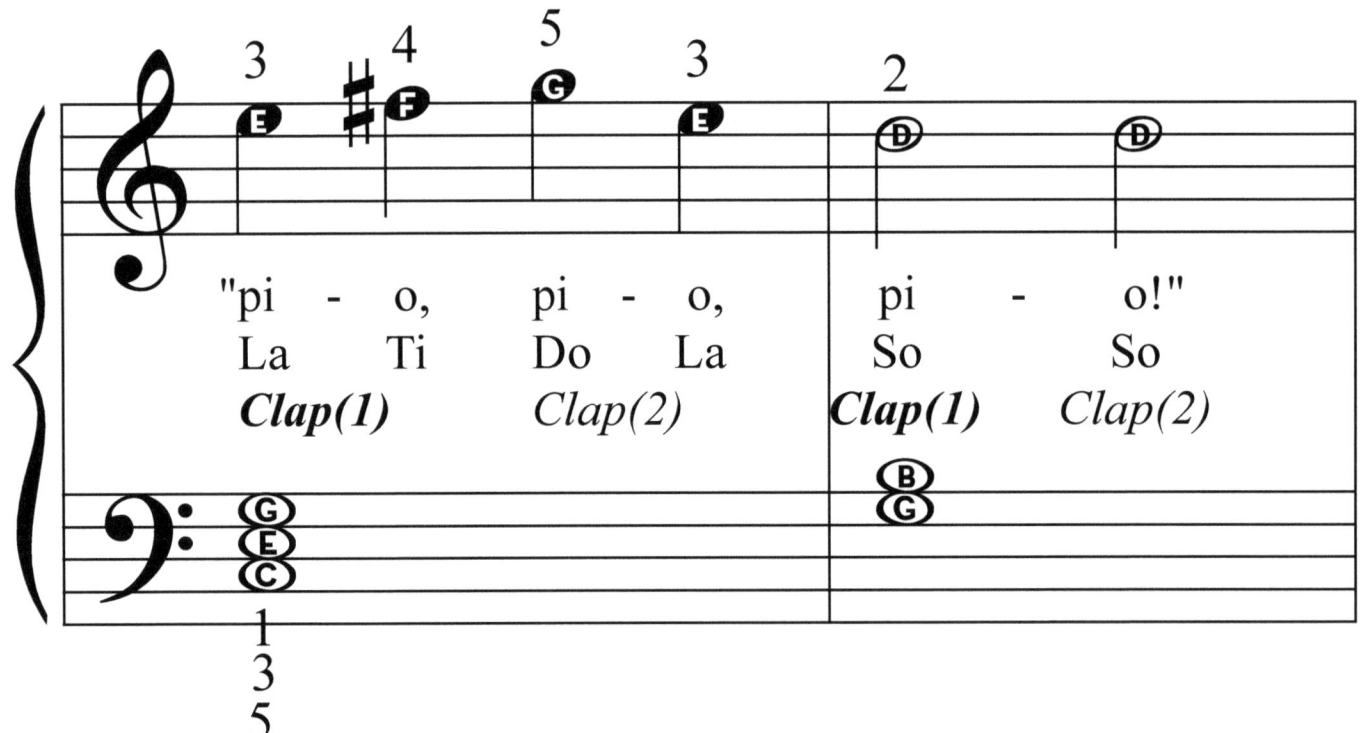

124

Los Pollitos (cont.)

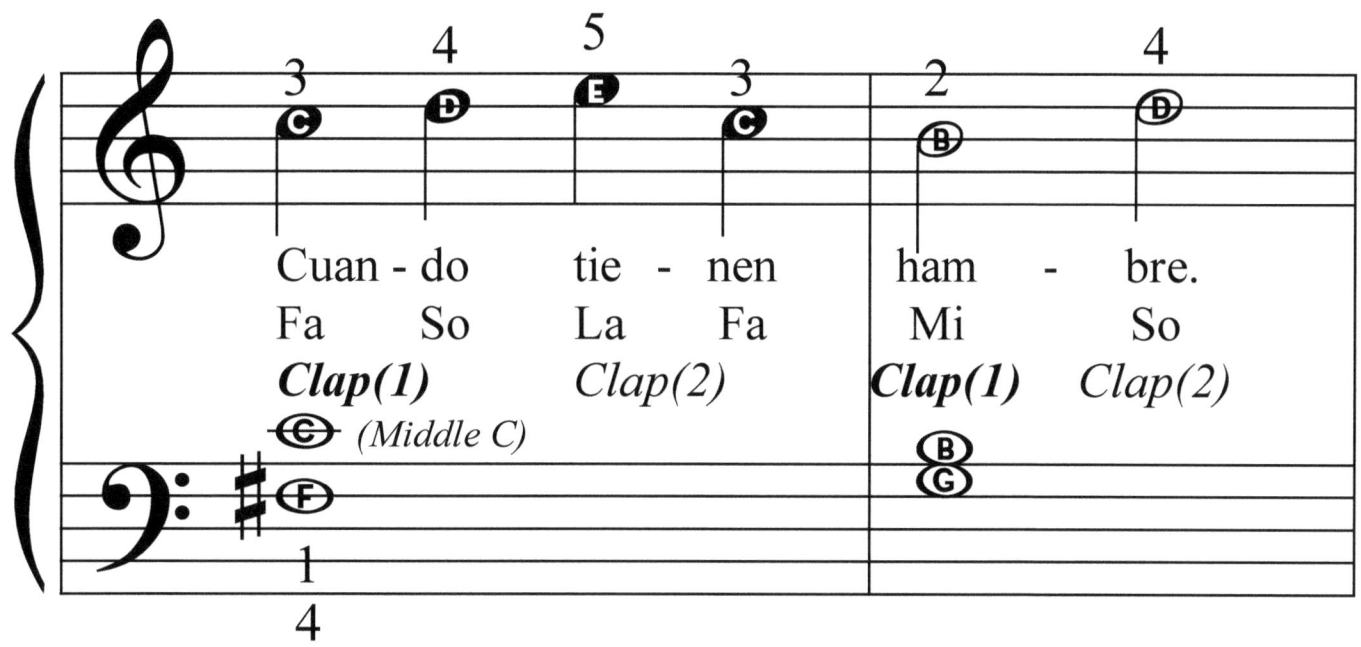

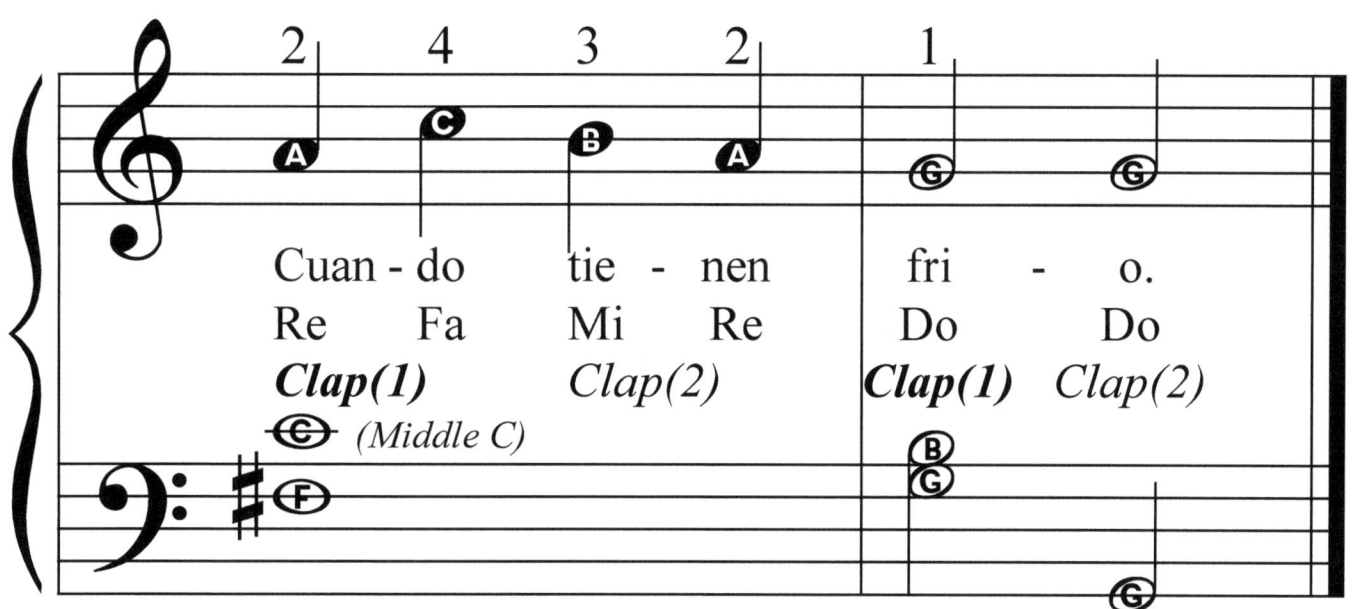

The Grand Staff

When we put the treble clef staff and the bass clef staff together, we call it the *Grand Staff*.

Notice that the treble clef staff and the bass clef staff are joined together with a vertical bar and a brace.

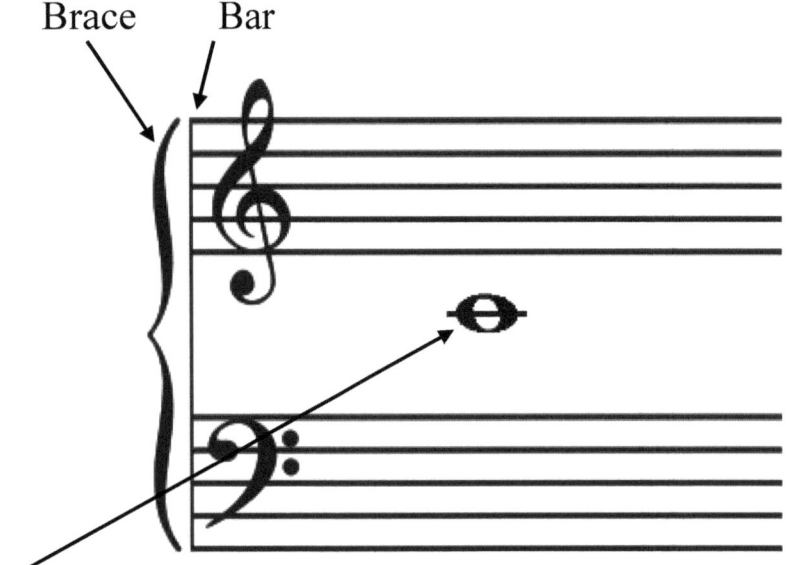

Middle C joins the treble and bass clefs together on the grand staff.

Middle C isn't on either the treble clef staff or the bass clef staff. It's on a special line of its own, just below the treble clef staff, and just above the bass clef staff. This line is called a *ledger line*.

The grand staff in a piece of music is often referred to as a *system*.

Each page of music contains one or more systems. Each system, or grand staff, ends with the bar line of the last measure in the system. The very last system, or grand staff, in the piece of music typically ends with a *double bar*.

LEDGER LINES

When we need to play notes in the music that are higher or lower than the lines and spaces of the staff, we put the notes on additional lines called *ledger lines*.

Ledger lines can be placed above a staff for higher notes, and below a staff for lower notes.

Grand Staff

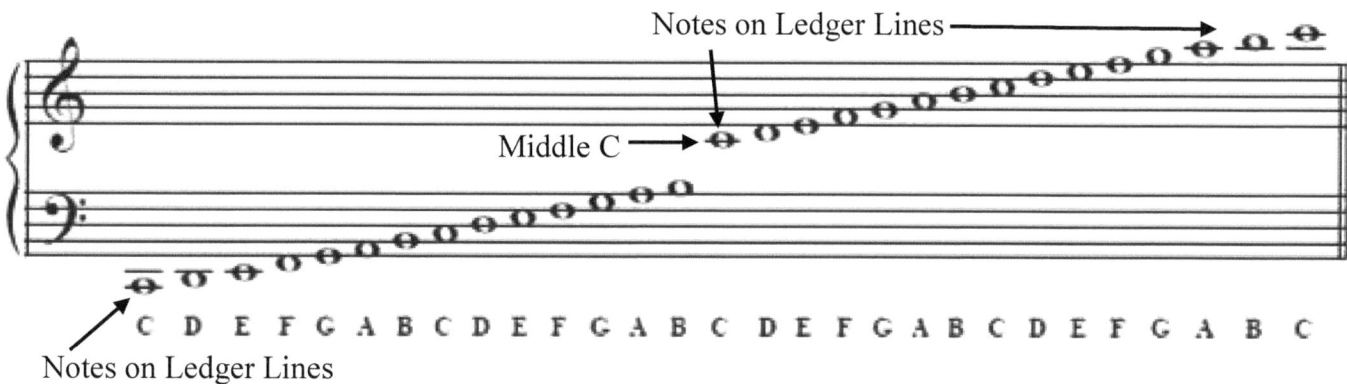

As on a staff, notes using ledger lines can be on lines or spaces.

The note can be *on the ledger line* (line note), or *on the space above or below the ledger line* (space note).

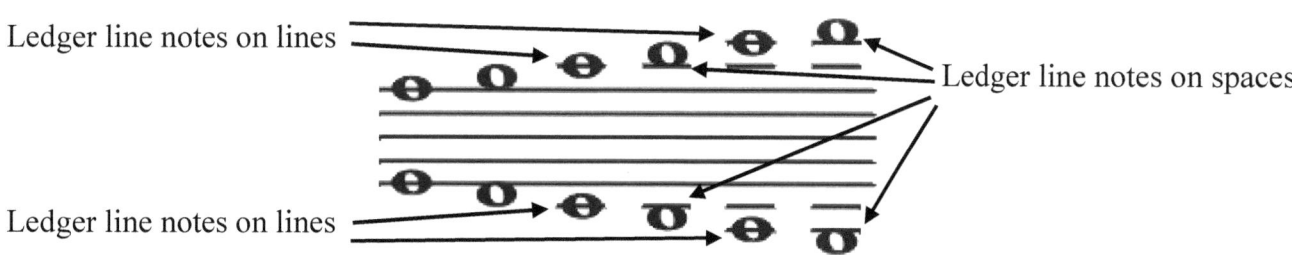

Middle C is on a ledger line (and it is a line note).

The second C above Middle C is on the second ledger line above the treble clef staff. The second C below Middle C is on the second ledger line below the bass clef staff. (This makes an interesting pattern to remember!)

Duérmete, Mi Niño

Using notes from the F Major Scale

Spanish and Latin American Lullaby

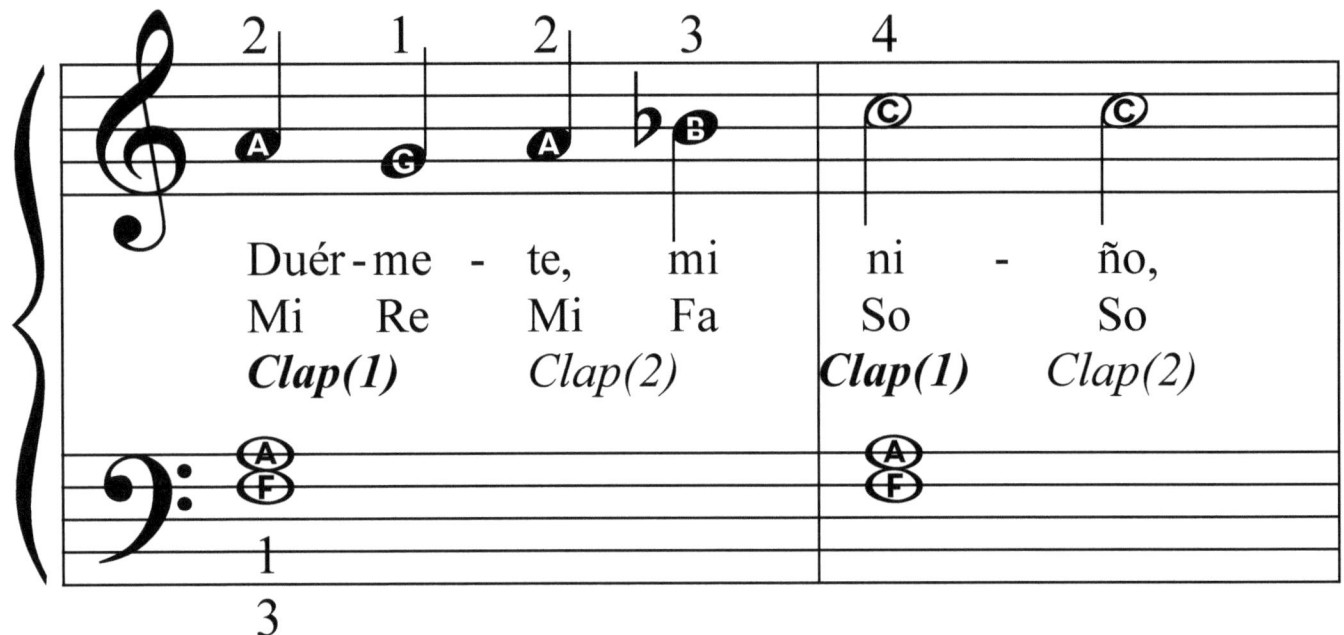

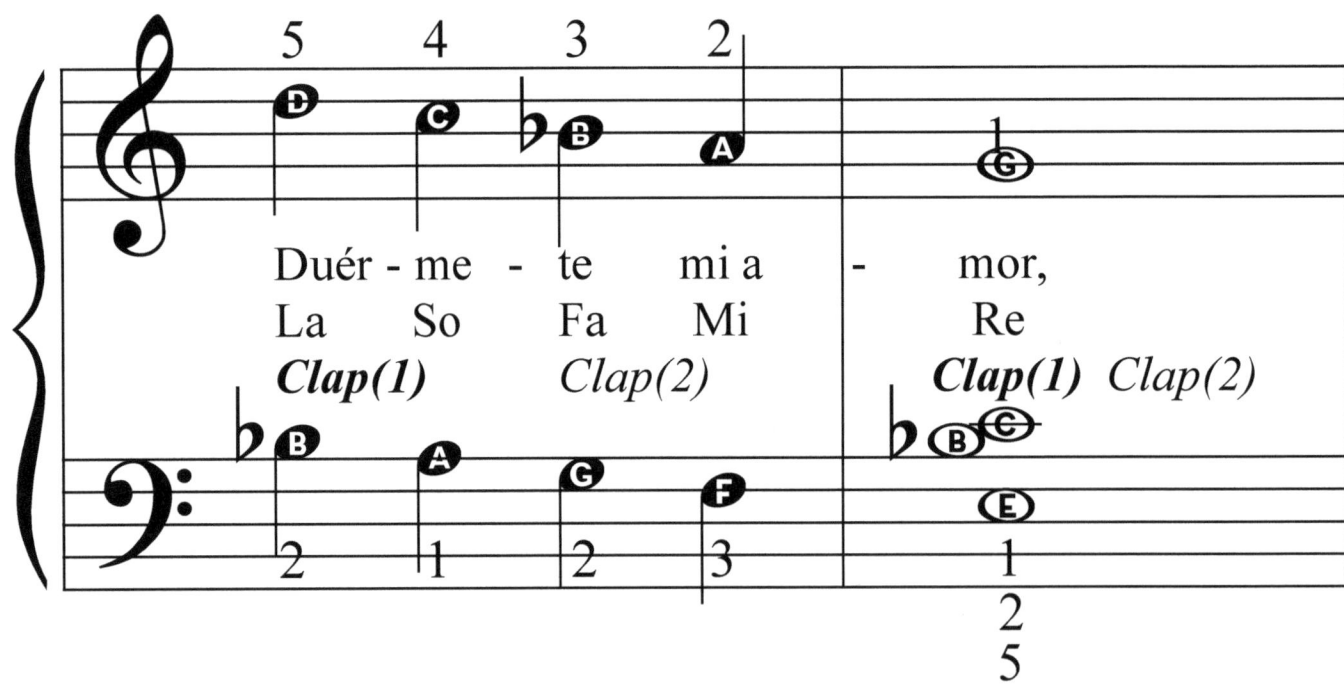

Duérmete, Mi Niño (cont.)

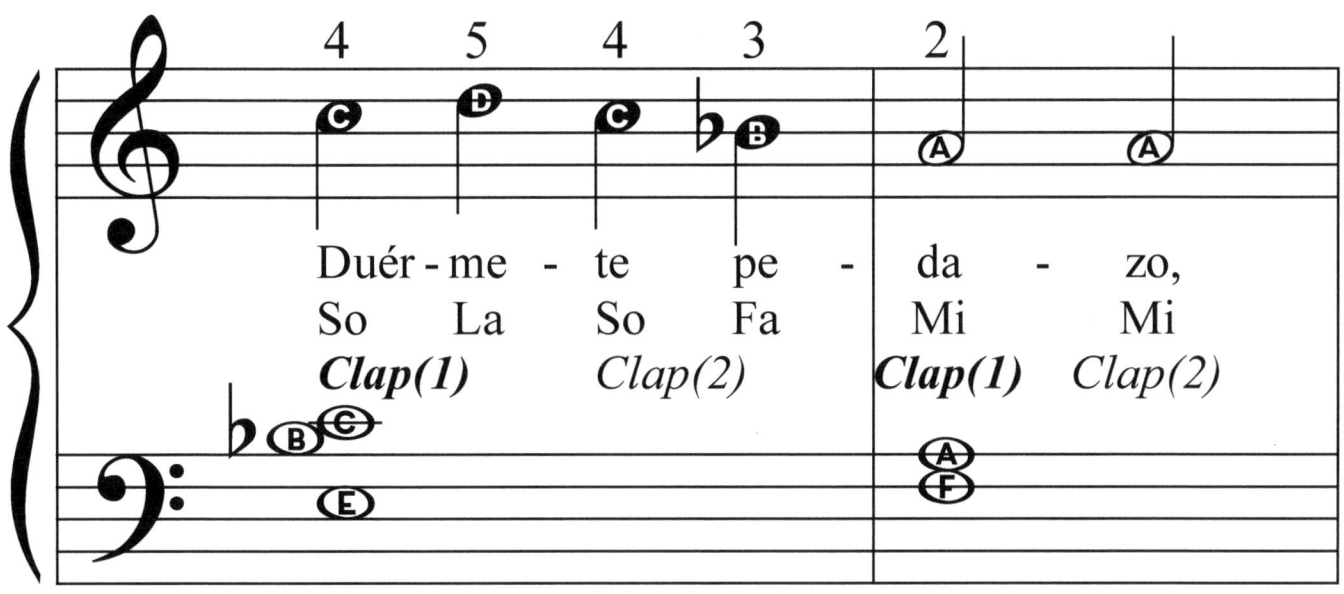

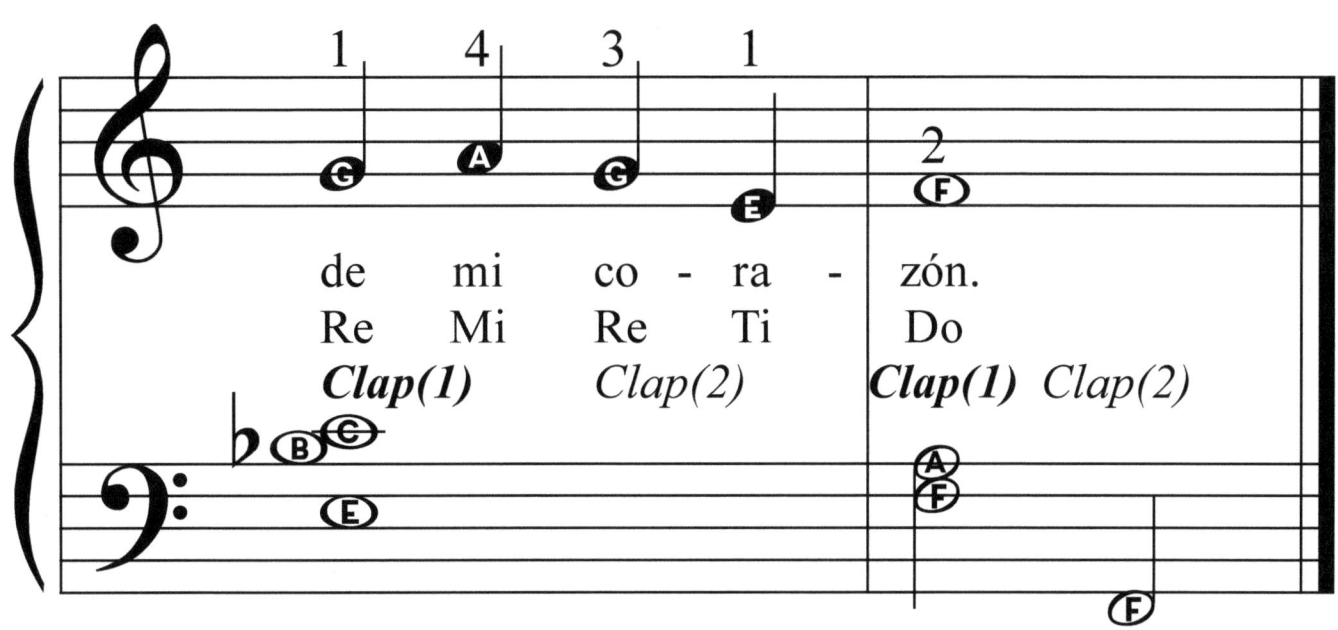

GRAND STAFF PRACTICE

Draw a <u>single</u> bar at the end of this grand staff.

Draw the bar, brace, and <u>double</u> bar for each grand staff below.

Now, go back up and draw a Middle C, on a ledger line, where it belongs, in between the treble clef and bass clef of each grand staff above.

A grand staff consists of a _____ clef and a _____ clef.

Another word for <u>grand staff</u> in a piece of music is _____.

Note and Ledger Line Practice

Draw the notes indicated below on the correct lines or spaces:

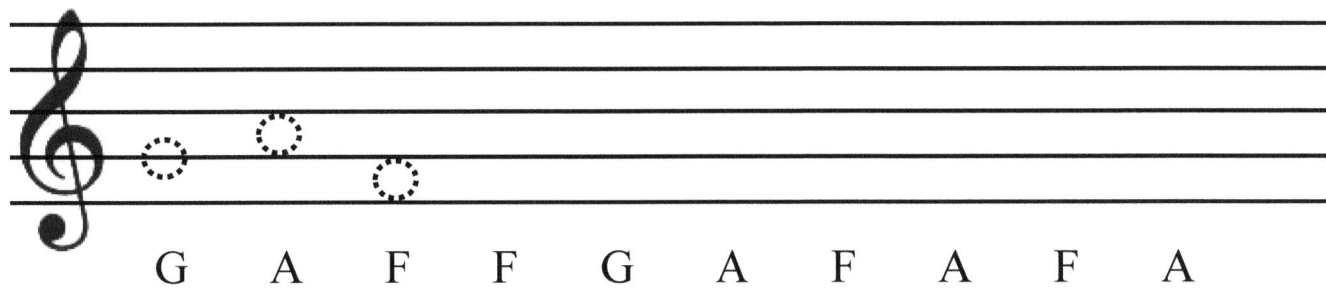

G A F F G A F A F A

Draw the notes indicated below on the correct lines or spaces:

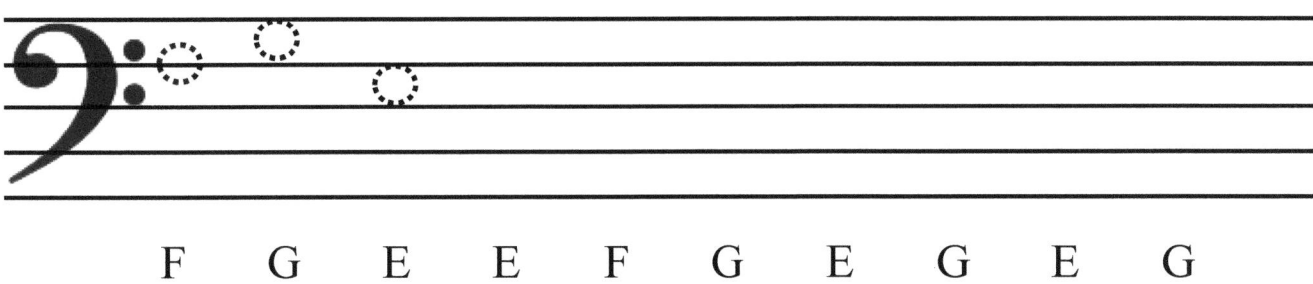

F G E E F G E G E G

Draw a ledger line with Middle C on it, in between the treble and bass clef of the grand staff below. Then draw a <u>double bar</u> at the end of the system.

Au Clair De La Lune

Using notes from the C Major Scale

French Folk Song

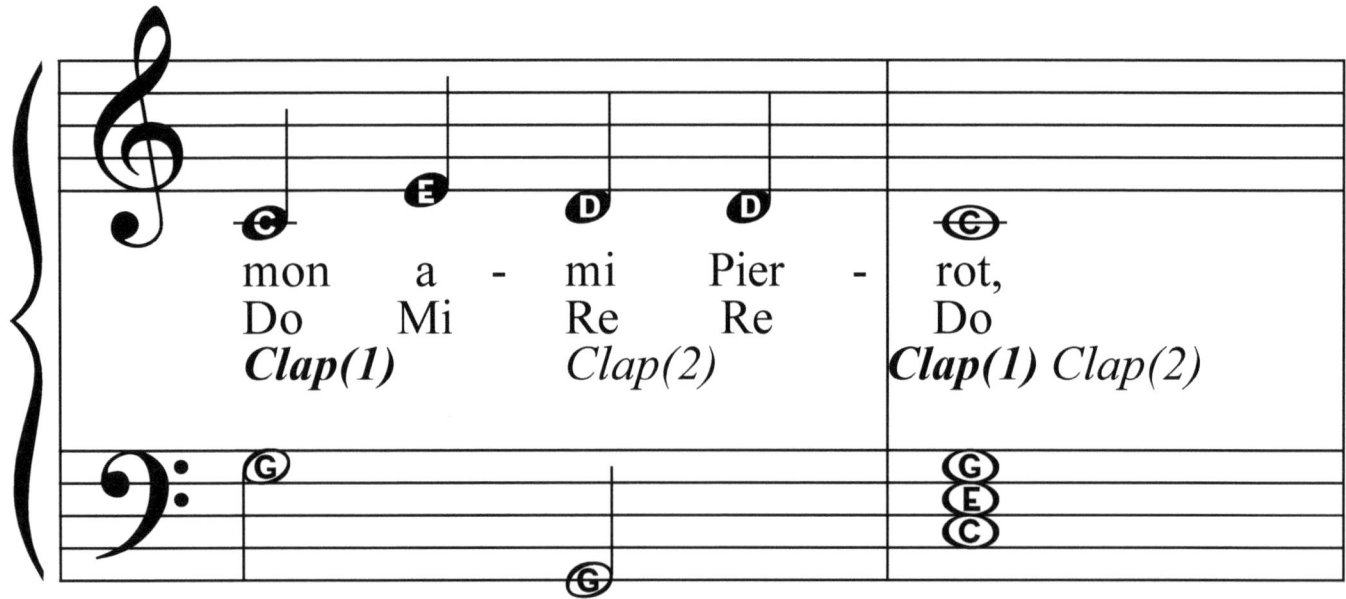

Au Clair De La Lune (cont.)

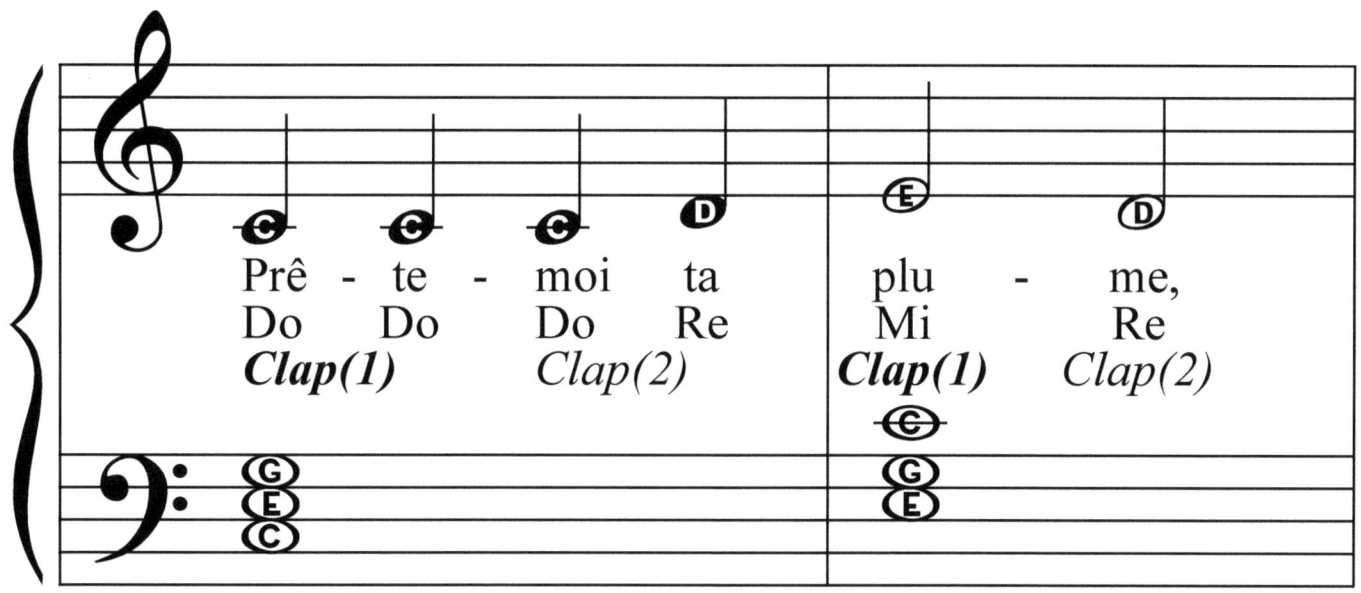

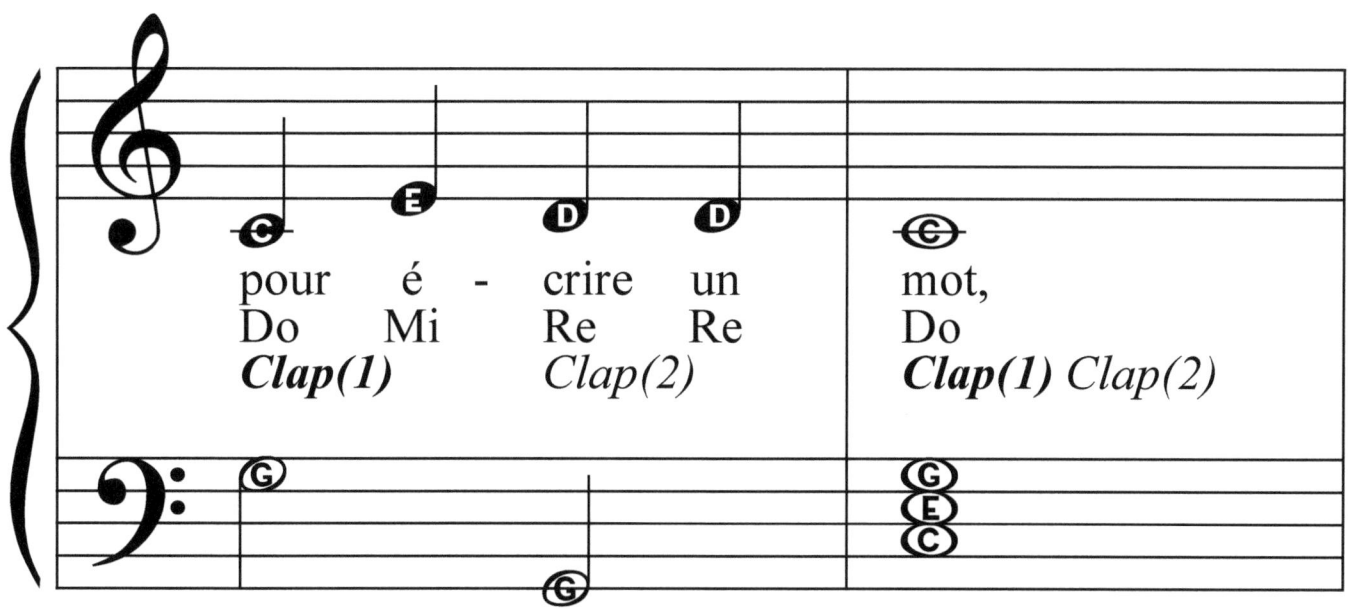

Au Clair De La Lune (cont.)

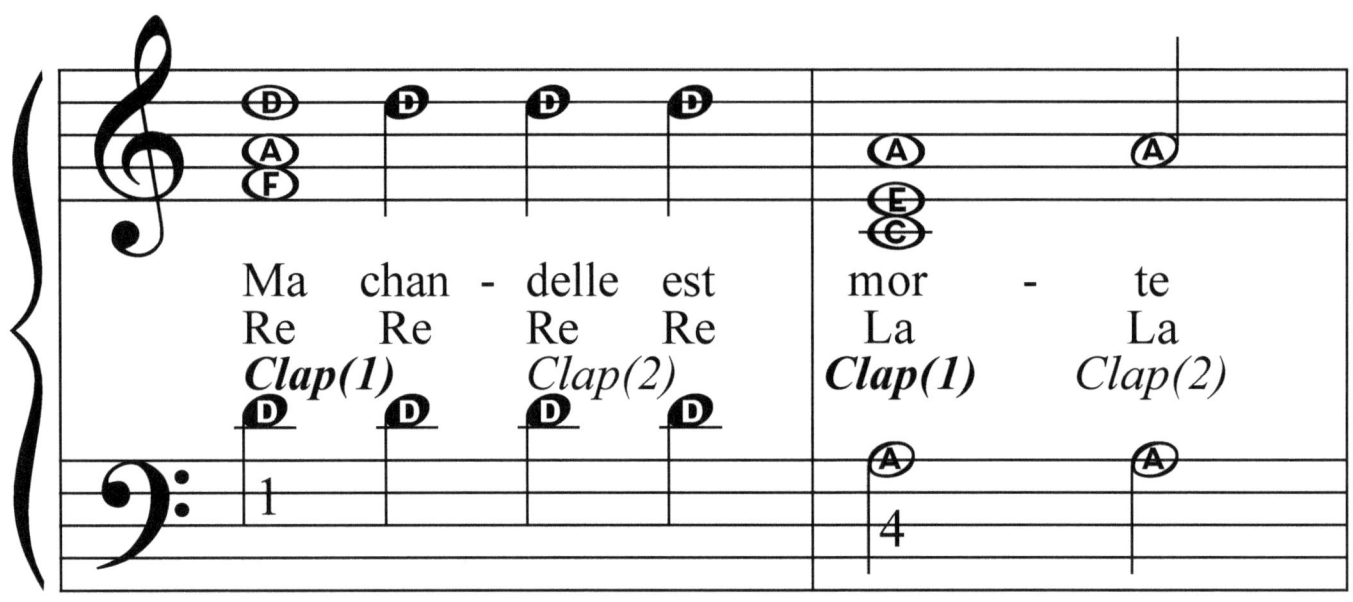

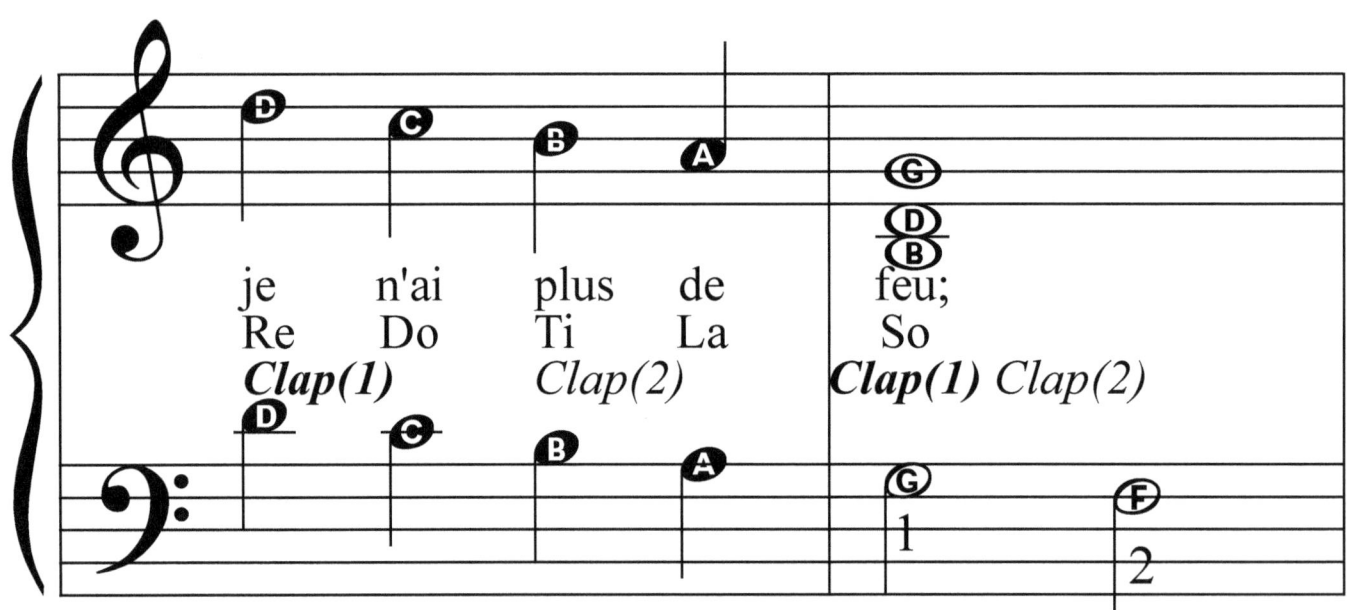

Au Clair De La Lune (cont.)

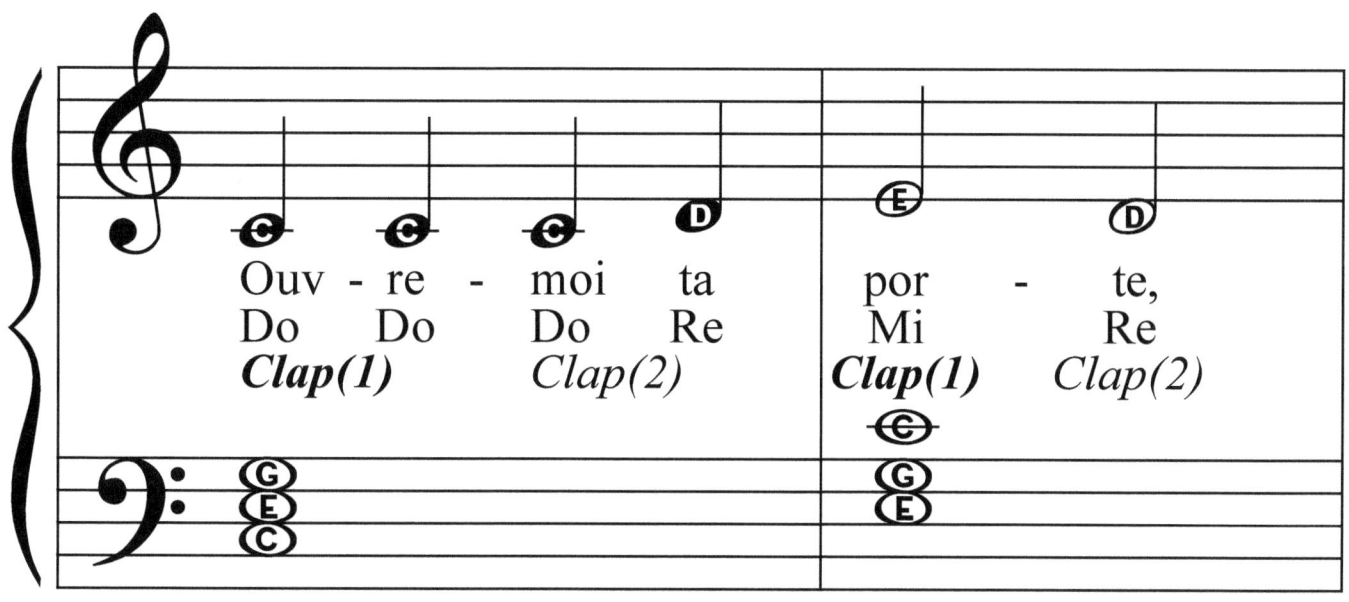

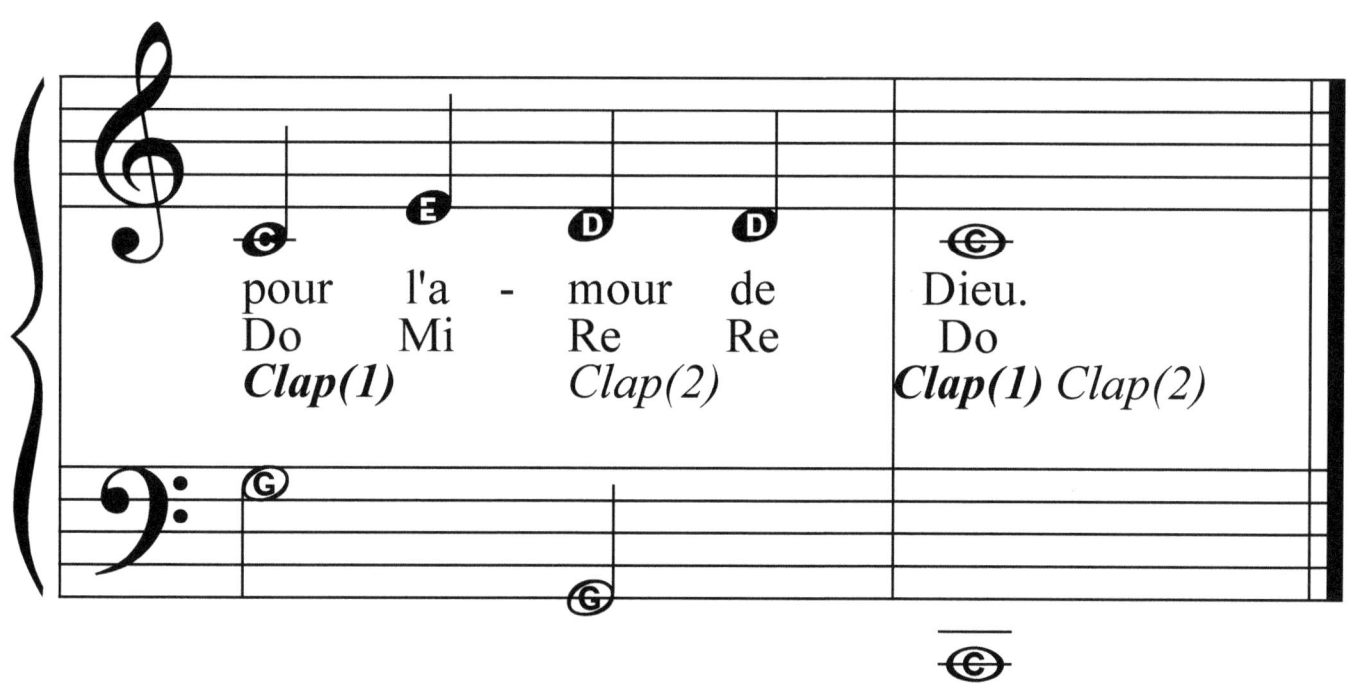

NOTE IDENTIFICATION PRACTICE

The middle line of the treble clef staff is B (the first B above Middle C), and the bottom line of the treble clef staff is E (the first E above Middle C).

Draw the notes indicated below on the correct lines or spaces:

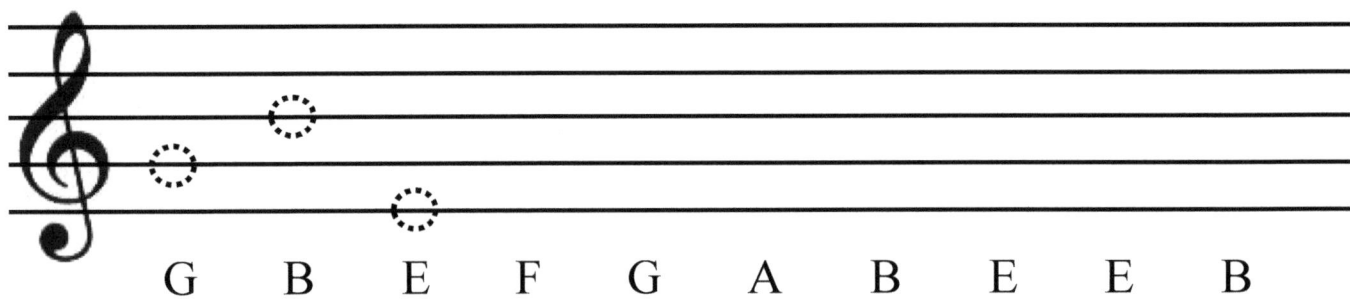

G　B　E　F　G　A　B　E　E　B

The middle line of the bass clef staff is D (the first D below Middle C), and the top line of the bass clef staff is A (the first A below Middle C).

Draw the notes indicated below on the correct lines or spaces:

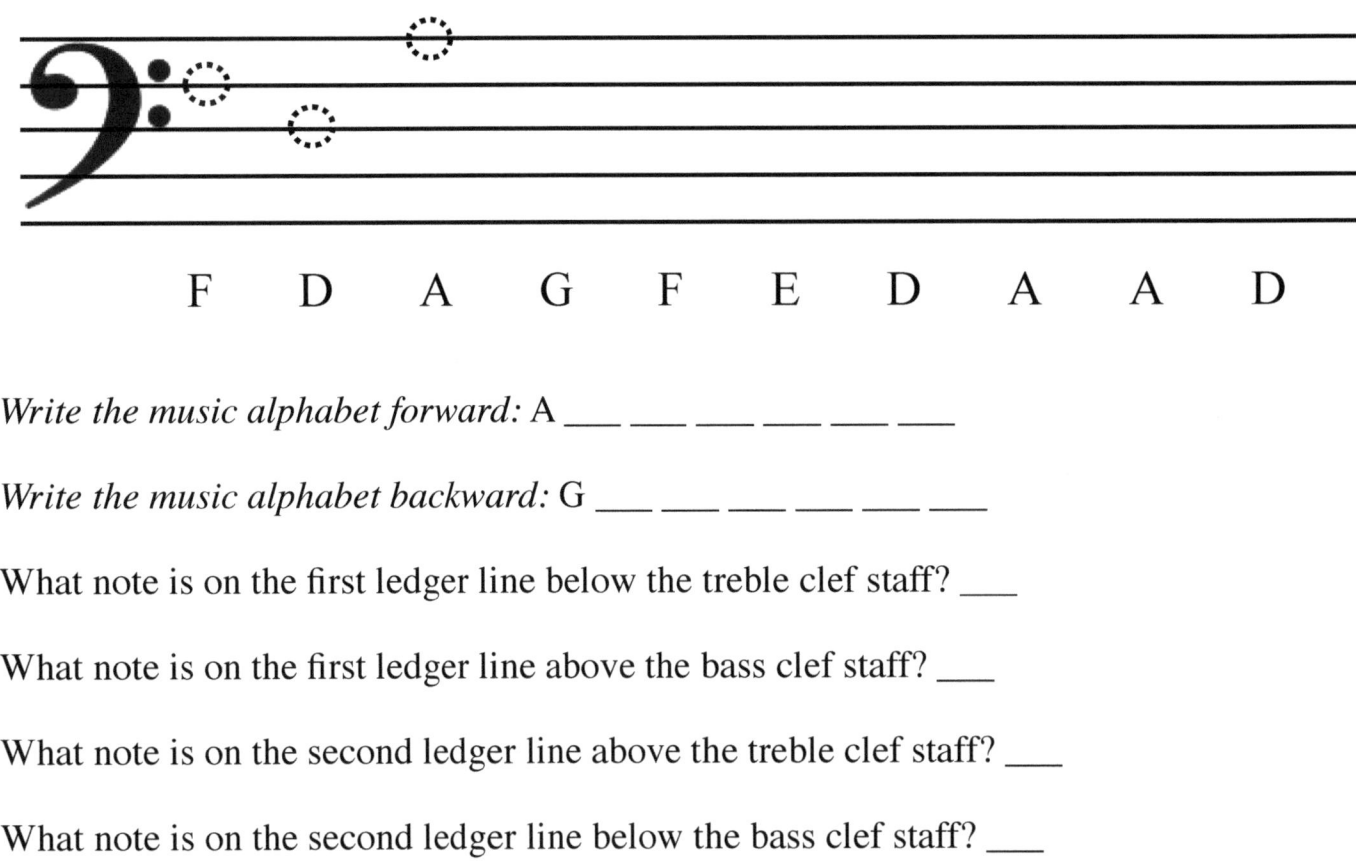

F　D　A　G　F　E　D　A　A　D

Write the music alphabet forward: A ___ ___ ___ ___ ___ ___

Write the music alphabet backward: G ___ ___ ___ ___ ___ ___

What note is on the first ledger line below the treble clef staff? ___

What note is on the first ledger line above the bass clef staff? ___

What note is on the second ledger line above the treble clef staff? ___

What note is on the second ledger line below the bass clef staff? ___

NOTE IDENTIFICATION PRACTICE (CONT.)

The treble clef sign points to ___, which is the second line from the bottom of the staff.

The middle line of the treble clef staff is ___.

The bottom line of the treble clef staff is ___.

The first ledger line below the treble clef staff is _____.

The bass clef sign points to ___, which is the second line from the top of the staff.

The middle line of the bass clef staff is ___.

The top line of the bass clef staff is ___.

The first ledger line above the bass clef staff is _____.

The second ledger line above the treble clef staff is ___.

The second ledger line below the bass clef staff is ___.

The space below the middle line of the treble clef staff is ___.

Write the letter names of the notes in the spaces below:

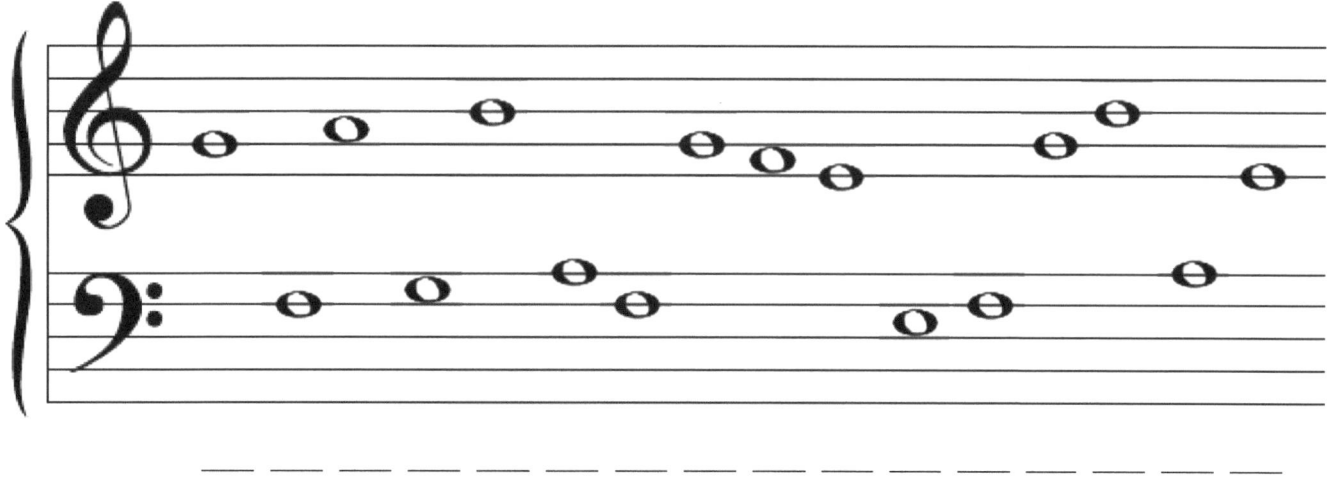

Draw a Middle C on the grand staff above.

Go Down, Moses

Using notes of the E Minor Scale

African-American Spiritual

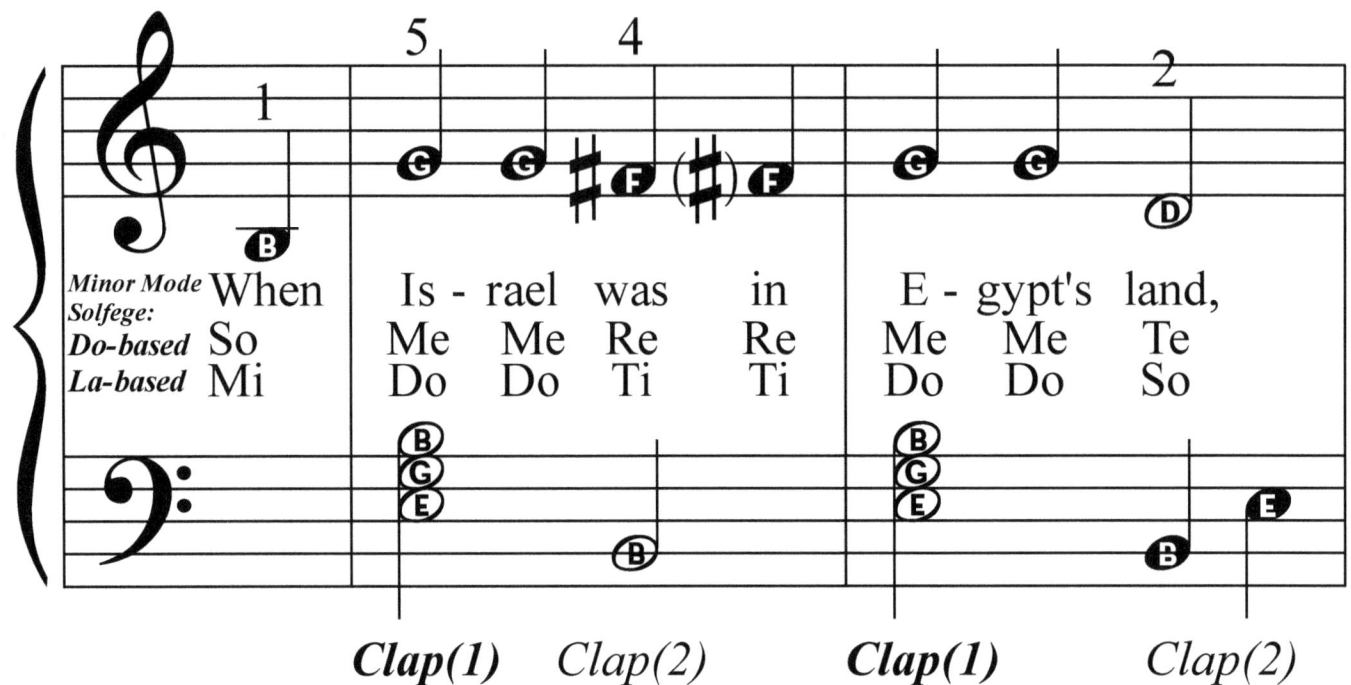

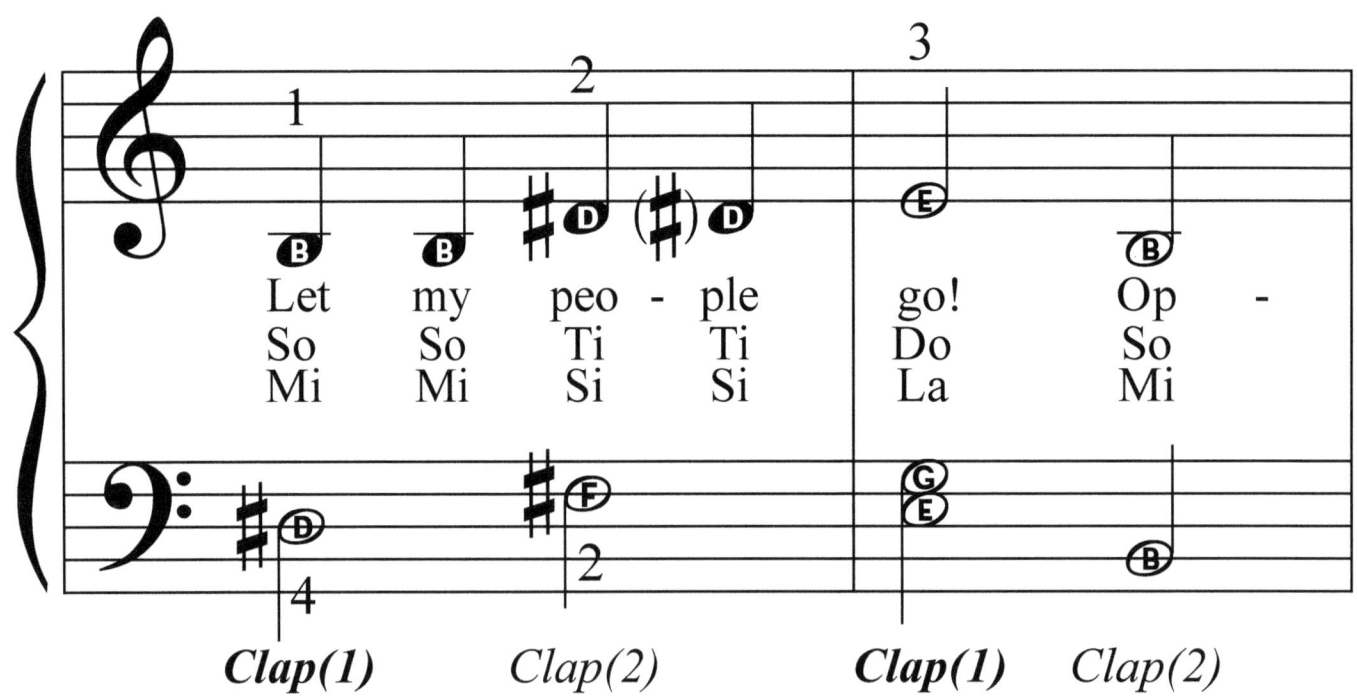

Go Down, Moses (cont.)

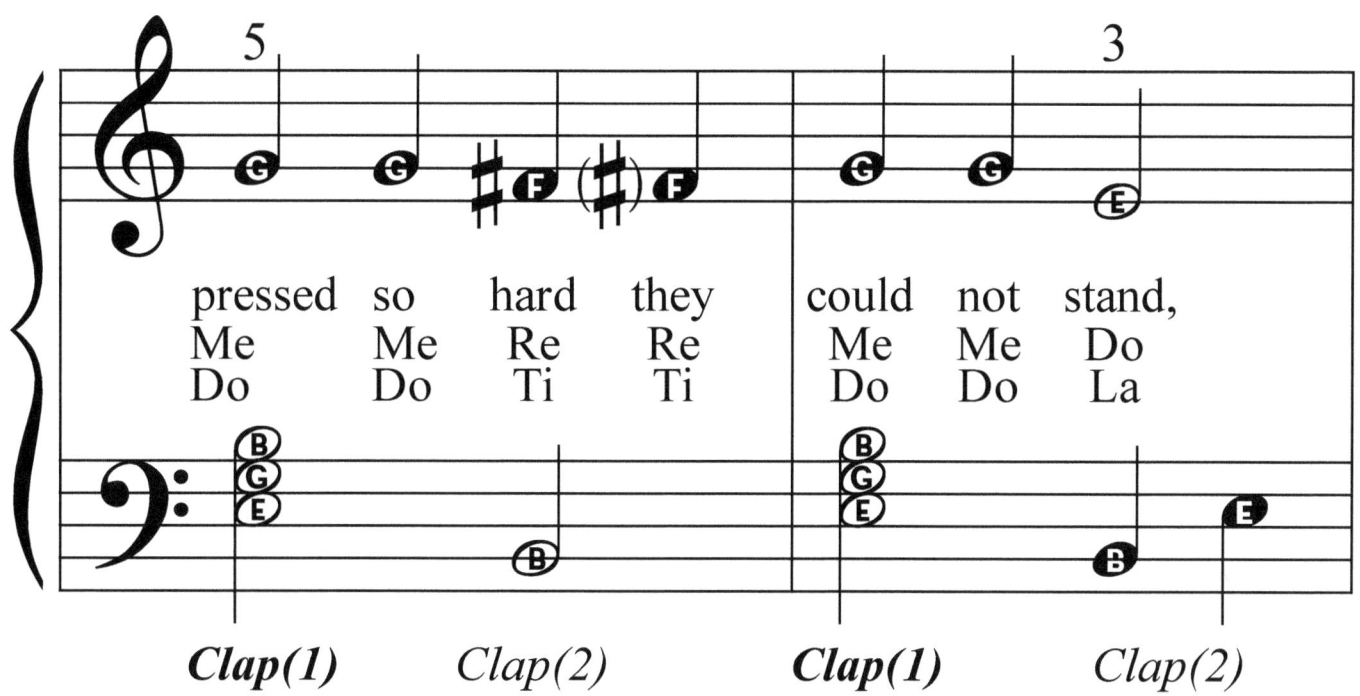
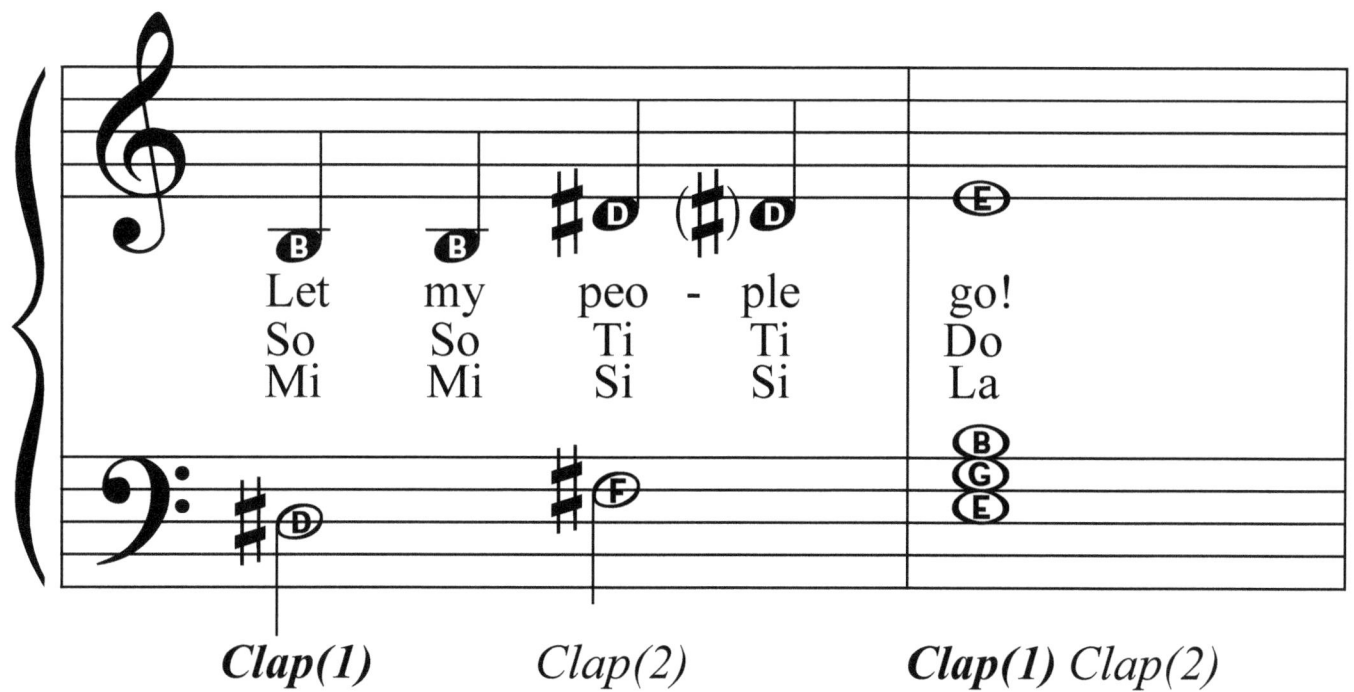

Go Down, Moses (cont.)

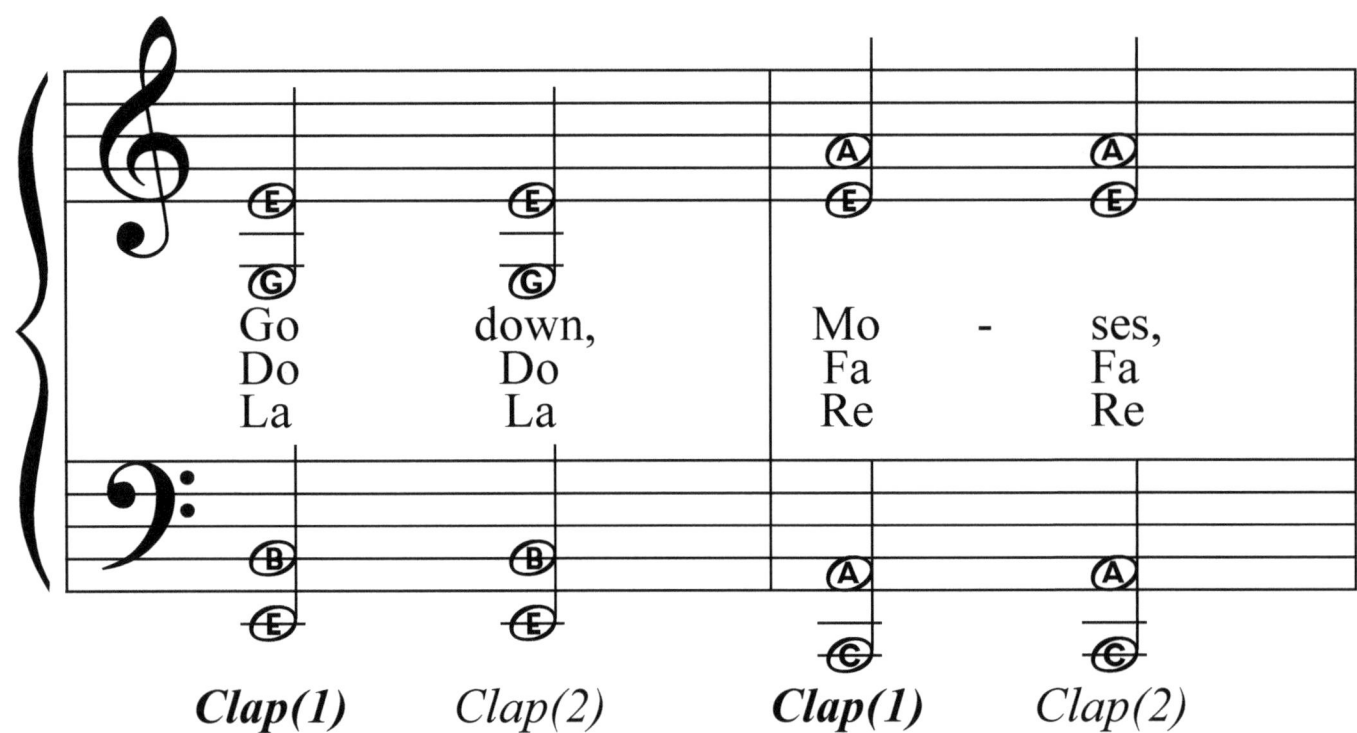
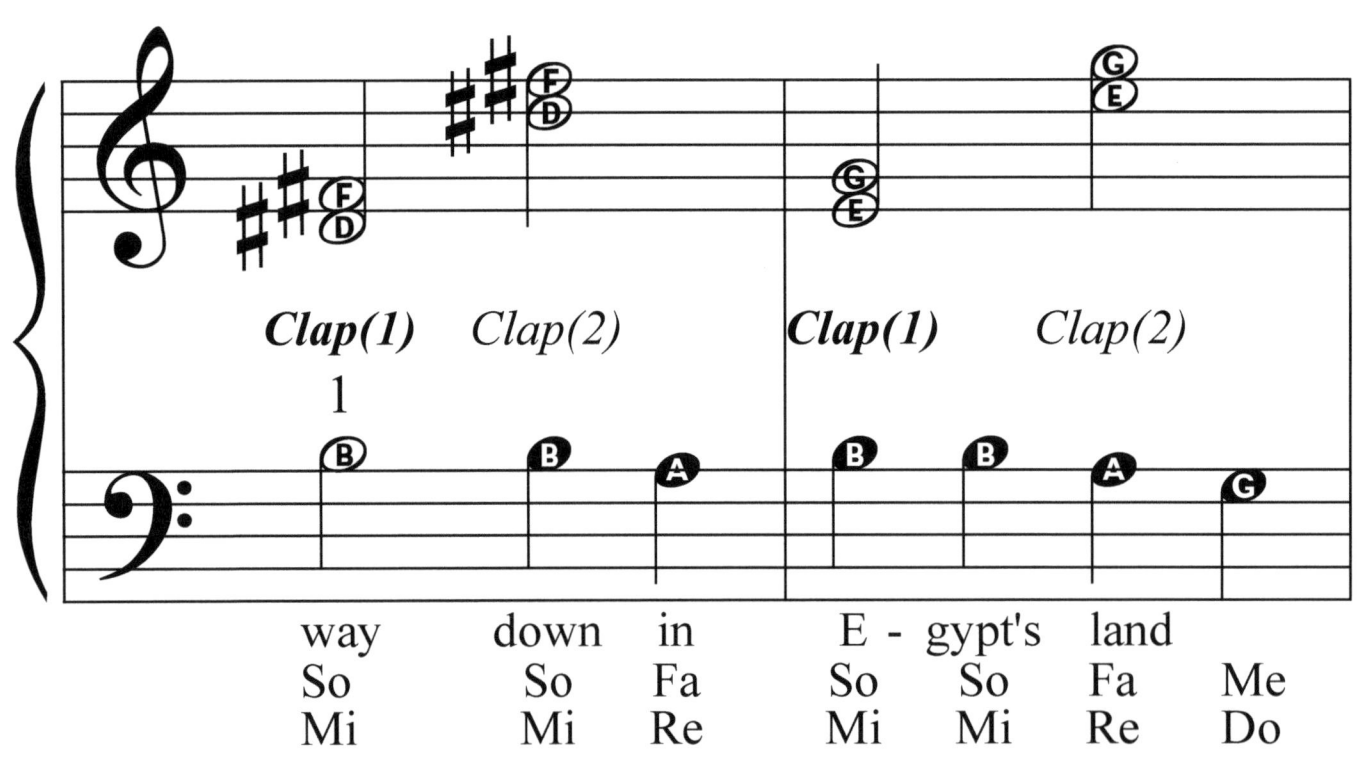

Go Down, Moses (cont.)

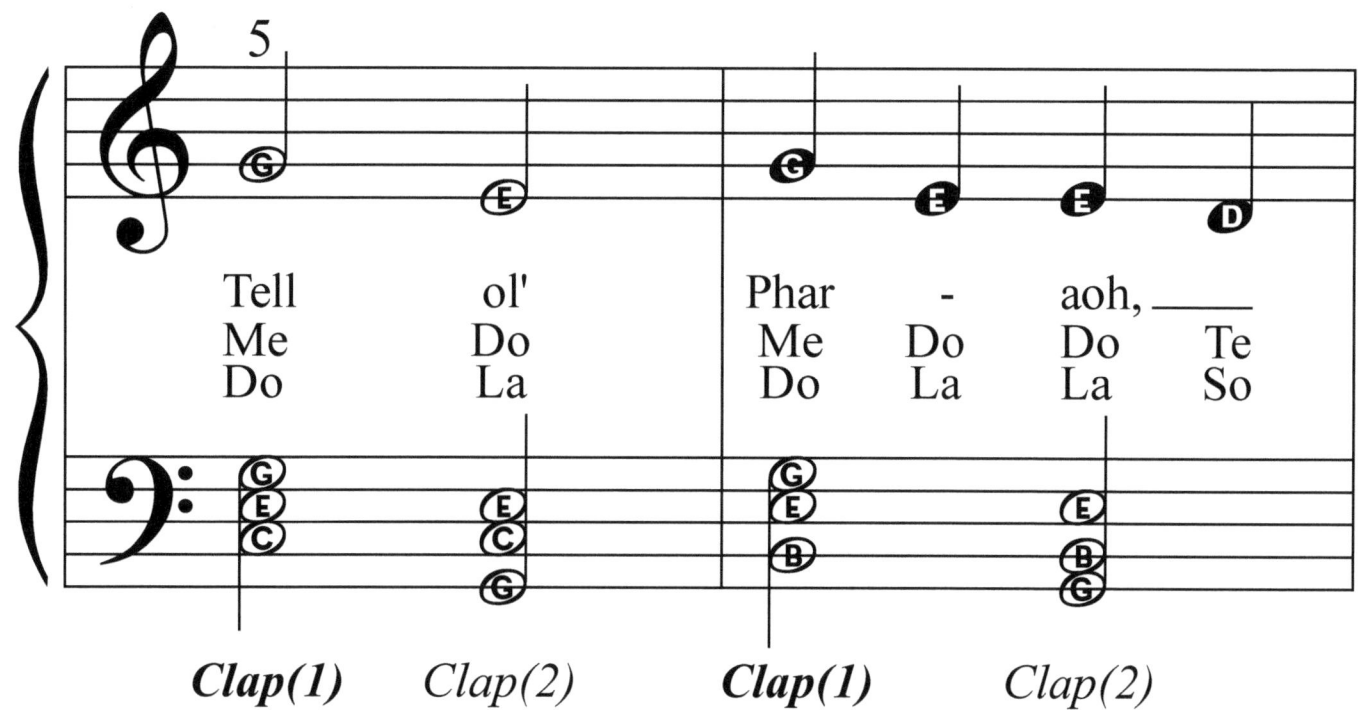
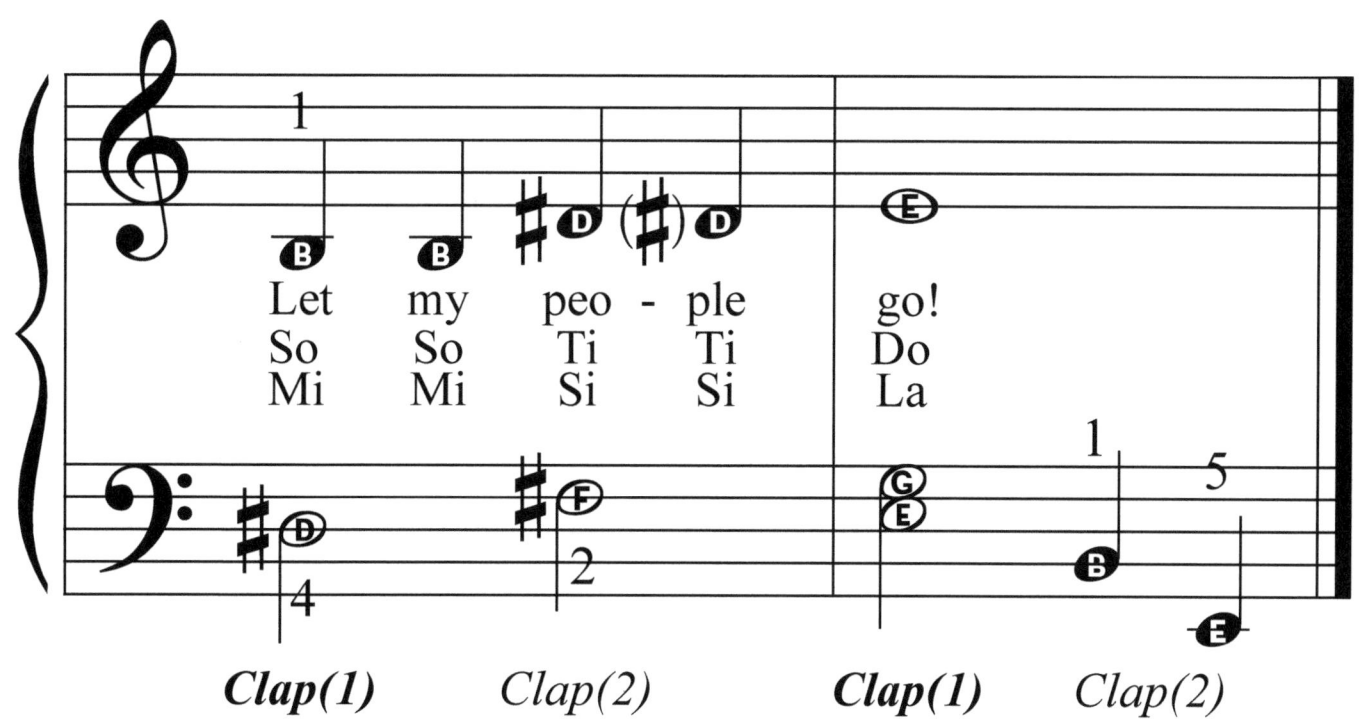

NOTE IDENTIFICATION PRACTICE

The top line of the treble clef staff is F (the second F above Middle C). The space below the top line F is E, and the space above the top line F is G (the second E and G above Middle C).

Draw the notes indicated below on the correct lines or spaces:

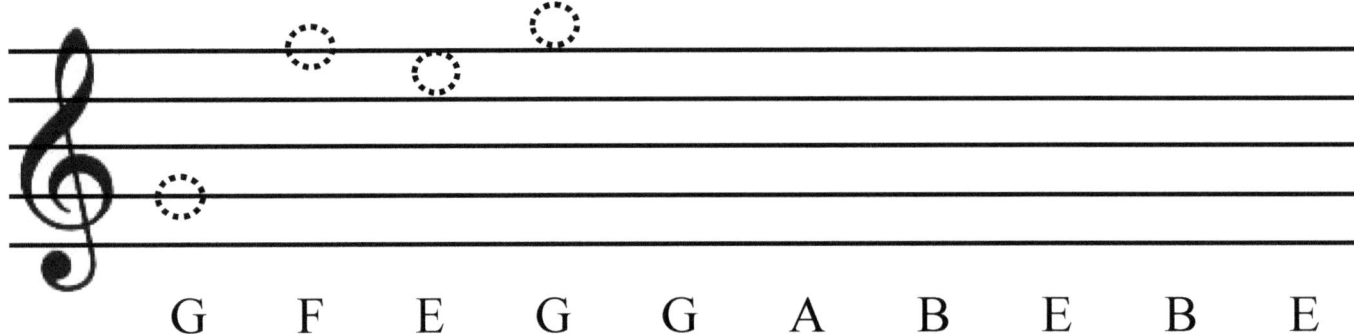

G F E G G A B E B E

The bottom line of the bass clef staff is G (the second G below Middle C). The space above the bottom line G is A, and the space below the bottom line G is F (the second A and G below Middle C).

Draw the notes indicated below on the correct lines or spaces:

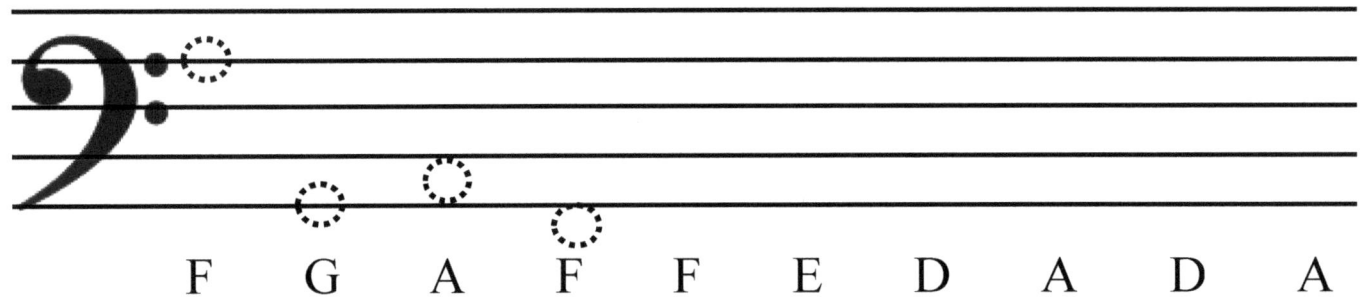

F G A F F E D A D A

Write the music alphabet forward: A ___ ___ ___ ___ ___ ___

Write the music alphabet backward: G ___ ___ ___ ___ ___ ___

What note is on the first ledger line below the treble clef staff? ___

What note is on the first ledger line above the bass clef staff? ___

What note is on the second ledger line above the treble clef staff? ___

What note is on the second ledger line below the bass clef staff? ___

NOTE IDENTIFICATION PRACTICE (CONT.)

The treble clef sign points to ___, which is the second line from the bottom of the staff.

The top line of the treble clef staff is ___.

The bottom line of the treble clef staff is ___.

The first ledger line below the treble clef staff is _____.

The bass clef sign points to ___, which is the second line from the top of the staff.

The bottom line of the bass clef staff is ___.

The top line of the bass clef staff is ___.

The first ledger line above the bass clef staff is _____.

The second ledger line above the treble clef staff is ___.

The second ledger line below the bass clef staff is ___.

The space below the top line of the treble clef staff is ___.

Write the letter names of the notes in the spaces below:

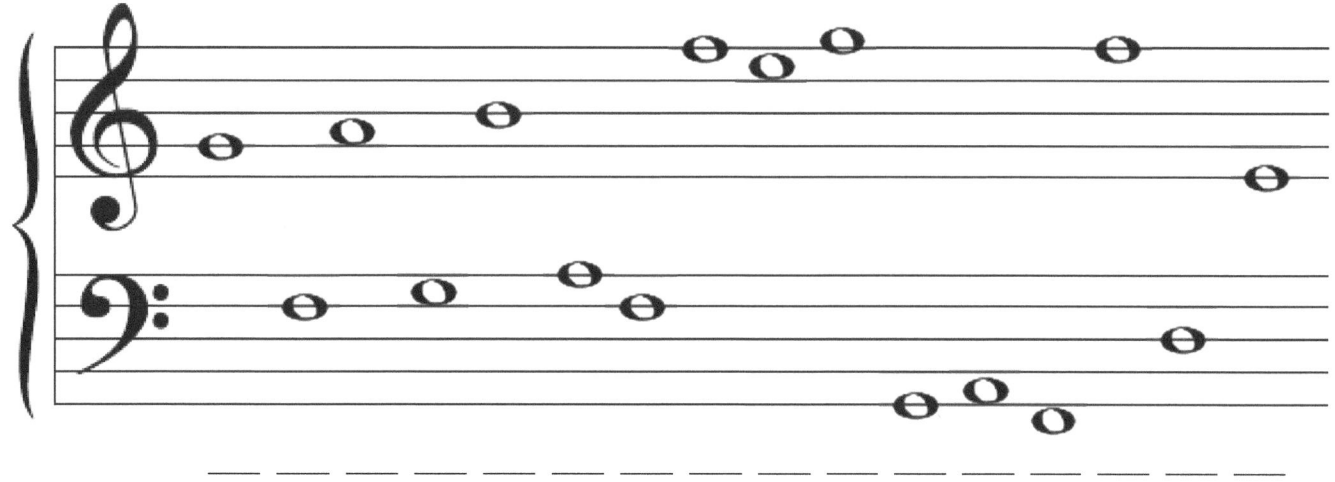

Draw a Middle C on the grand staff above.

Note Identification Practice (cont.)

The treble clef sign points to ___, which is the second line from the bottom of the staff.

The middle line of the treble clef staff is ___.

The top line of the treble clef staff is ___.

The first ledger line below the treble clef staff is _____.

The bass clef sign points to ___, which is the second line from the top of the staff.

The middle line of the bass clef staff is ___.

The bottom line of the bass clef staff is ___.

The first ledger line above the bass clef staff is _____.

The second ledger line above the treble clef staff is ___.

The second ledger line below the bass clef staff is ___.

The space below the top line of the bass clef staff is ___.

Write the letter names of the notes in the spaces below:

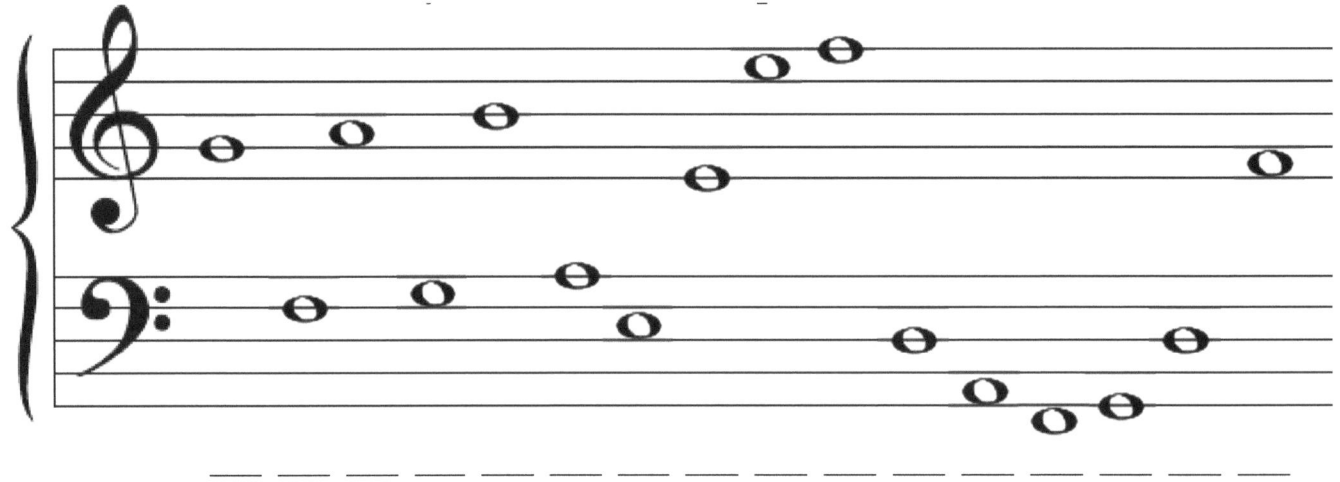

Draw a Middle C on the grand staff above.

First 5 Major Scales
Two Octaves

C Major

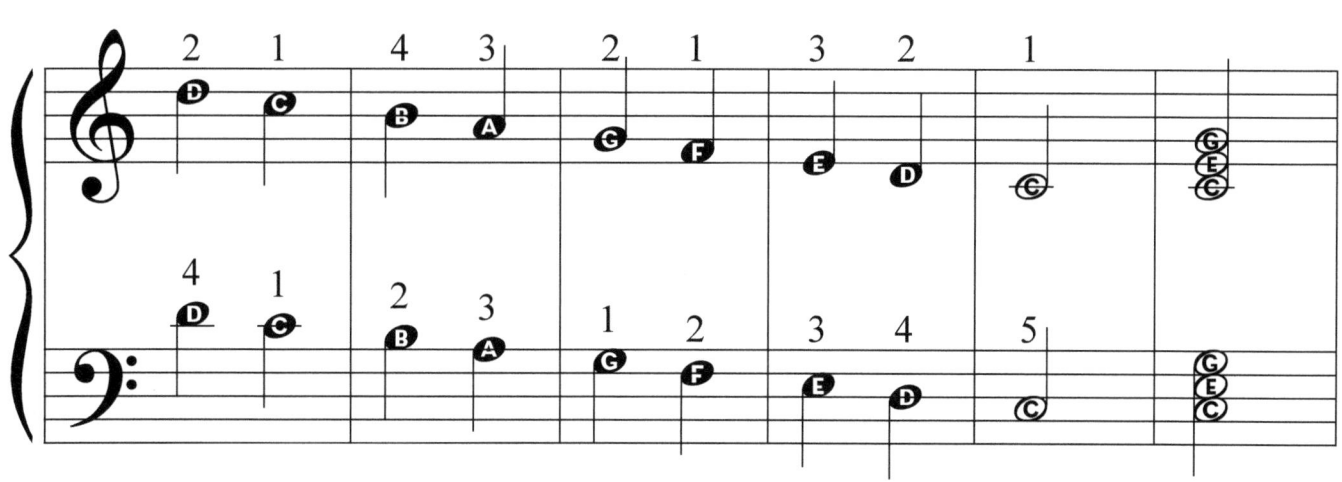

First 5 Major Scales (cont.)

G Major

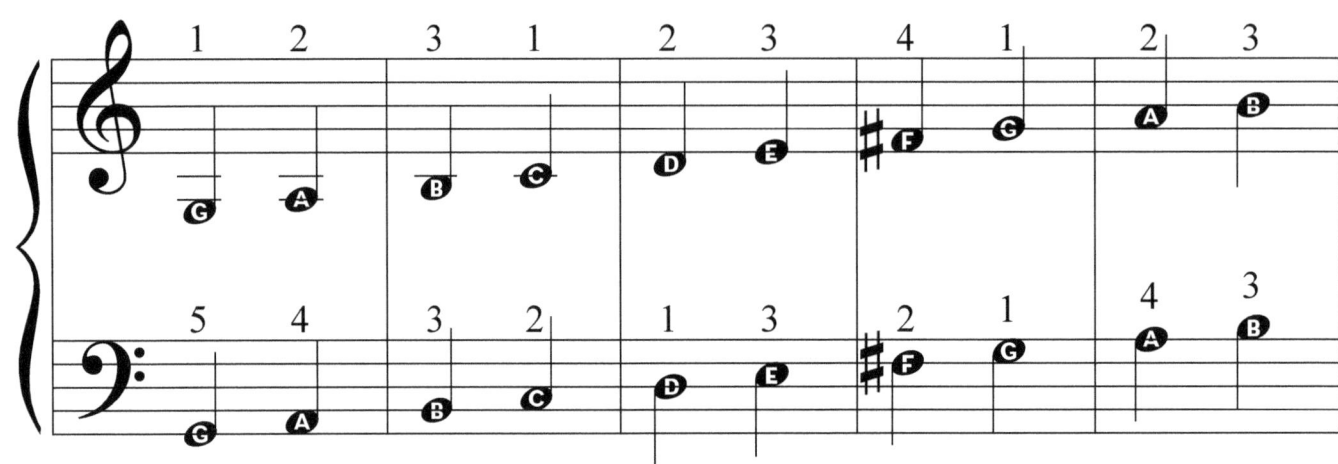

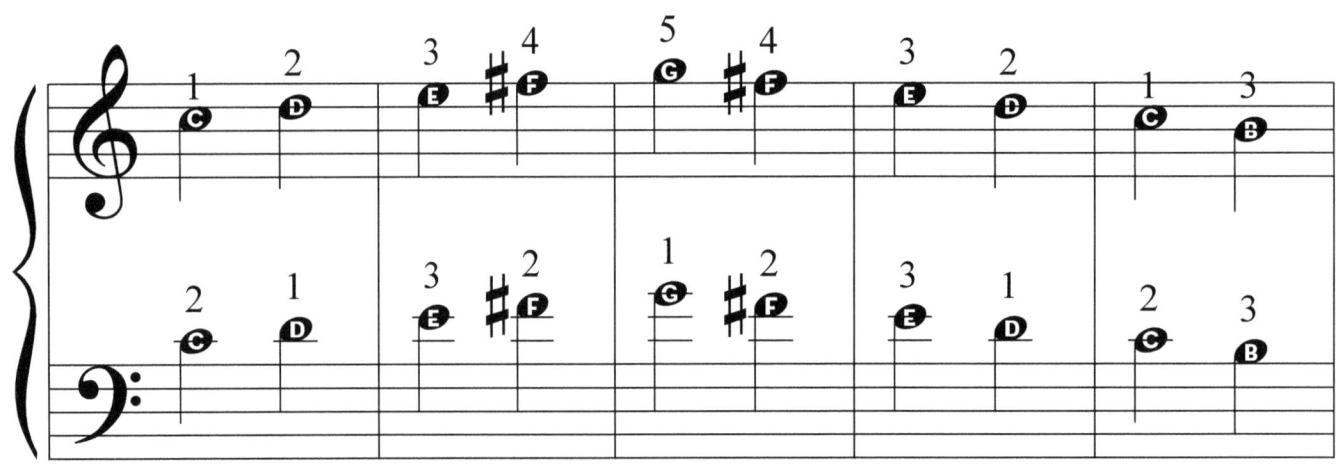

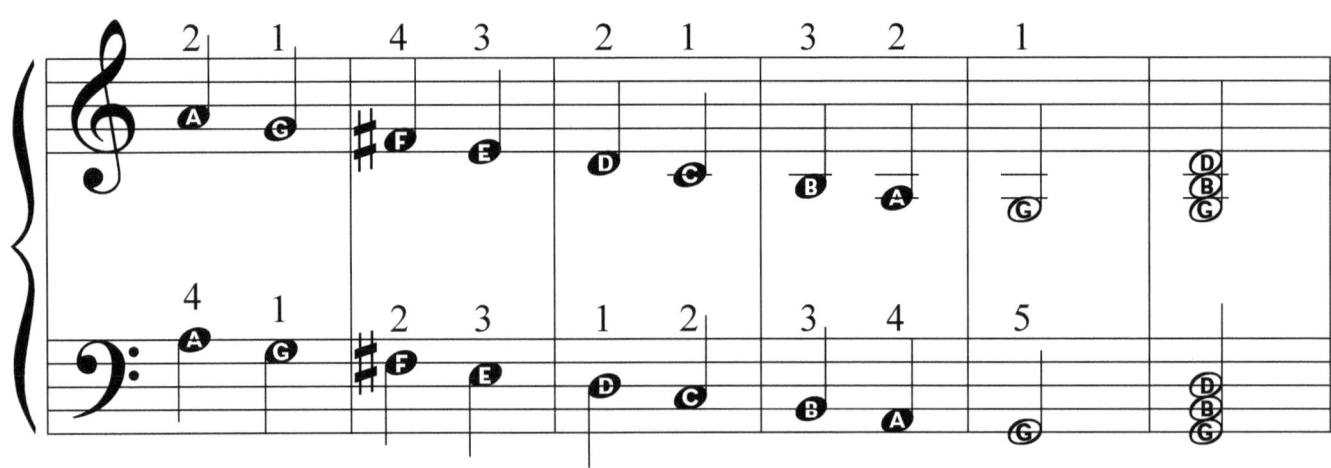

First 5 Major Scales (cont.)

D Major

First 5 Major Scales (cont.)

A Major

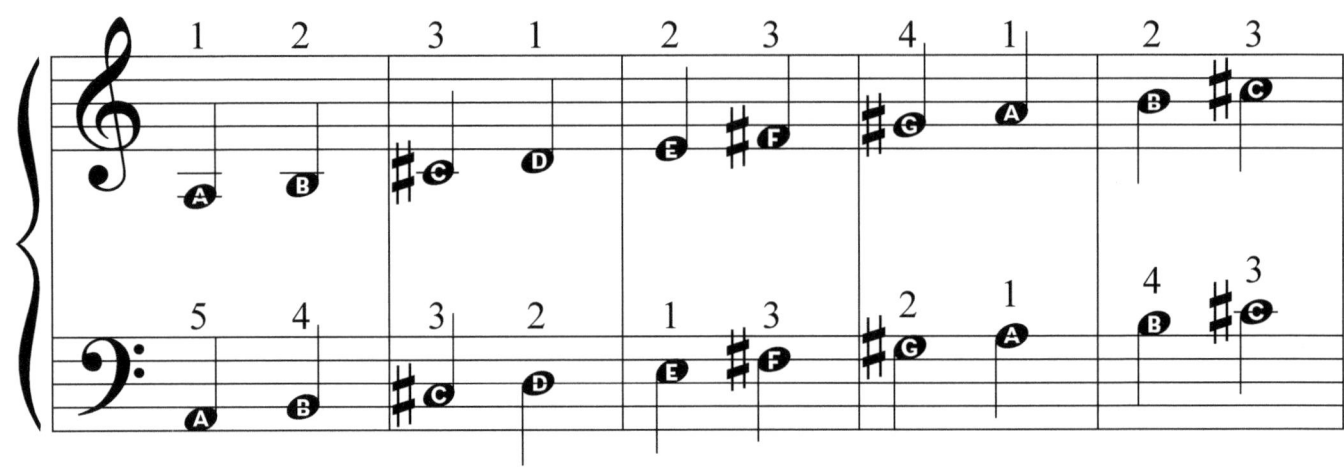

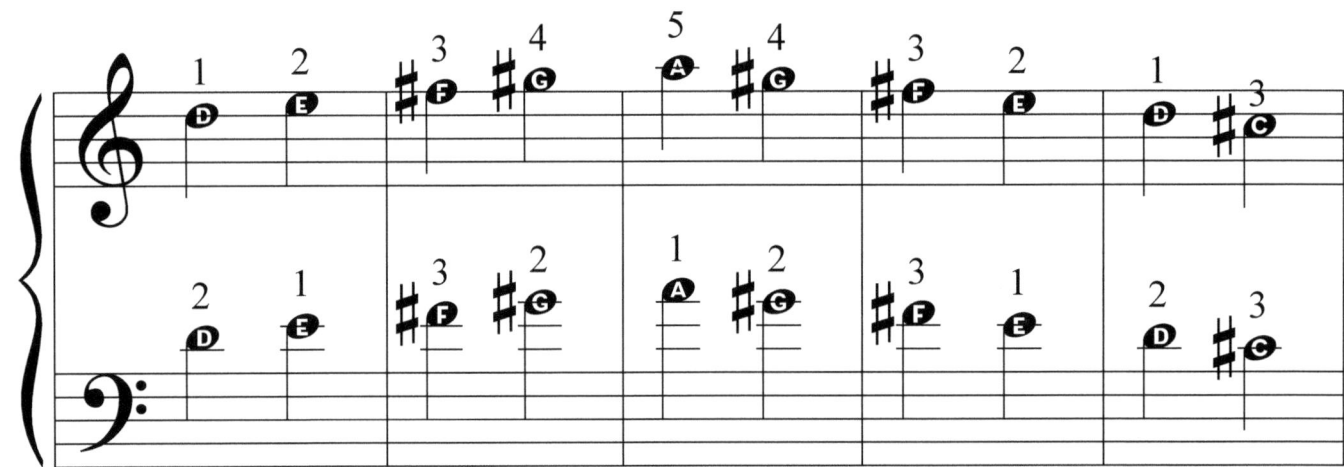

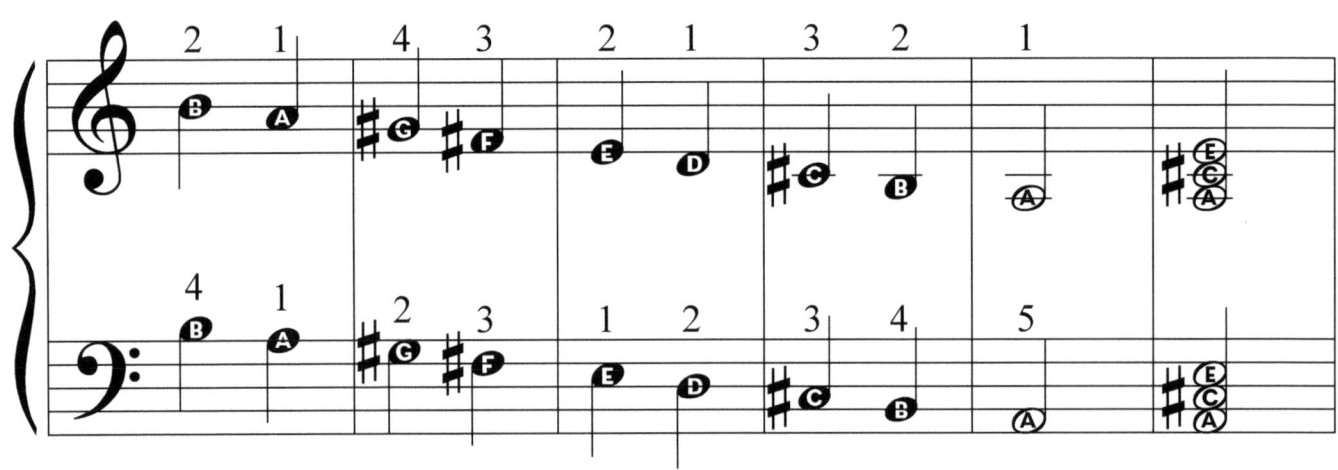

First 5 Major Scales (cont.)

E Major

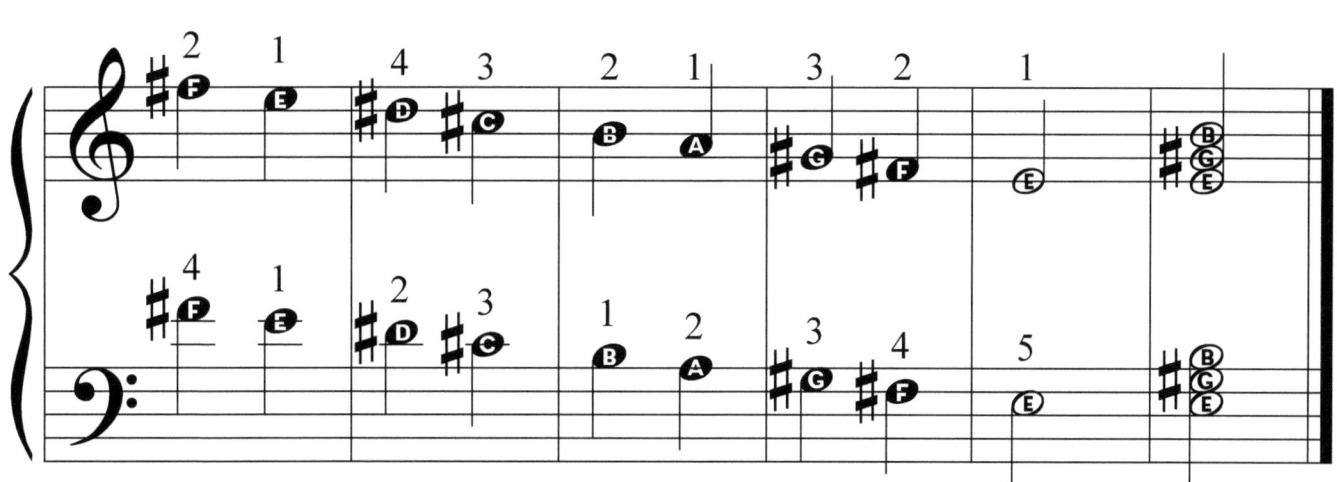

Wow! By now you've learned at least 24 songs! That is fantastic!

How many can you play from memory?
Strive for ten!

Also, continue to practice playing your two-octave scales every day. This is an important habit that will help you develop technical ability, improve your musicianship, and train your ears!

Here's a challenge:

Can you play the A Minor Scale, two octaves? Give it a try!

And...

Keep up the good work!

Little Birdie

Using notes from the G Major Scale
Southern Mountain Banjo Tune

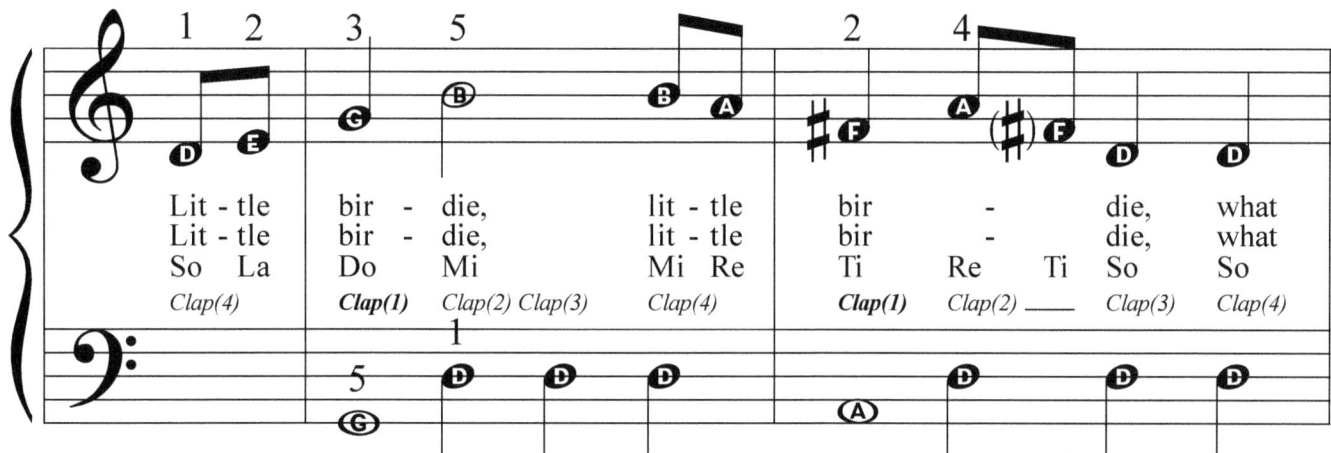

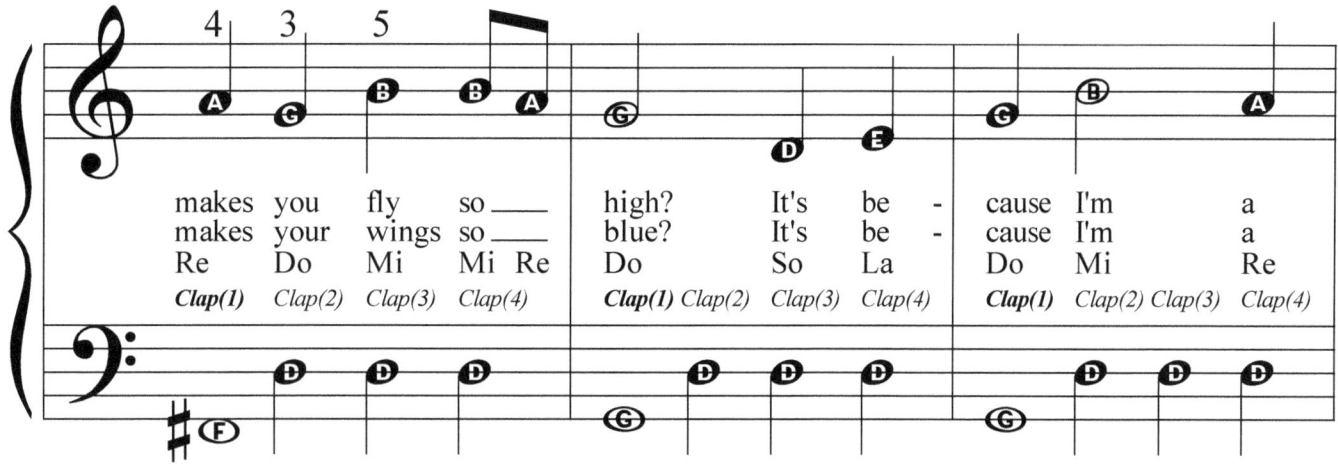

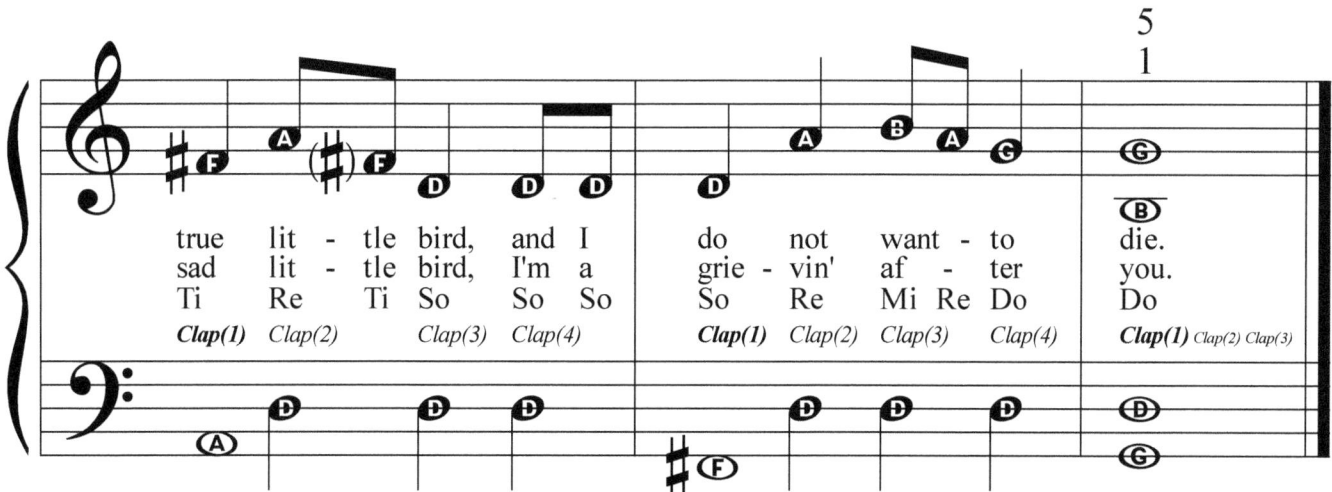

RHYTHM

Music has a beat, and the notes of a song are sung or played in various rhythms to the beat of the music.

Sometimes we clap, or tap our foot to the beat of a song while we sing or play the rhythmic melody.

Composers of music who use music notation to write down their songs show us what notes or pitches to sing or play, what rhythms to sing or play the notes in, and also what rhythms to sing or play the notes in.

We place notes on a staff to tell us the pitches. We use the *shape* of the notes to tell us the rhythms. We assign each note shape a *value* that refers to how long it is held, or its **duration**, in a rhythm.

To begin, we're going to learn about four different note values:

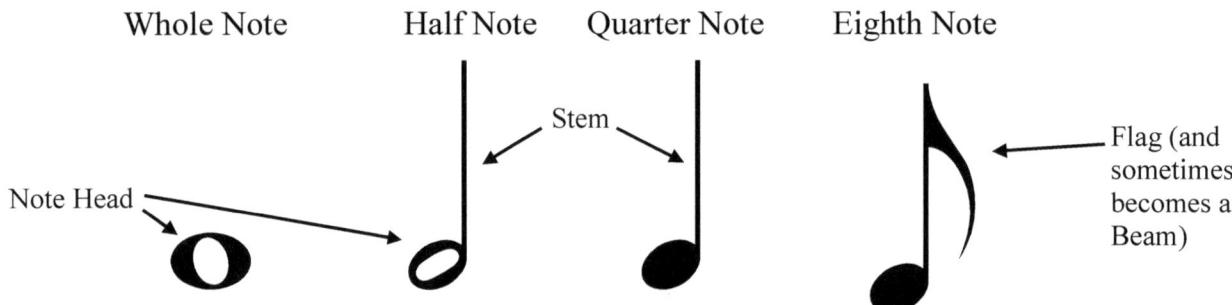

The shapes of the notes are determined by several features. The round or oval part of the note is called the **note head**. The stick part of the note is called the **stem**. The curly part of the note is called the **flag** (and sometimes the **beam**).

Some notes have hollow note heads, such as the whole note and the half note, and some notes have solid note heads, such as the quarter note and the eighth note. Often when two eighth notes are placed next side by side, they share the flag and it turns into a beam.

Two eighth notes *beamed together*

Rhythm (cont.)

When we count rhythms in music, we use the ***pulse*** and the ***beat***. The *pulse* is often the first beat of each grouping, which traditionally gets extra emphasis, and the *beat* is often the division of each grouping.

For example, we often count music in groupings of four beats, like this:

<u>4 Beats per Grouping</u>
One, two, three, four; **One**, two, three, four; **One**, two, three, four; **One**, two, three, four; **One**, two, three, four; etc.

Sometimes we count music in groupings of three beats, or two beats, or other numbers, such as six beats, or five beats (although five- and six-beat groupings are less common), like this:

<u>3 Beats per Grouping</u>
One, two, three; **One**, two, three; **One**, two, three; **One**, two, three; etc.

<u>2 Beats per Grouping</u>
One, two; **One**, two; **One**, two; **One**, two; etc.

<u>6 Beats per Grouping</u>
One, two, three, four, five, six; **One**, two, three, four, five, six; **One**, two, three, four, five, six; **One**, two, three, four, five, six; etc.

<u>5 Beats per Grouping</u>
One, two, three, four, five; **One**, two, three, four, five; **One**, two, three, four, five; **One**, two, three, four, five; etc.

Count the above groupings of beats aloud, speaking the numbers, while tapping your foot every time you say, "One."

The "One" beat, or beat one, or the first beat of each grouping, is called the ***down beat***. (When conducting a choir, band, or orchestra, the conductor makes a motion downward for beat one. The tradition of this conducting pattern is part of the reason why beat one is called the down beat.)

RHYTHM (CONT.)

Groupings of beats in music are called *measures*. When music is written down, the composer uses vertical lines, called *bar lines*, to separate each measure. For this reason, measures are often also called *bars*.

The piano music below consists of four measures (or four bars).

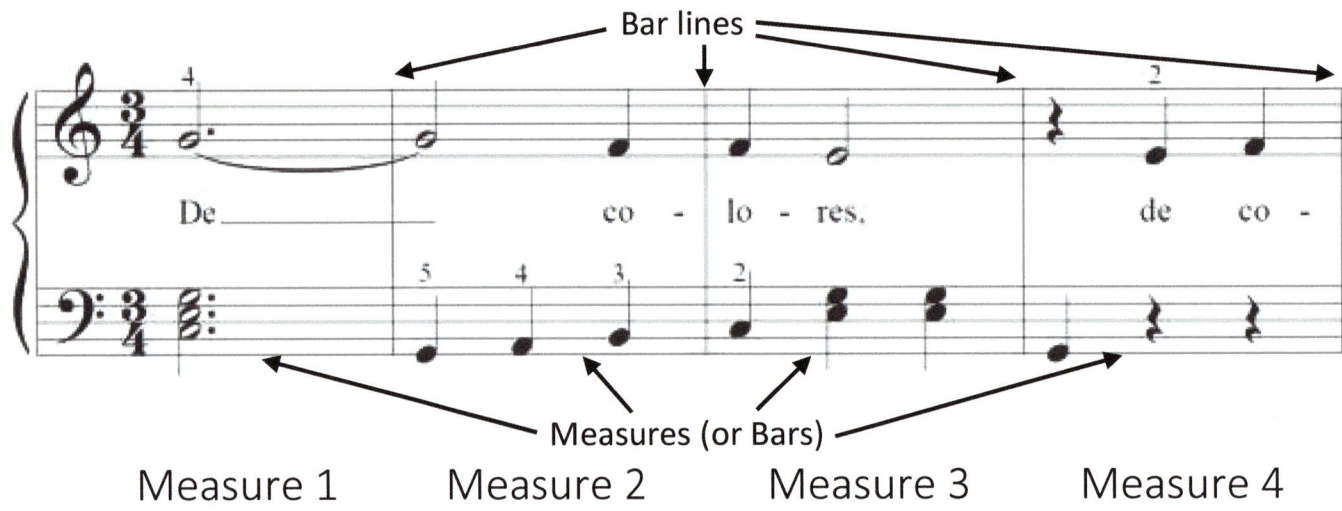

How many measures are in the excerpt of music by J.S. Bach below? ____

MINUET
BWV Anh. 114
from "Notebook for Anna Magdalena Bach"

Johann Sebastian Bach
(C. Petzold)
PS Urtext

Rhythm (cont.)

Each measure receives the exact number of beats in the grouping, whether there are 4 beats, 3 beats, 2 beats, 5 beats, etc. We refer to these groupings as **beats per measure**.

So, a song or a piano piece might get 4 beats per measure, or 3 beats per measure, or 2 beats per measure, or 5 beats per measure.

The way a composer writes down how many beats per measure there will be for a particular music composition is by using what we call a *time signature*.

Time signatures tell us how many beats per measure.

Time signatures consist of a number on the top, and a number on the bottom. The *top number* tells us *how many beats per measure*. The *bottom number* tells us *what kind of note gets one beat*. For now, we will use the number four (4) for the bottom number, which represents a quarter note (♩).

If the top number is a 4, and the bottom number is a 4, then we say, "There are four beats per measure and a quarter note gets one beat."

If the top number is a 3, and the bottom number is a 4, then we say, "There are three beats per measure and a quarter note gets one beat."

If the top number is a 2, and the bottom number is a 4, then we say, "There are two beats per measure and a quarter note gets one beat."

4/4 This time signature specifies ____ beats per measure and a quarter note gets one beat.

3/4 This time signature specifies ____ beats per measure and a quarter note gets one beat.

RHYTHM (CONT.)

Each type of note receives a certain number of beats. When the bottom number of a time signature is 4, representing a quarter note, then the note types receive the following number of beats:

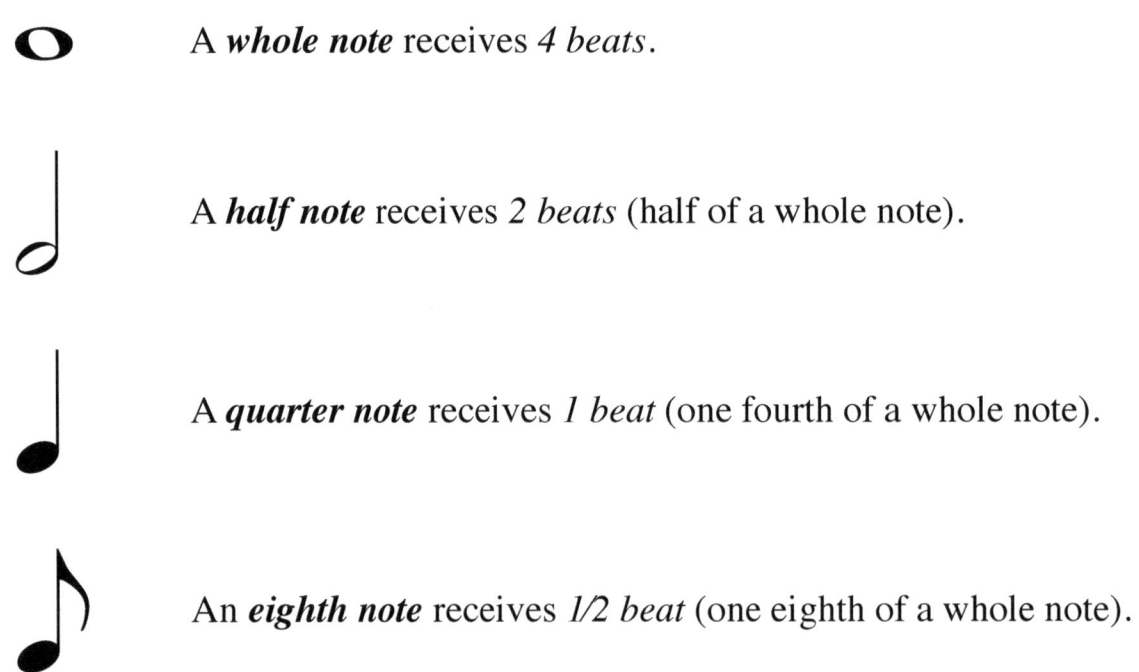

A *whole note* receives *4 beats*.

A *half note* receives *2 beats* (half of a whole note).

A *quarter note* receives *1 beat* (one fourth of a whole note).

An *eighth note* receives *1/2 beat* (one eighth of a whole note).

Let's do some math!

If the time signature is $\frac{4}{4}$, then there are four beats per measure and a quarter note gets one beat. This means that there can be four quarter notes in one measure. Or, there could be one whole note in one measure (since a whole note gets four beats). How many half notes could there be in one measure? ___

If the time signature is $\frac{2}{4}$, then there are two beats per measure and a quarter note gets one beat. This means that there can be two quarter notes in one measure. Or, there could be one half note in one measure (since a half note gets two beats). Could there be a whole note in one measure (knowing that a whole note gets four beats)? Yes / No *(circle one)*

Write the time signature for three beats per measure, quarter note gets one beat: ____

RHYTHM PRACTICE

Draw bar lines to divide the grand staff below into three measures:

Write the time signature for four beats per measure, a quarter note gets one beat: ___

Write the time signature for three beats per measure, a quarter note gets one beat: ___

Write the time signature for two beats per measure, a quarter note gets one beat: ___

The top number of a time signature tells us how many _____ per _____.

Write the rhythmic name of each note below:

_____ Note   _____ Note   _____ Note   _____ Note

Rhythm Practice (cont.)

When the bottom number of a time signature is 4, representing a quarter note, then the note types receive the following number of beats:

A *whole note* gets _____ beat(s).

A *half note* gets _____ beat(s).

A *quarter note* gets _____ beat(s).

An *eighth note* gets _____ beat(s).

4/4 This time signature means there are _____ beats per measure, and a _____ note gets one beat.

2/4 This time signature means there are _____ beats per measure, and a _____ note gets one beat.

3/4 This time signature means there are _____ beats per measure, and a _____ note gets one beat.

In **4/4** time, there could be up to _____ whole note(s) in one measure.

In **3/4** time, there could be up to _____ quarter note(s) in one measure.

In **2/4** time, there could be up to _____ half note(s) in one measure.

In **4/4** time, there could be up to _____ half note(s) in one measure.

In **4/4** time, there could be up to _____ eighth note(s) in one measure.

Rhythm Practice (cont.)

Draw ten whole notes on the G line of the treble clef, and ten half notes on the F line of the bass clef:

Draw ten quarter notes on the G line of the treble clef, and ten eighth notes on the F line of the bass clef:

Play the following rhythm games; see how long you can keep going:

1. With four beats per measure, tap your foot on beat one, and clap on beats one, two, three, and four.

2. With four beats per measure, tap your left knee with your left hand on beat one, and tap your right knee with your right hand on beats one, two, three, and four.

3. With three beats per measure, play Middle C on the piano with the third finger of your Left Hand on beat one, and speak, "Ta" with your voice on beats one, two, and three.

Song of Happiness

Using notes from the C Major Scale — Navajo Song for Feasts and Joyous Occasions

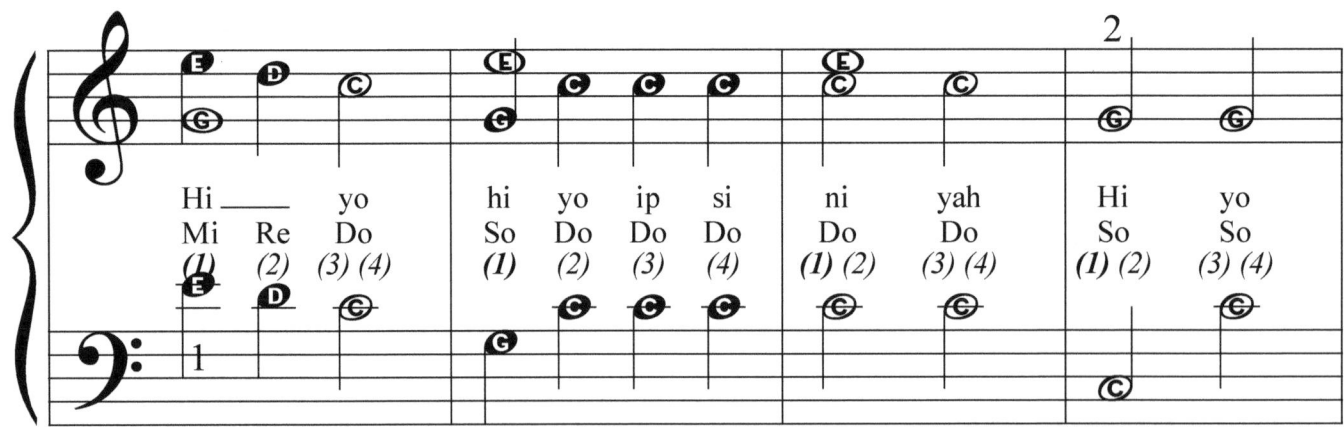

Song of Happiness (cont.)

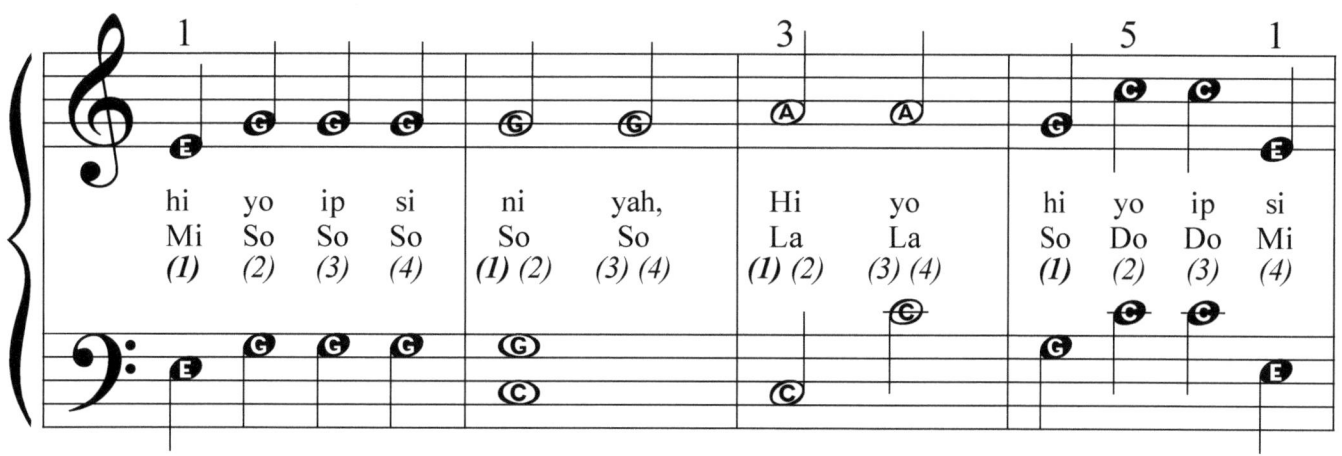
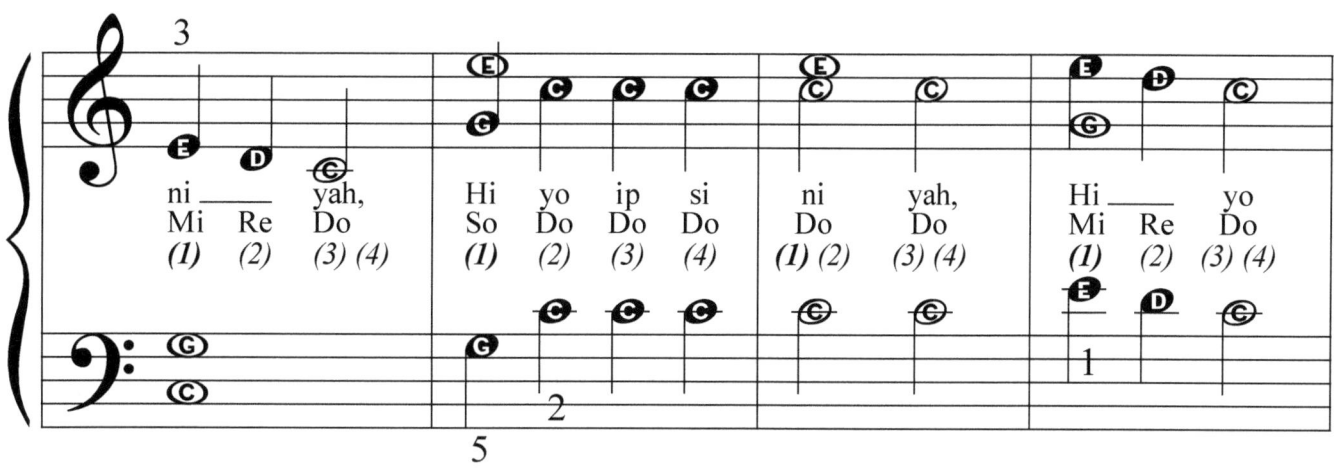
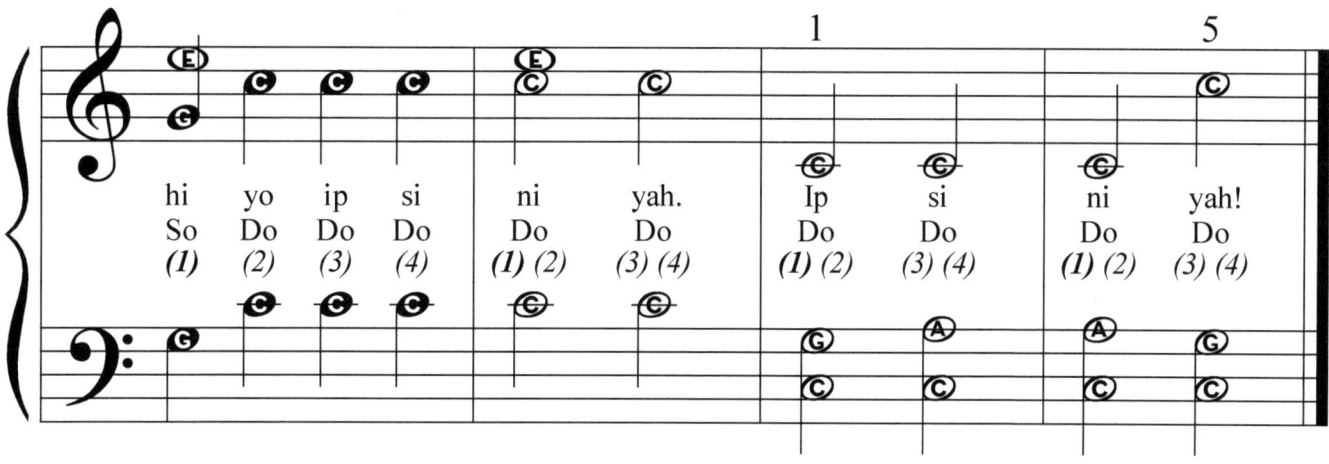

More Rhythm Practice

Draw bar lines to divide the grand staff below into four measures:

Write the time signature for three beats per measure, a quarter note gets one beat: ___

Write the time signature for two beats per measure, a quarter note gets one beat: ___

Write the time signature for four beats per measure, a quarter note gets one beat: ___

The top number of a time signature tells us how many _____ per _____.

Write the rhythmic name of each note below:

Note   Note   Note   Note

More Rhythm Practice (cont.)

When the bottom number of a time signature is 4, representing a quarter note, then the note types receive the following number of beats:

A *quarter note* gets ____ beat(s).

A *half note* gets ____ beat(s).

A *whole note* gets ____ beat(s).

An *eighth note* gets ____ beat(s).

3/4 This time signature means there are ____ beats per measure, and a _____ note gets one beat.

4/4 This time signature means there are ____ beats per measure, and a _____ note gets one beat.

2/4 This time signature means there are ____ beats per measure, and a _____ note gets one beat.

In **4/4** time, there could be up to ____ half note(s) in one measure.

In **3/4** time, there could be up to ____ quarter note(s) in one measure.

In **2/4** time, there could be up to ____ quarter note(s) in one measure.

In **4/4** time, there could be up to ____ whole note(s) in one measure.

In **4/4** time, there could be up to ____ eighth note(s) in one measure.

More Rhythm Practice (cont.)

Draw ten whole notes on the G line of the treble clef, and ten half notes on the F line of the bass clef:

Draw ten quarter notes on the G line of the treble clef, and ten eighth notes on the F line of the bass clef:

Play the following rhythm games; see how long you can keep going:

1. With two beats per measure, tap your foot on beat one, and clap on beats one and two.

2. With four beats per measure, tap your right knee with your right hand on beat one, and tap your left knee with your left hand on beats one, two, three, and four.

3. With three beats per measure, play Middle C on the piano with the third finger of your Right Hand on beat one, and speak, "Ta" with your voice on beats one, two, and three.

MORE NOTE IDENTIFICATION PRACTICE

The second line from the top of the treble clef staff is D (the second D above Middle C). The space below that line D is C, and the space above that line D is E (the first C and the second E above Middle C).

Draw the notes indicated below on the correct lines or spaces:

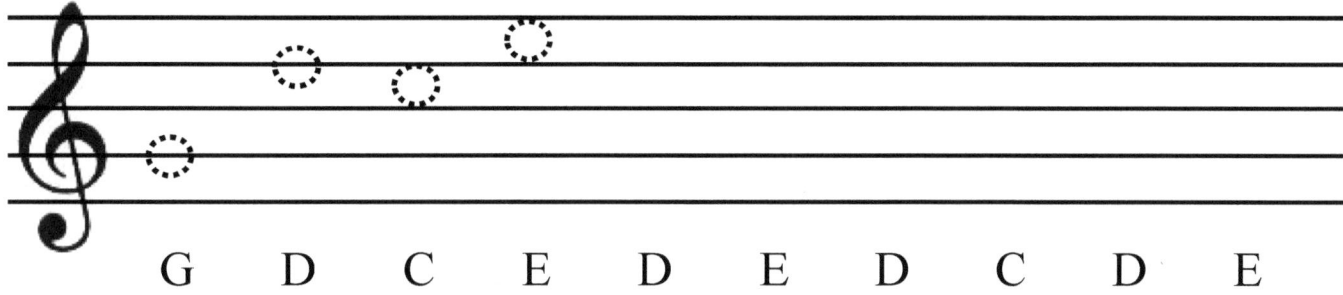

G   D   C   E   D   E   D   C   D   E

The second line from the bottom of the bass clef staff is B (the second B below Middle C). The space above that line B is C, and the space below that line B is A (the first C and second A below Middle C).

Draw the notes indicated below on the correct lines or spaces:

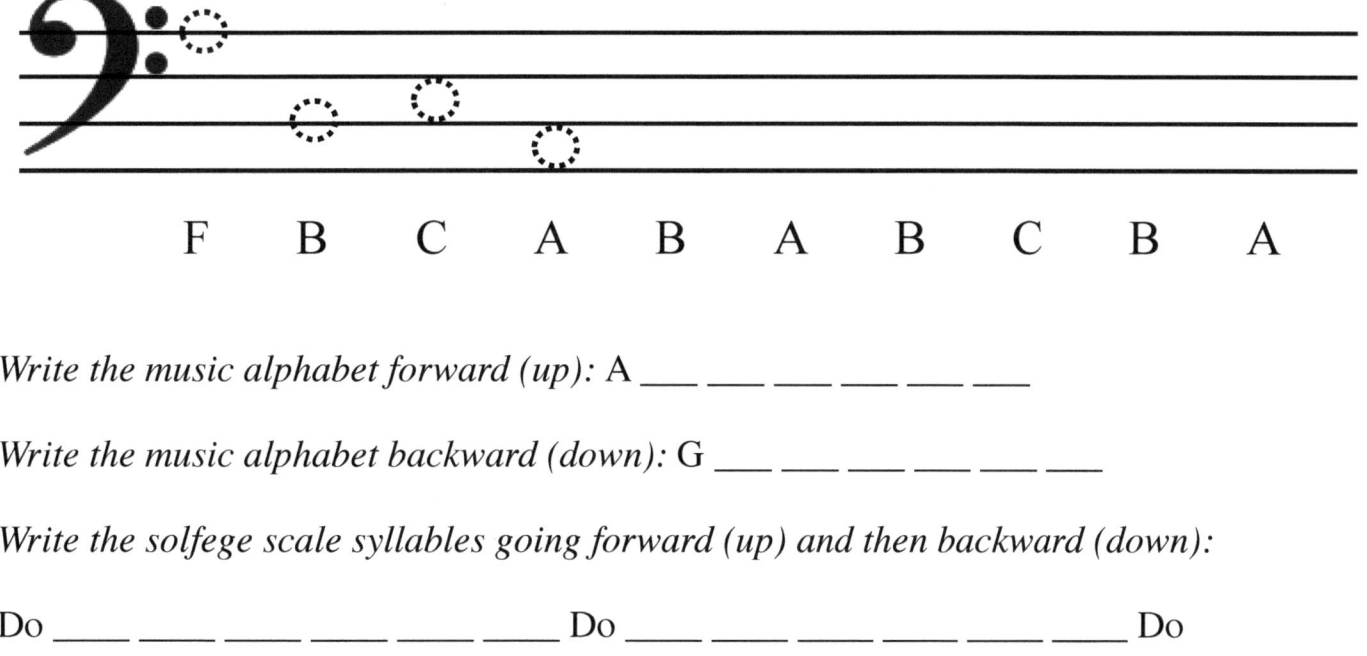

F   B   C   A   B   A   B   C   B   A

Write the music alphabet forward (up): A ___ ___ ___ ___ ___ ___

Write the music alphabet backward (down): G ___ ___ ___ ___ ___ ___

Write the solfege scale syllables going forward (up) and then backward (down):

Do ___ ___ ___ ___ ___ ___ Do ___ ___ ___ ___ ___ ___ Do

MORE NOTE IDENTIFICATION PRACTICE (CONT.)

The treble clef sign points to ___, which is the second line from the bottom of the staff.

The bottom line of the treble clef staff is ___.

The top line of the treble clef staff is ___.

The first ledger line below the treble clef staff is _____.

The bass clef sign points to ___, which is the second line from the top of the staff.

The top line of the bass clef staff is ___.

The bottom line of the bass clef staff is ___.

The first ledger line above the bass clef staff is _____. The second ledger line above the treble clef staff is ___.

The second ledger line below the bass clef staff is ___.

The space above the bottom line of the bass clef staff is ___.

Write the letter names of the notes in the spaces below:

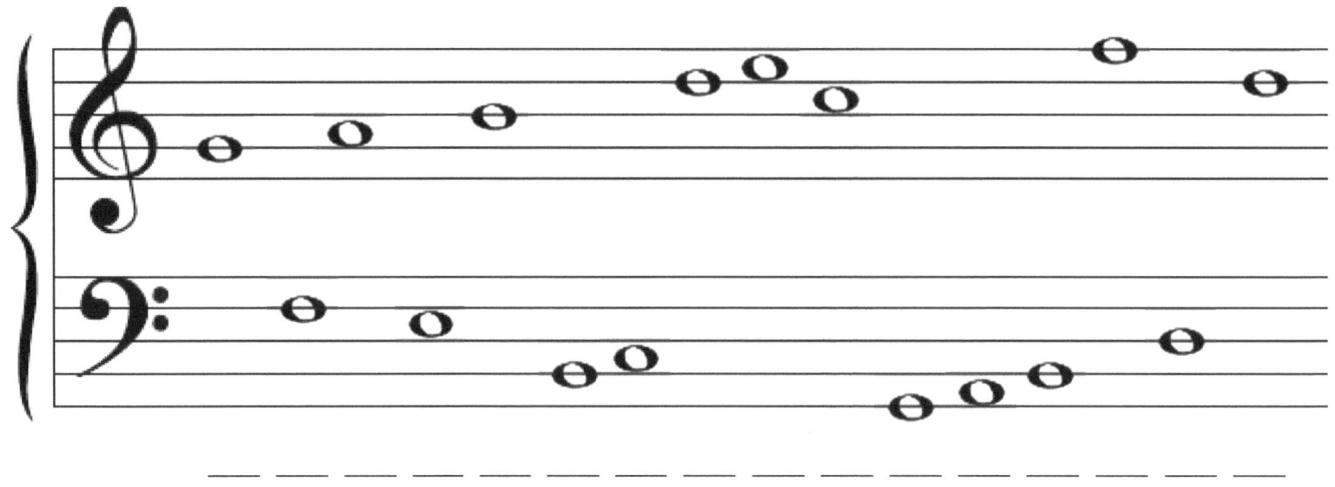

Draw a Middle C on the grand staff above.

More Note Identification Practice (cont.)

The treble clef sign points to ___, which is the second line from the bottom of the staff.

The middle line of the treble clef staff is ___.

The bottom line of the treble clef staff is ___.

One ledger line below the treble clef staff is _____.

The bass clef sign points to ___, which is the second line from the top of the staff.

The middle line of the bass clef staff is ___.

The top line of the bass clef staff is ___.

One ledger line above the bass clef staff is _____. The first ledger line above the treble clef staff is ___.

The first ledger line below the bass clef staff is ___.

The space below the top line of the treble clef staff is ___.

The space above the bottom line of the bass clef staff is ___.

Write the letter names of the notes in the spaces below:

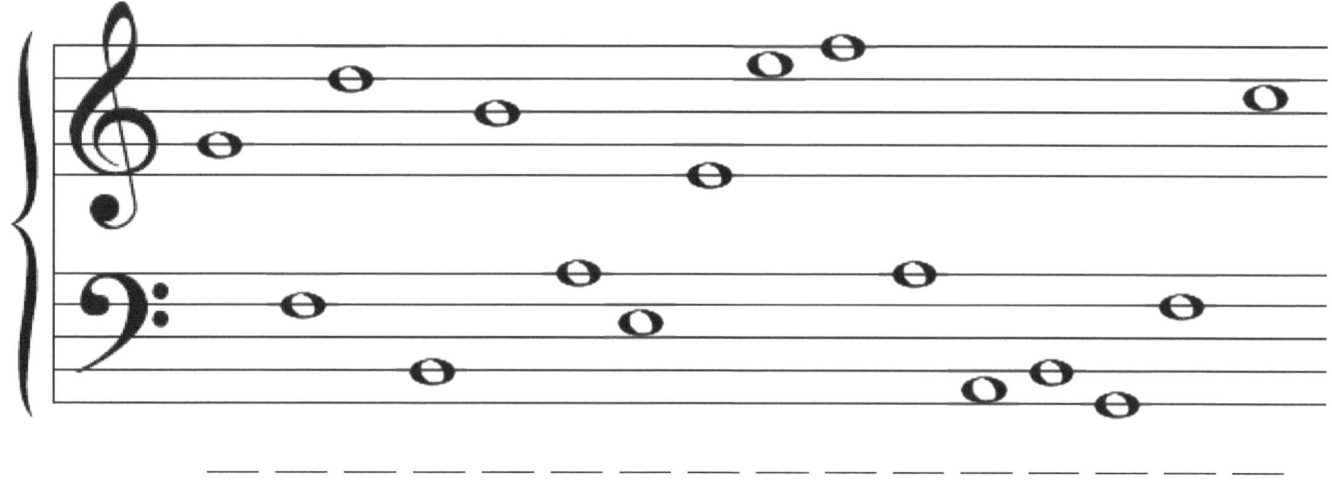

Draw a Middle C on the grand staff above.

Bought Me A Cat

Using notes from the C Major Scale   Traditional

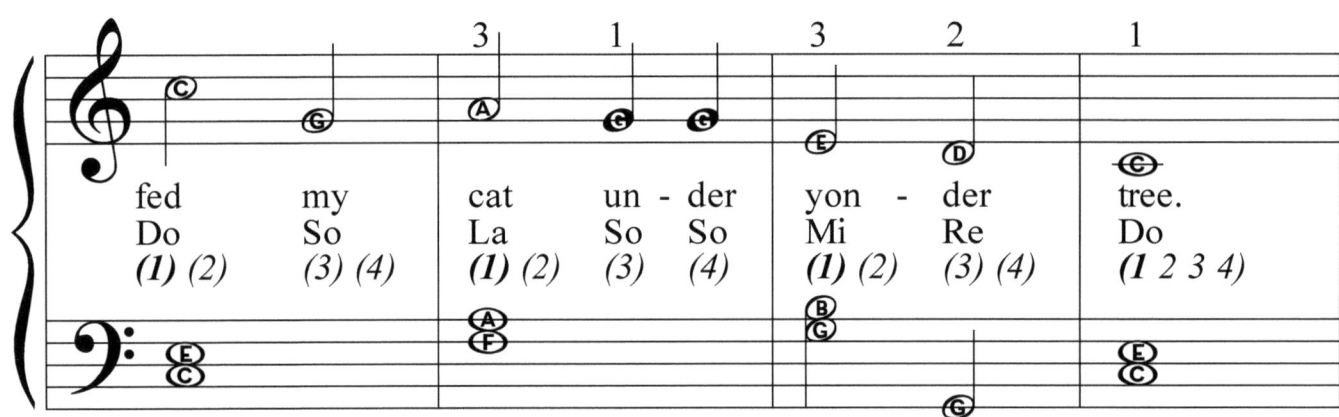

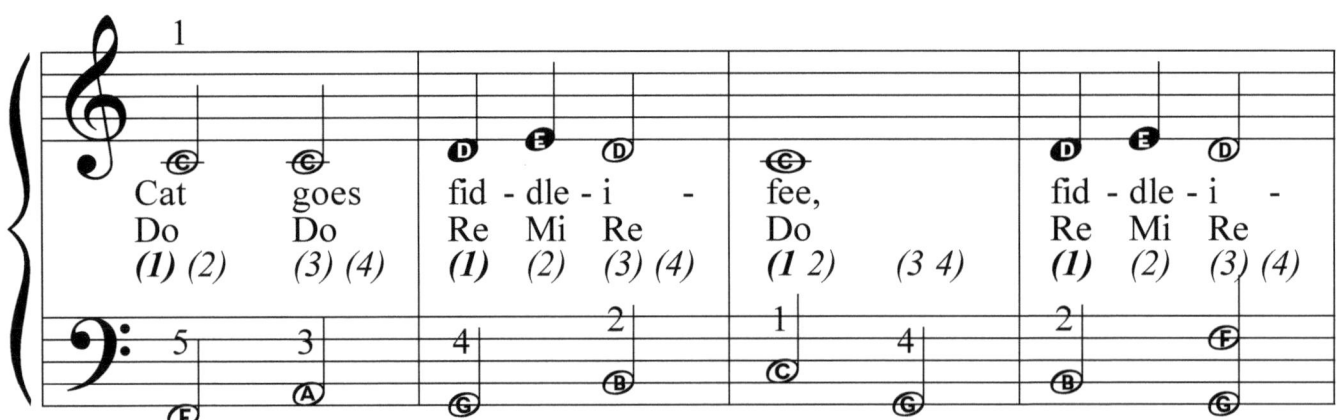

BOUGHT ME A CAT (CONT.)

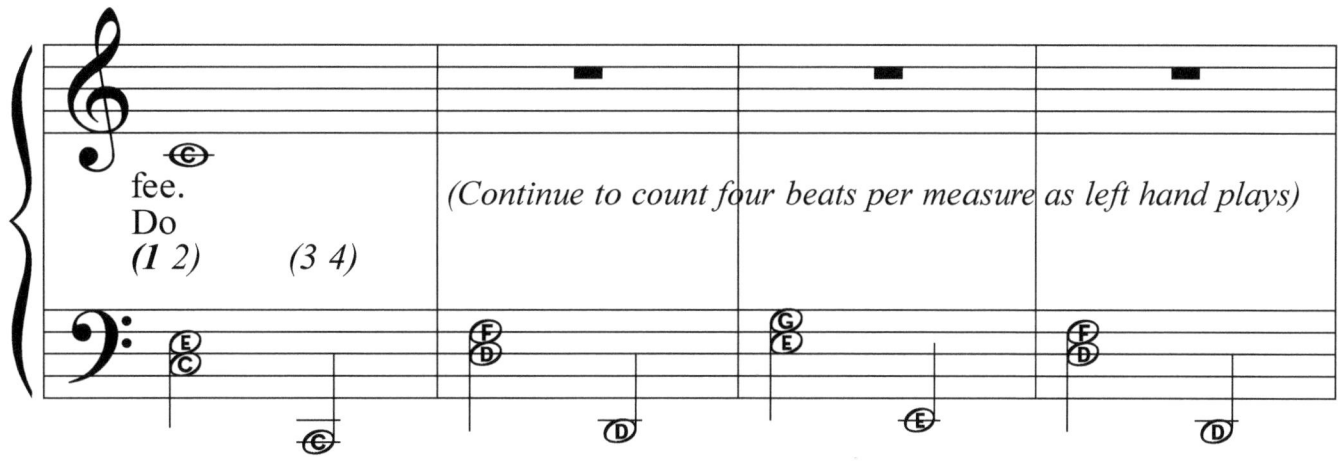

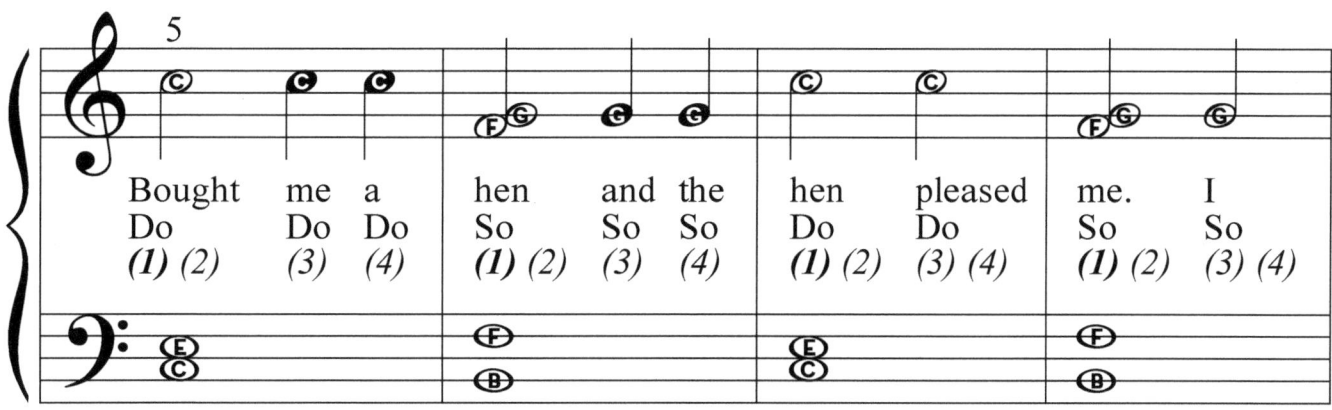

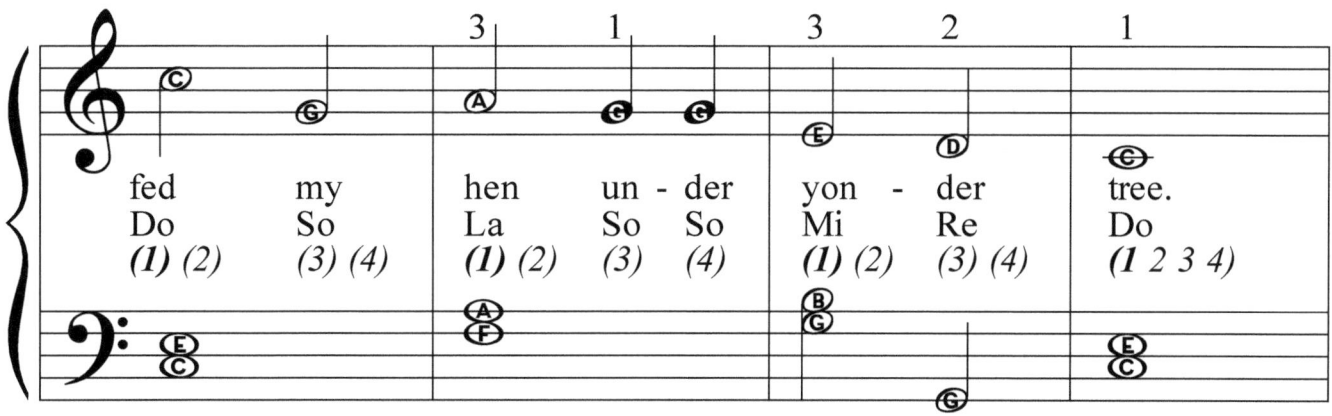

BOUGHT ME A CAT (CONT.)

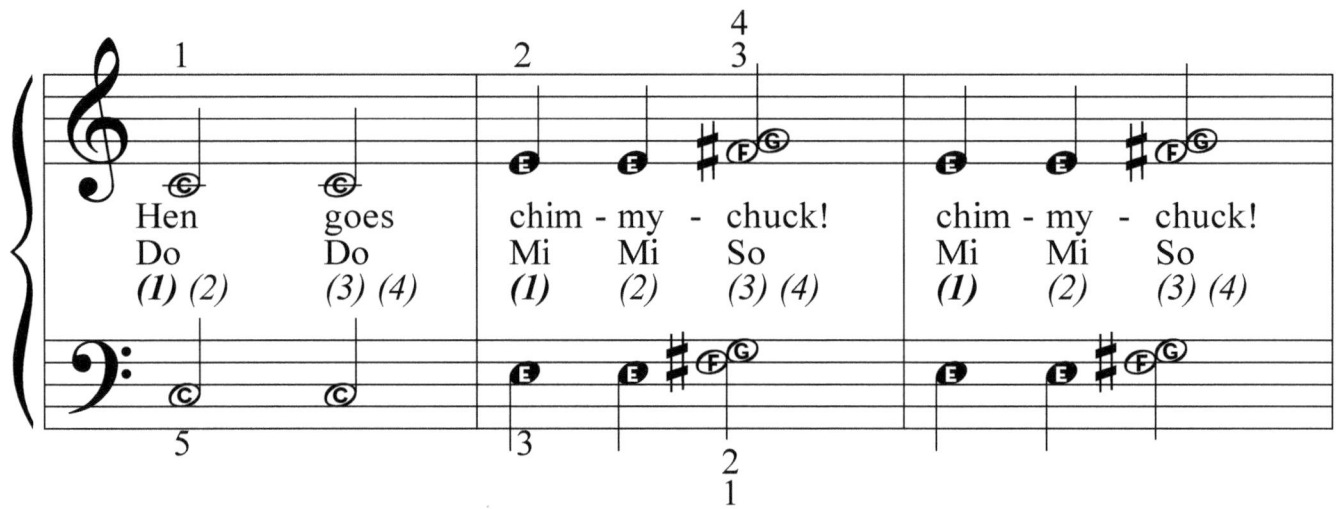

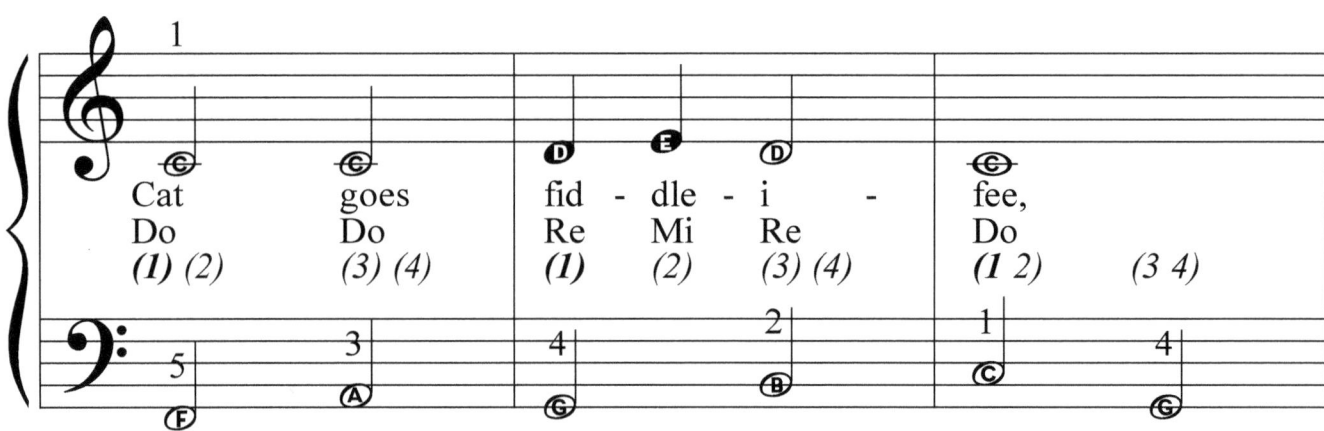

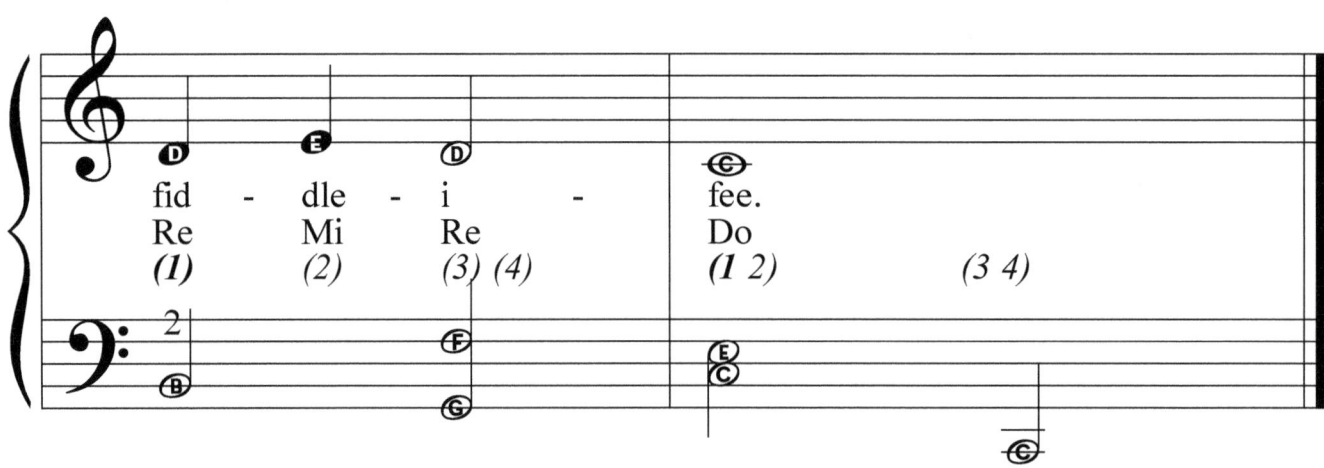

Pick-up Measure

Songs don't always start on beat one. This means that songs can begin on beats other than the down beat.

For example, if a song has four beats per measure, it could start on beat two, beat three, or beat four. These starting beats would come before the first down beat.

Four; *One*, Two, Three, Four; *One*, Two, Three, Four; *One*, Two, Three, Four; *One*, Two, Three, Four; etc.

Three, Four; *One*, Two, Three, Four; *One*, Two, Three, Four; etc.

Another example, if a song has three beats per measure, it could start on beat two, or beat three. These starting beats would come before the first down beat.

Three; *One*, Two, Three; *One*, Two, Three; etc.

Two, Three; *One*, Two, Three; *One*, Two, Three; etc.

Songs that start on a beat other than beat one are said to have a ***pick-up measure***. This unique measure at the very beginning of a piece will have fewer beats than the other measures in the piece.

What beat does this song start on in the pick-up measure? Beat ____

THE HERRING SONG

Using notes from the F Major Scale — English Folk Song

The Herring Song (cont.)

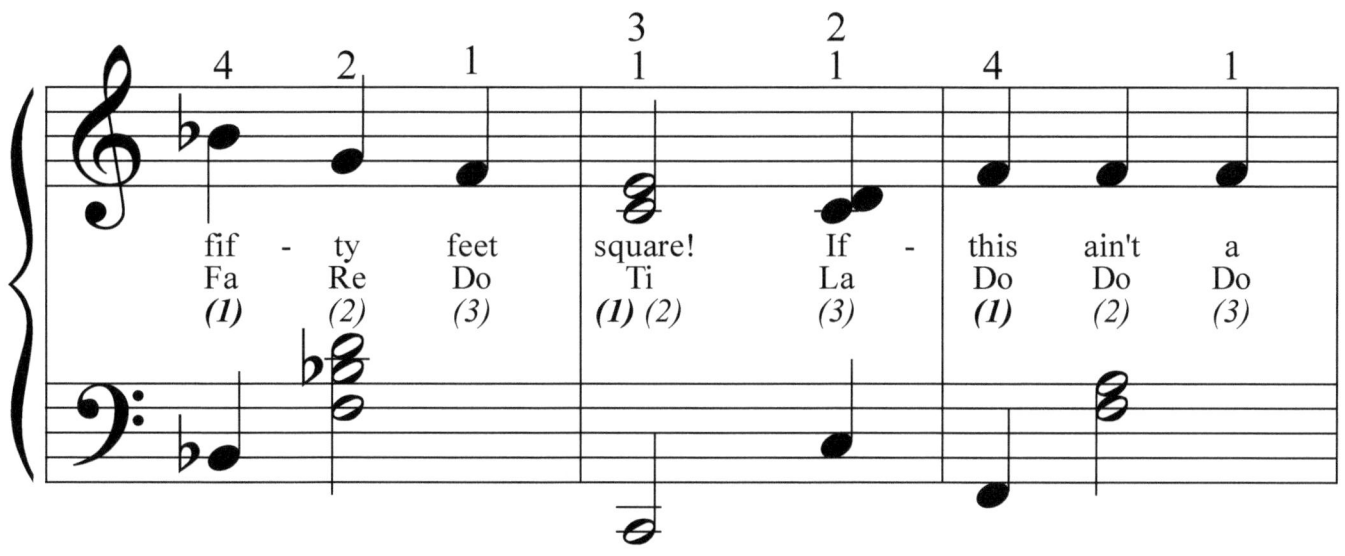
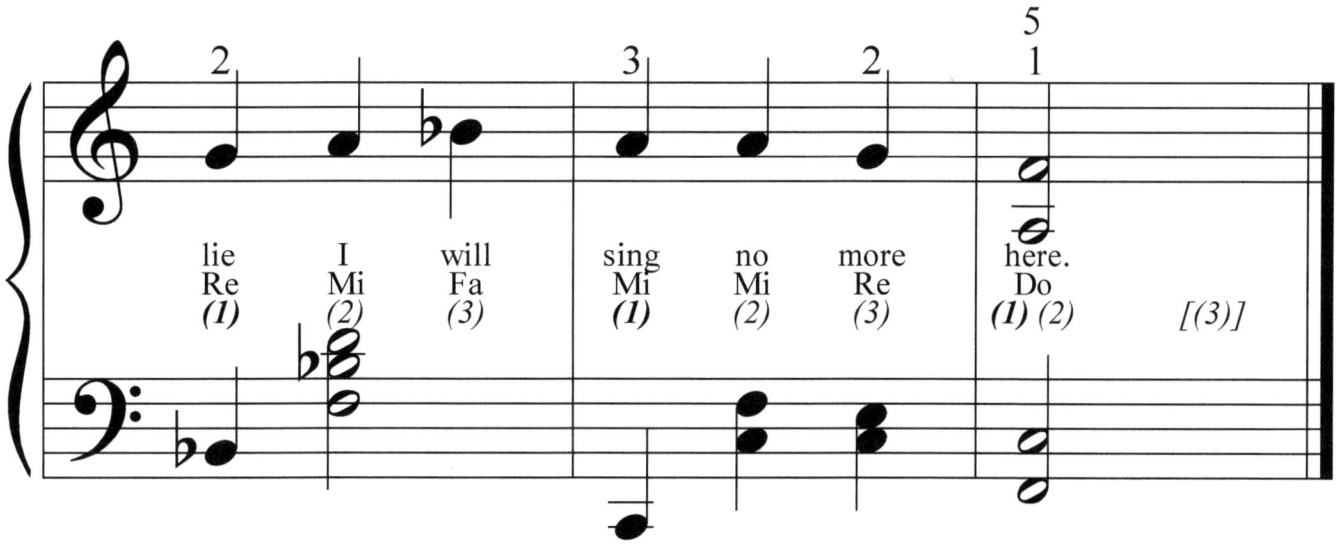

Dotted Notes and Ties

Sometimes we want to write a note that has one and a half beats.

For example, in $\frac{3}{4}$ time, where there are three beats per measure and a quarter note gets one beat, we can fill up the measure with quarter notes and half notes like this:

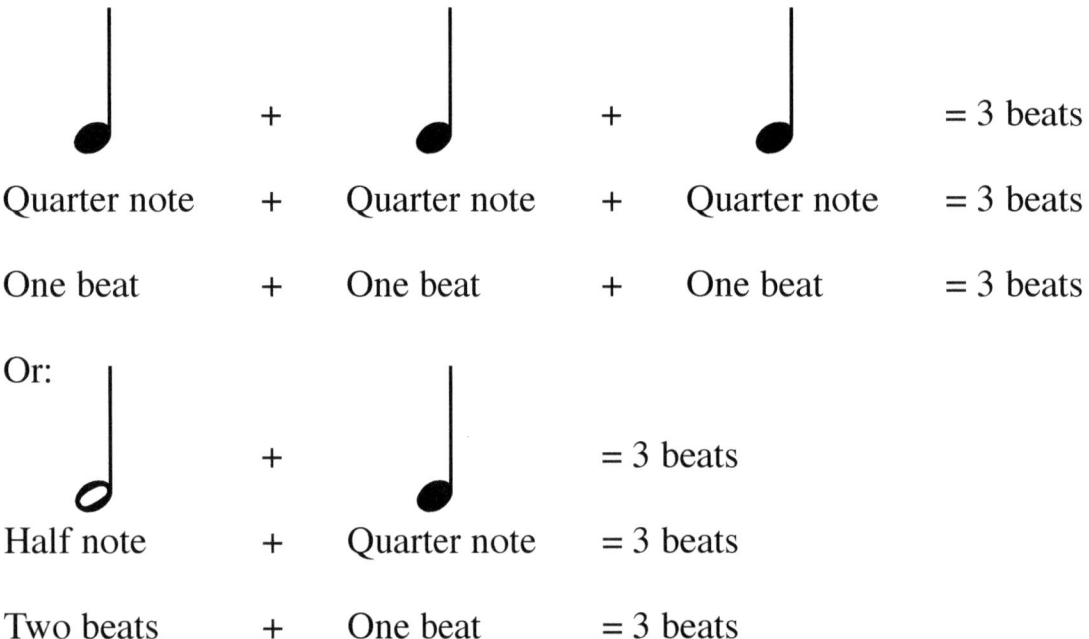

| Quarter note | + | Quarter note | + | Quarter note | = 3 beats |
| One beat | + | One beat | + | One beat | = 3 beats |

Or:

| Half note | + | Quarter note | = 3 beats |
| Two beats | + | One beat | = 3 beats |

What if you want to fill up the measure (3 beats) with just *one* note? So far, there isn't one note that has 3 beats. A whole note has too many beats (4), and two half notes also have too many beats (2 + 2 = 4).

We use a dot (•) placed just to the right of a note to indicate "plus half the duration of the note." So, it's much like, a note-and-a-half. We call them ***dotted notes***.

A dotted half note is the same as a half note plus a quarter note (but it is just one note, not two).

| Dotted half note = | Half note + | Quarter note *(but you play just one note)* |
| Three beats = | Two beats + | One beat |

A dotted half note has *3 beats*.

DOTTED NOTES AND TIES (CONT.)

Sometimes we want to write a note that is longer than one measure.

For example, in $\frac{4}{4}$ time, where there are four beats per measure and a quarter note gets one beat, the largest note value that can fit into the measure is a whole note, which gets all four beats. What if we wanted one note to fill up two measures, or get eight beats?

We can use a *tie*. A *tie* is a curved line or an arc that connects two notes together so that the first note receives the full duration of both notes, but the note is only sung or played once.

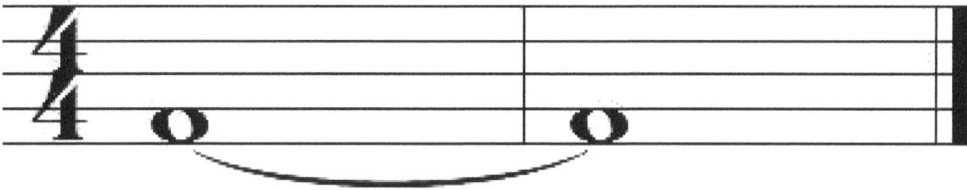

In this example, the first whole note is sung or played, and is held for four beats. Then, since it is tied to a whole note in the next measure, the first note is held for four more beats, but is not sung or played a second time (it is just held for that long).

We can tie many combinations of notes together, depending on the needs of the composer and the music.

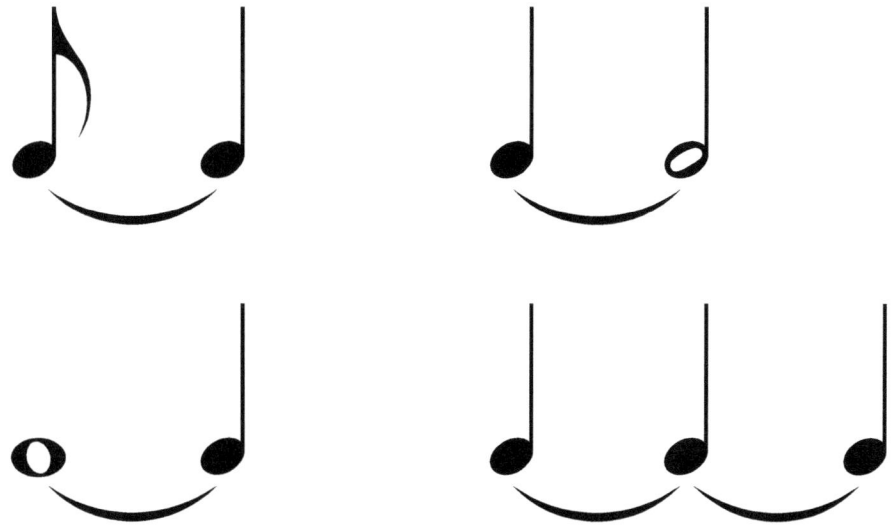

How many beats would each of the above combinations receive?

175

DOTTED NOTES AND TIES (CONT.)

Another creative way a composer can specify to hold a note longer than its usual value is by using a *fermata*.

A fermata over a note tells the performer to hold out the note longer than the number of beats normally assigned to that note. It is often used at the end of a song or piece, so that the final note(s) are held longer to add intensity to the finish. It is sometimes used in the middle of piece to add dramatic or emotional effect in the music.

Aus meines Herzens Grunde

JOHANN SEBASTIAN BACH

How many fermatas can you find in the chorale by J.S. Bach above? _____

DOTTED NOTES AND TIES PRACTICE

A ___ next to a note means to add one half of the note's value to the duration of the note.

A half note with a dot after it is called a _____ half note.

When there are four beats per measure, and a quarter note gets one beat, then a dotted half note receives: *(circle one)*

        one beat / two beats / three beats / four beats.

A dotted quarter note is equal to: *(check one)*

    ___ a quarter note plus a half note
    ___ a quarter note plus an eighth note
    ___ two quarter notes

A curved line or arc that connects two notes together so that the first note receives the full duration of both notes is called a _____.

How many beats should we hold the whole note below? ____

How many beats does this half note tied to a quarter note receive? ____

This symbol 𝄐 placed over or under notes in music tells a performer to hold out the note longer than the number of beats normally assigned to that note, and is called a _____.

Draw a fermata here:

DE COLORES

Using notes from the C Major Scale

Spanish Song of Celebration

Anthem of the United Farmworkers of America (founded by Cesar Chavez)

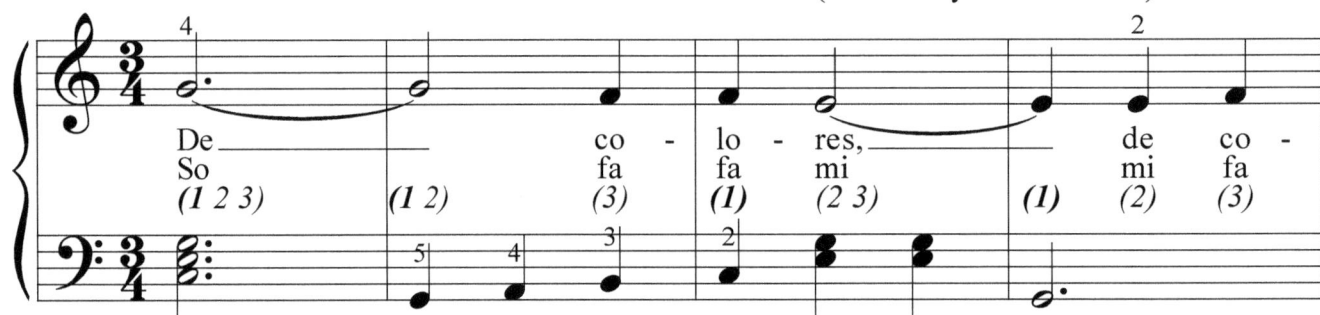
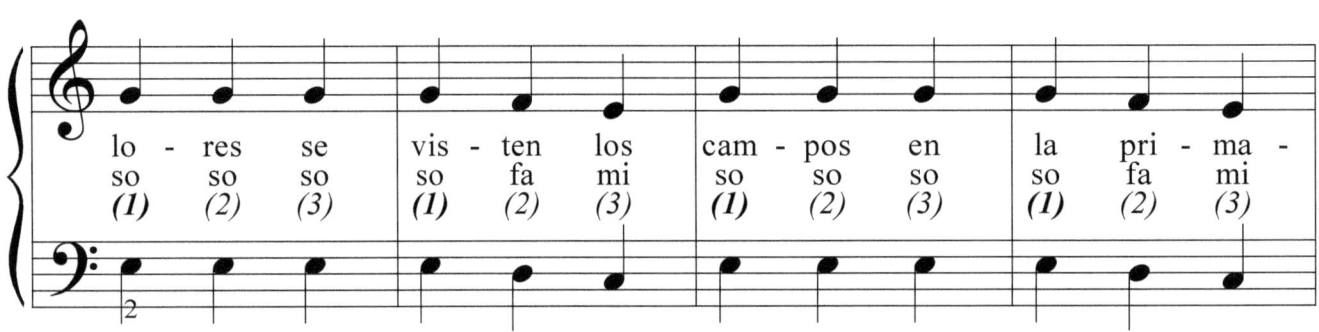
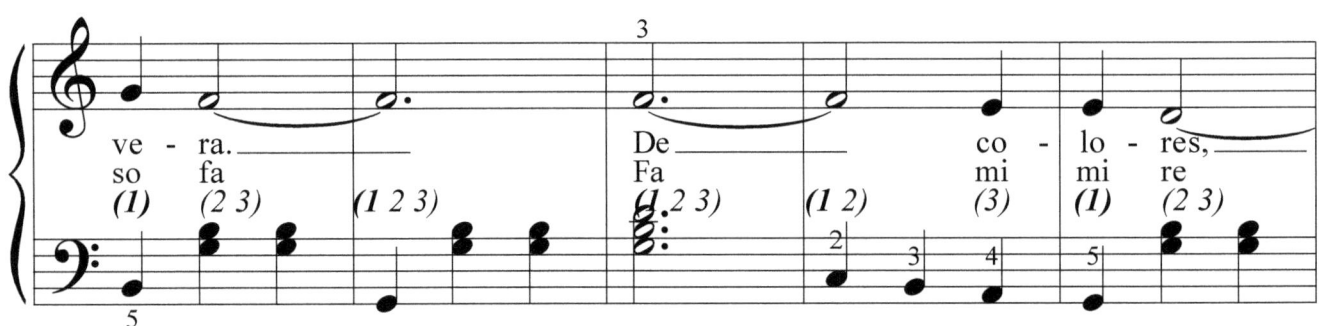

DE COLORES (CONT.)

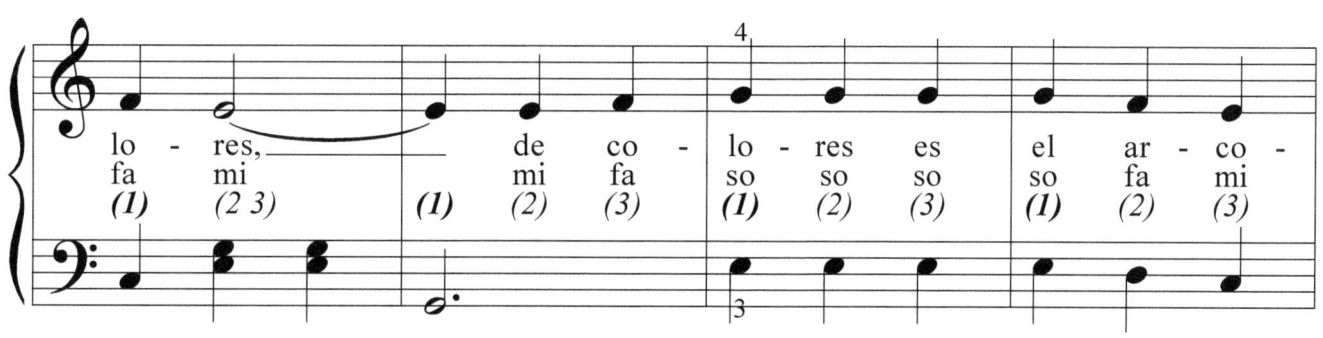
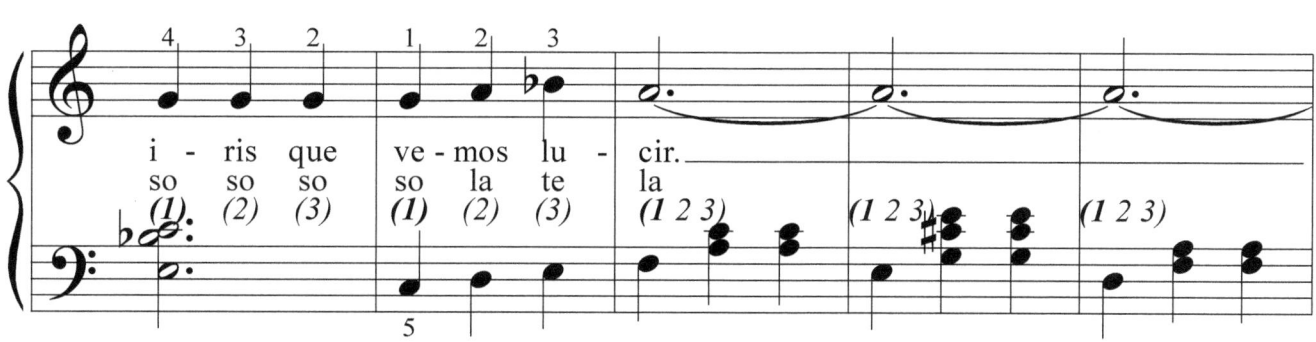

De Colores (cont.)

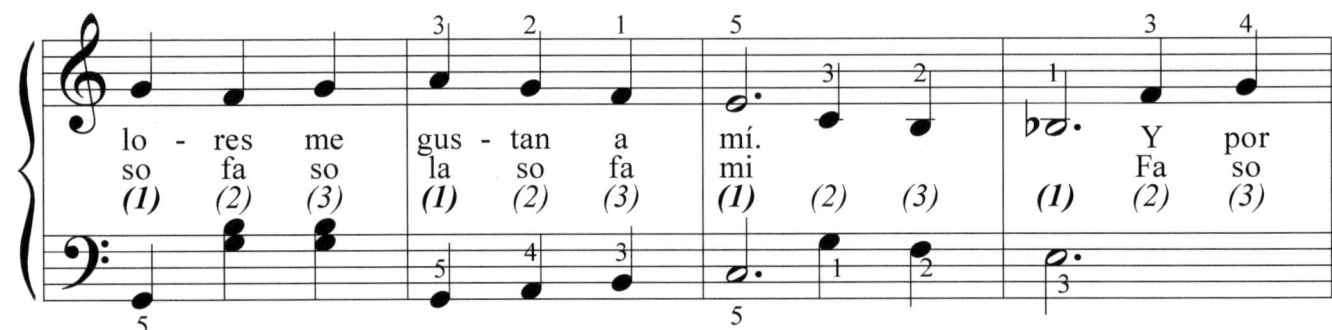

Can you hold down the dotted half notes while you play the quarter notes with other fingers? Try it!

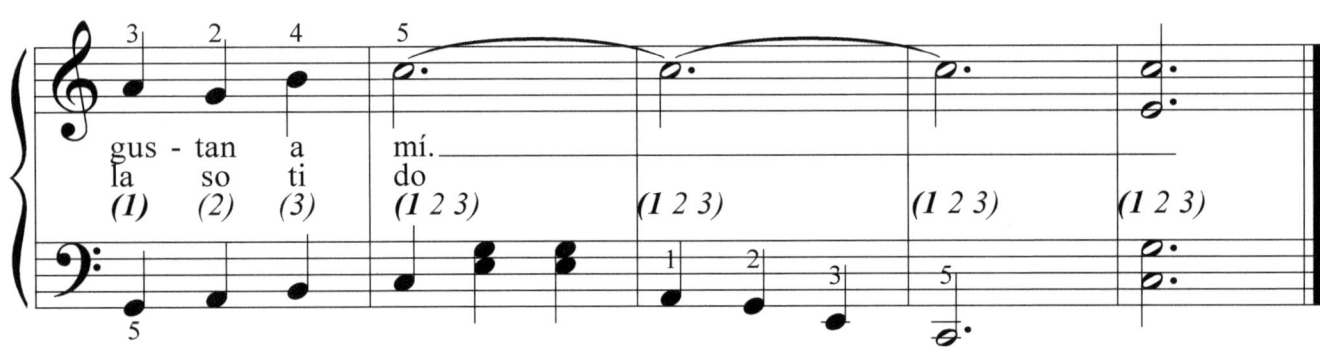

FINAL REVIEW

Going from one note to the very next note is a _____ step.

Going from one note to another note, skipping over one note is a _____ step.

An _____ is the distance between two notes.

An _____ is an interval of eight, and goes from one note to the same note, such as A to A, or C to C, or F♯ to F♯.

A _____ raises a note by a half step.

A _____ lowers a note by a half step.

A _____ cancels out a previously altered note.

Sharps, flats, and naturals are called _____.

The G clef is also called the _____ clef and points to ___.

The F clef is also called the _____ clef and points to ___.

The staff consists of how many lines? ___

The top line of the treble clef staff is ___.

The bottom line of the bass clef staff is ___.

The special note that falls between the two clefs of the grand staff, and sits on one ledger line below the treble clef staff, and on one line above the bass clef staff, is _____.

The numbers at the beginning of a piece of music that tell us how many beats per measure and what kind of note gets one beat are called the _____.

When there are four beats per measure and a quarter note gets one beat,

   a whole note gets ____ beat(s),
   a half note gets ____ beat(s),
   a quarter note gets ____ beat(s),
   an eighth note gets ____ of a beat.

Final Review (cont.)

A _____ next to a note means to add one half of the note's value to the duration of the note.

A half note with a dot after it is a _____ note.

When there are four beats per measure, and a quarter note gets one beat, then a dotted half note receives: *(circle one)*

        one beat / two beats / three beats / four beats.

A dotted quarter note is equal to: *(check one)*
- ___ a quarter note plus a half note
- ___ a quarter note plus an eighth note
- ___ two quarter notes

A curved line or arc that connects two notes together so that the first note receives the full duration of both notes is a _____.

The symbol 𝆑 placed over or under notes in music tells a performer to hold out the note longer than the number of beats normally assigned to that note, and is called a _____.

In the song, *De colores*, the first note of the second measure in the bass clef is ___. The first note of the third measure in the bass clef is ___.

In the song, *De colores*, in measures 9 and 10, the treble clef F followed by F consists of a _____ note tied to a _____ note.

In the song, *De colores*, all the notes of the last measure, before the double bar, are _____ notes.

In the final song, *For S/He's a Jolly Good Fellow*, the first measure only has one beat (quarter notes). This measure is called a _____ measure, and starts on beat ____.

In the final song, *For S/He's a Jolly Good Fellow*, in measure 13, the three dotted half notes in the bass clef are _____, _____, and _____.

In the final song, *For S/He's a Jolly Good Fellow*, there is a fermata in which measure? _____

For S/He's a Jolly Good Fellow

Using notes from the G Major Scale Popular Song of Congratulations

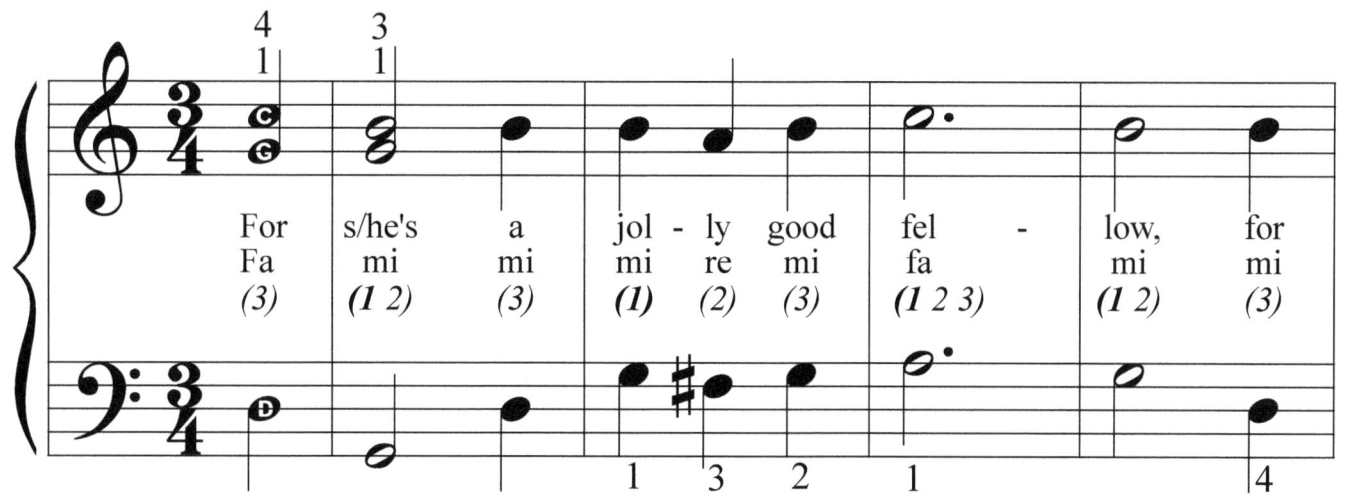
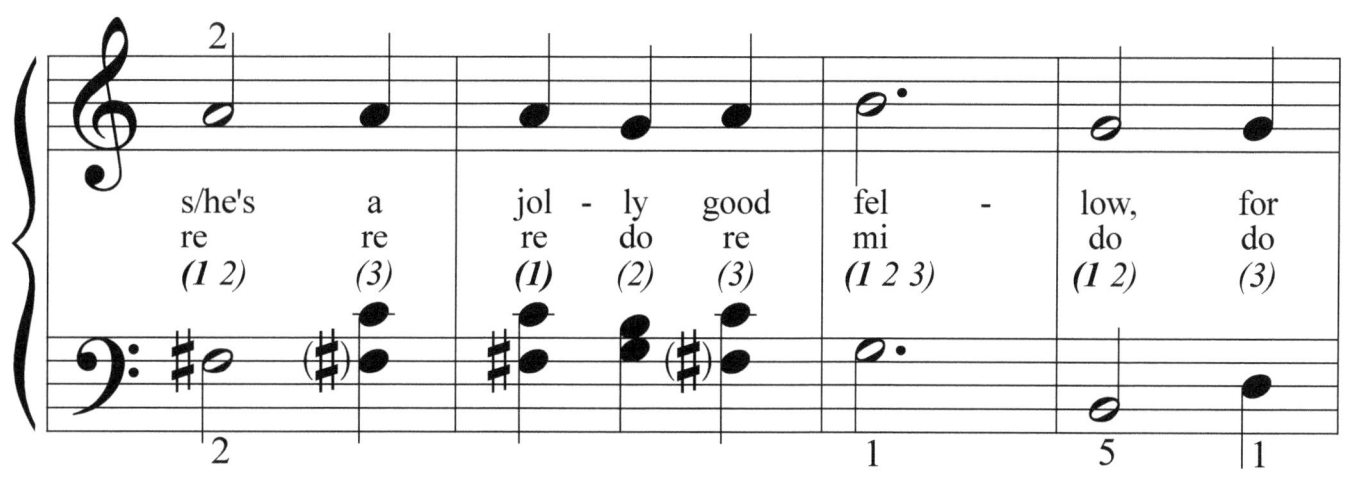
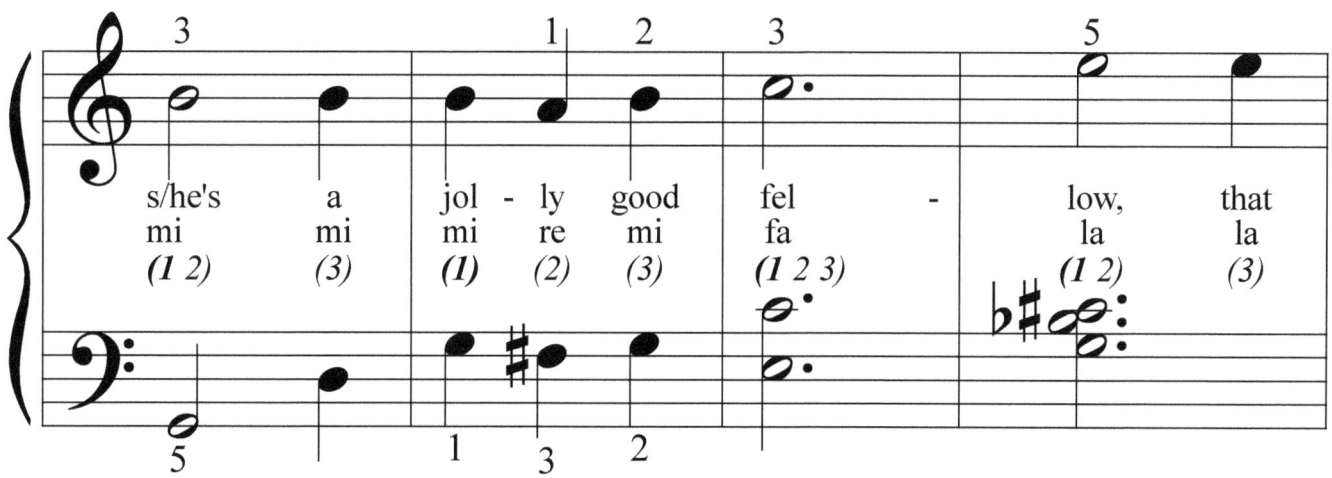

For S/He's a Jolly Good Fellow (cont.)

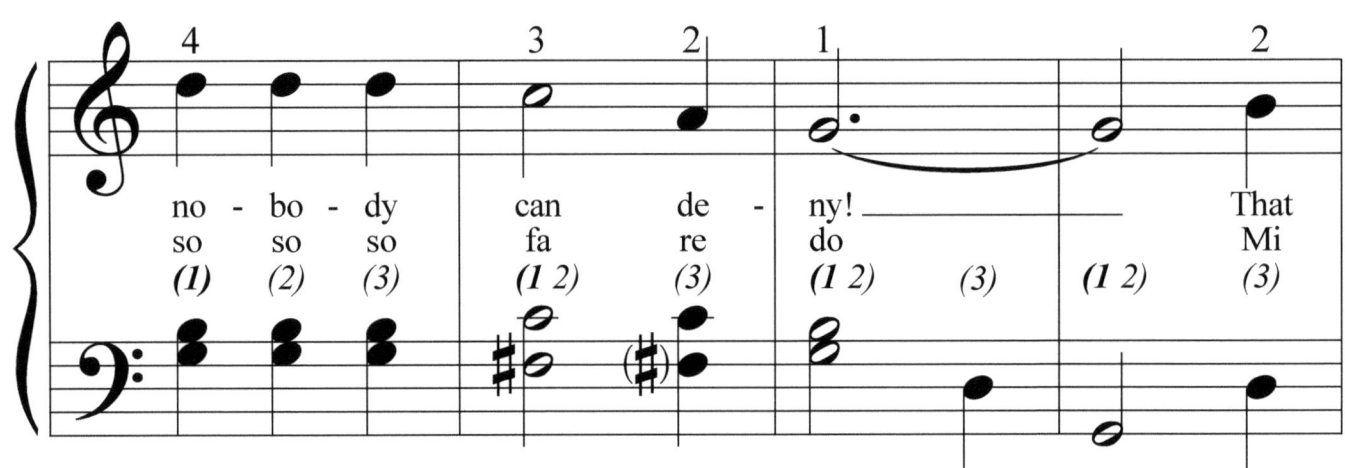
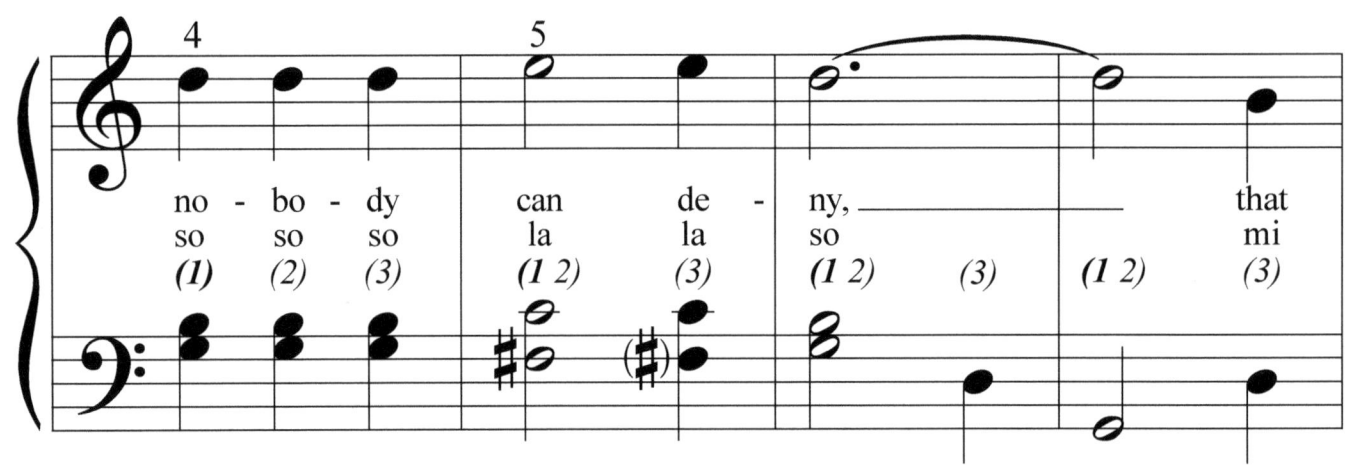
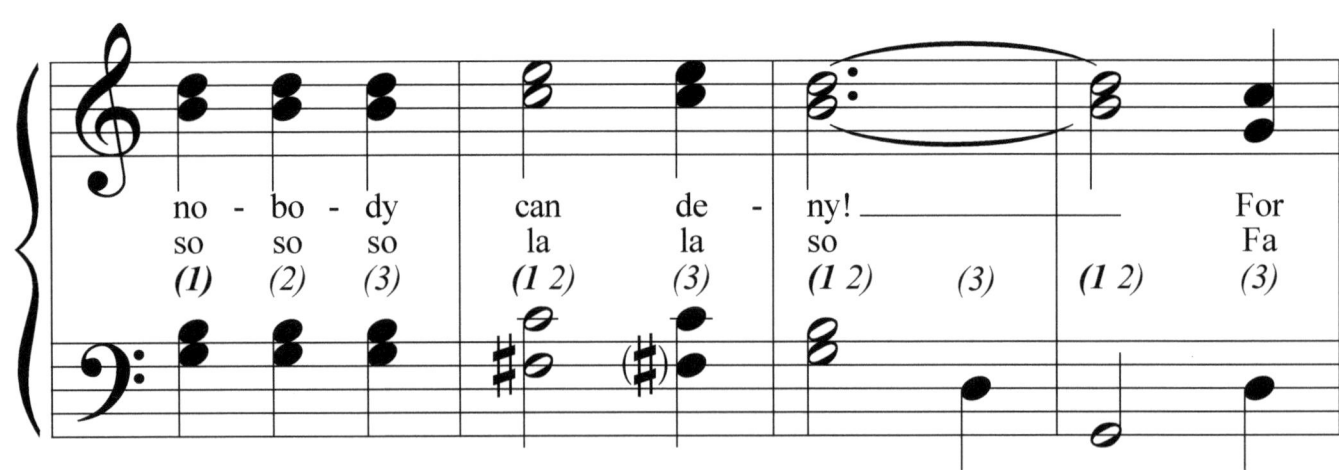

For S/He's a Jolly Good Fellow (cont.)

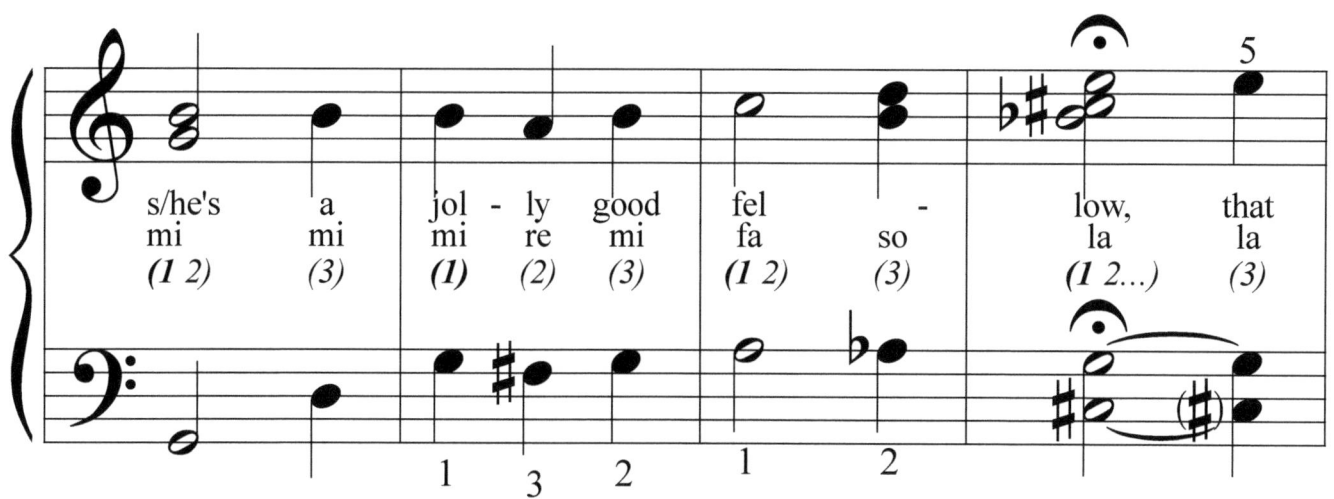
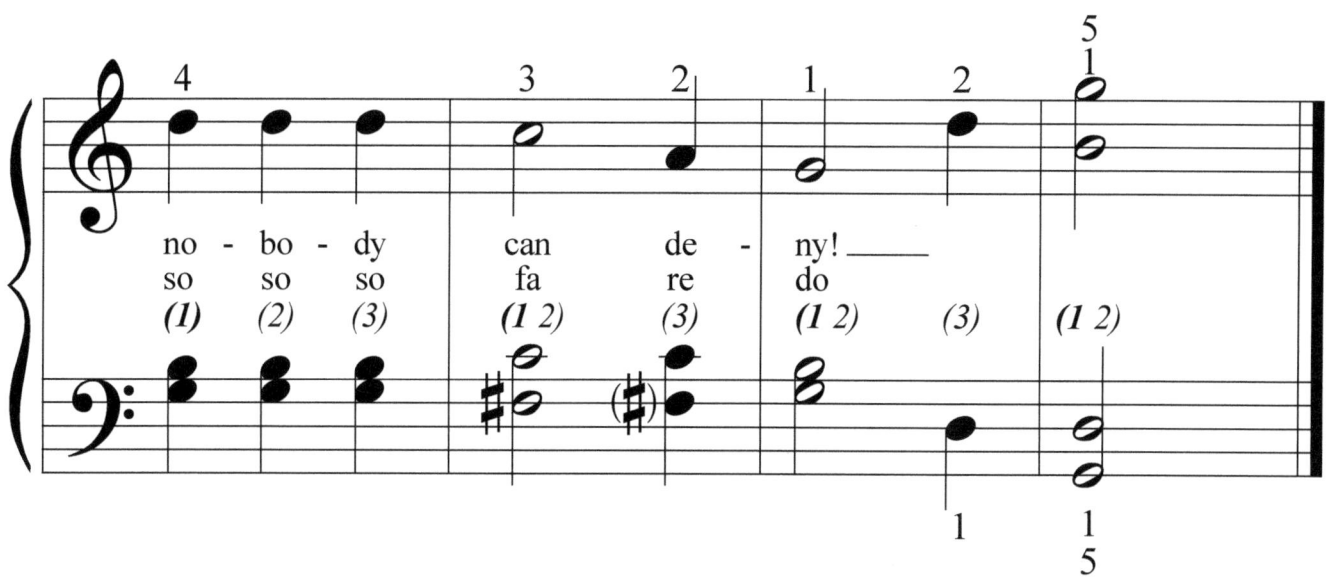

YOU DID IT!

CONGRATULATIONS!

You have completed Part Four

of your first piano lesson book!

This is the final part, so you are done!
And now you earn a prize!

You should be very proud of yourself for completing your piano book!

To get your prize and certificate, complete the order form on the next page.

Circle your favorite choice for your prize, and be sure to include your name and address, or the name and address of your parent or w.

You can mail the order form to me, or you can scan it and email it to me from your computer or device.

Guess what?

You're ready for Book 2!

In *Presto, It's Piano Magic! Book 2*, you'll learn more about playing the piano, reading music, rhythm, scales, piano technique, music theory, ear training, transposing music, improvising, and composing music. I can't wait to see you there!

Keep up the good work!

COMPLETION!

Prize and Certificate Order Form

To: Presto! It's Music Magic Publishing Company   Date: _____

Dear Presto,

Student _____ has successfully completed *Presto! It's Piano Magic, Book 1*, having mastered the concepts and skills, played all the songs and pieces from memory, sung the songs on solfege and words, clapped the rhythms, and answered all the questions in the worksheets and reviews.

Please send a Certificate of Completion and the selected prize to address:

_____
(Please print name, address, telephone number, and email address clearly.)

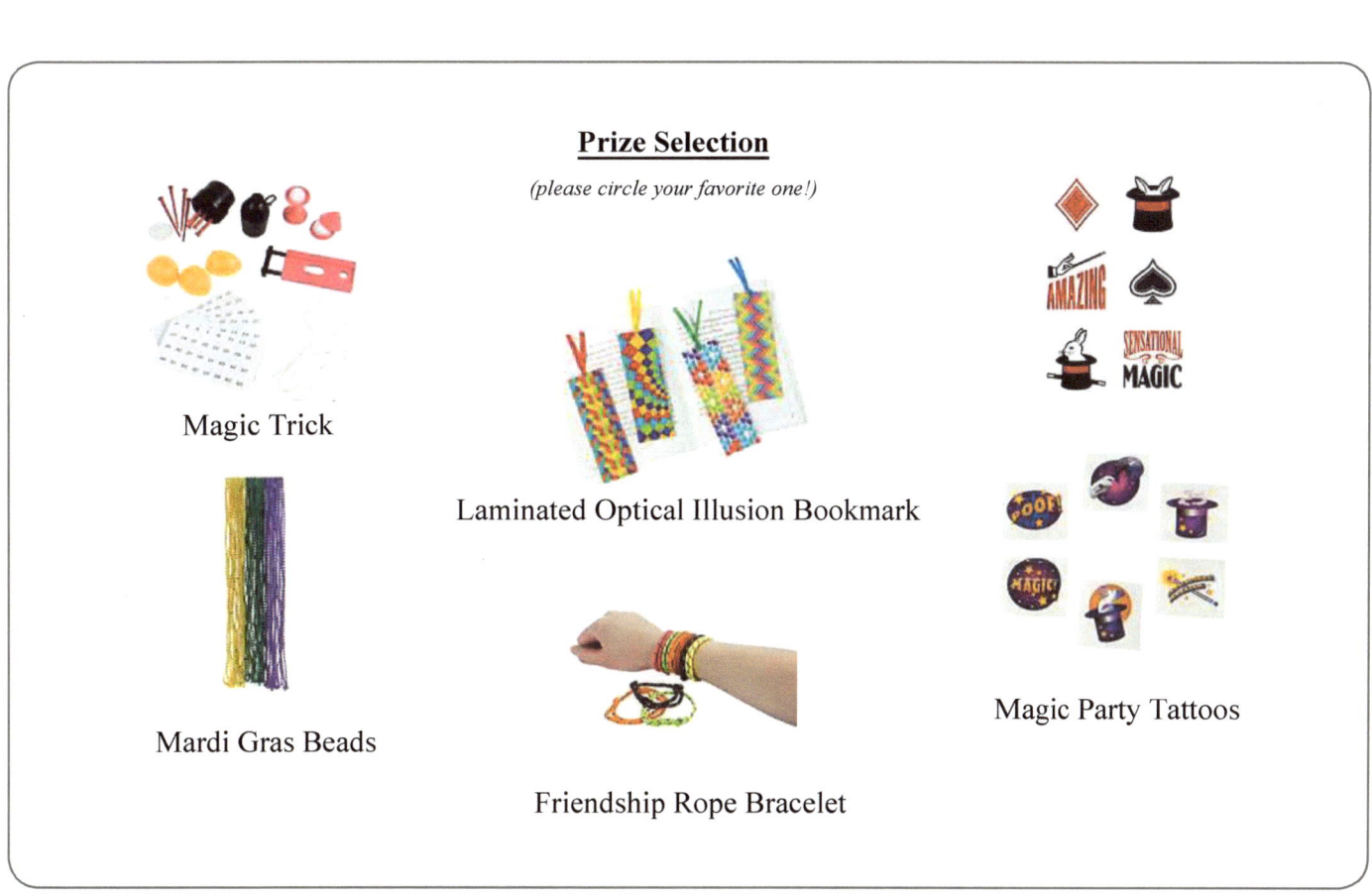

Prize Selection

(please circle your favorite one!)

Magic Trick

Laminated Optical Illusion Bookmark

Mardi Gras Beads

Friendship Rope Bracelet

Magic Party Tattoos

To receive your prize and certificate, complete and mail this form to:

Presto Music Magic Publishing
36068 Hidden Springs Rd., Ste. C178
Wildomar, CA 92595

Or, scan and email this form to:

customerservice@prestopianomagic.com